Sexual Enslavement of Girls and Women Worldwide

Sexual Enslavement of Girls and Women Worldwide

Andrea Parrot and Nina Cummings

Practical and Applied Psychology
Judy Kuriansky, Series Editor

Westport, Connecticut
London

Library of Congress Cataloging-in-Publication Data

Parrot, Andrea.
    Sexual enslavement of girls and women worldwide / Andrea Parrot and Nina Cummings.
        p. cm. — (Practical and applied psychology, ISSN 1938–7725)
    Includes bibliographical references and index.
    ISBN-13: 978–0–275–99291–0 (alk. paper)
    1. Human trafficking. 2. Slave trade. 3. Slavery. 4. Women slaves. 5. Child
slaves. 6. Prostitution. 7. Child prostitution. 8. Women—Crimes against. 9. Children—
Crimes against. I. Cummings, Nina, 1955– II. Title.
HQ281.P37 2008
364.15'3—dc22   2008015122

British Library Cataloguing in Publication Data is available.

Library of Congress Catalog Card Number: 2008015122
ISBN: 978–0–275–99291–0
ISSN: 1938–7725

First published in 2008

Praeger Publishers, 88 Post Road West, Westport, CT 06881
An imprint of Greenwood Publishing Group, Inc.
www.praeger.com

Printed in the United States of America

The paper used in this book complies with the
Permanent Paper Standard issued by the National
Information Standards Organization (Z39.48–1984).

10 9 8 7 6 5 4 3 2 1

We dedicate this book to all the women who had the courage to share their stories so others could better understand the personal toll of sexual slavery.

Contents

Series Foreword

Sex slavery, trafficking of women and girls, forced marriage, and prostitution—the very words can send chills up and down our spines. These are age-old practices and abuses that modern-day people are thankfully, finally, willing to face and take action against. In this book, authors Andrea Parrot and Nina Cummings confront us with shocking stories of such abuses of women and girls. They draw us, for example, close to a 14-year-old Congolese girl whipped and raped by rebels; a 12-year-old Indian girl married off to a man twice her age who forced her into domestic servitude and a life of torture; and a young Chinese girl so desperate to support her infant that she was lured into an escort service by a gang member promising her an escape from her current abusive life. These authors expose us to many horrific incidences of sexploitation, but they do not leave us mired in the misery. They document myriad efforts, from individual and collective civil society actions to legislation, to stop the violence against women and girls. As such, this revealing book is a heroic effort in support of females' freedom and rights.

The issue of violence against women is one that none of us should ignore, and one that I've become increasingly keenly aware of in many aspects of my work. As a representative of several international psychological organizations to the United Nations, I attend many briefings and meetings, such as the annual Commission on the Status of Women, focused on abuse and violence against women around the world. As a relief worker in war zones and after natural disasters, I've seen the devastating conditions women in particular suffer, from poverty to prostitution and rape. . . . And as a psychologist, too, I have been the proud peer applauding so many global colleagues doing courageous work to combat violence against women in their own countries, setting up hotlines, awareness campaigns, and rehabilitation programs. Yes, in the face of this world of violence against women described in these pages, one can become discouraged and enraged, yet readers can also become encouraged and heartened that people are so dedicated—that they often put their own lives on the line—to help these women, rescue victims, rehabilitate survivors, stop the abuses, and ultimately prevent the onset of these problems for future generations of girls. This book is an invaluable tool for the awareness and advocacy of such efforts, and, as such,

should be circulated through all levels of society to spotlight these horrific situations, so we can see ways to work more fervently, and effectively, toward solutions
and prevention.

Dr. Judy Kuriansky, PhD
Series Editor, Practical and Applied Psychology

Preface

The sexual slavery of women is a difficult and complicated topic. Researching the social, cultural, economic, and political threads that run throughout its many manifestations shows a convoluted path to women's enslavement. The predominant theme, however, is that women's enslavement for sexual exploitation is most certainly a result of ongoing patriarchal systems that institutionalize women's diminished worth in the world. The root cause of the abuse of women is the inequitable power relations between genders fueled by misogyny. This leads to situations where sexual exploitation of women for sexual pleasure and profit supersedes women's worth as human beings. Researching sexual slavery practices that have existed and do exist confirms that the world continues to be a dangerous place for women as paradigm shifts and equitable political and economic distribution are a long way off.

In order to write a book about sexual slavery, we had numerous discussions about what constitutes sexual slavery. Prostitution in and of itself does not create slavery conditions unless certain contexts exist. Some women voluntarily go to work in both legal and illegal brothels, for example, but may then become bound to conditions of debt bondage or involuntary sexual servitude. Many women argue that they have chosen sex work as a profession and that they are by no means subservient to or enslaved by the customers who seek their services. While some individuals believe prostitution cannot be separated from the exploitation of women, others argue that denying sex work as a legitimate livelihood infringes on one's individual liberty (Chuang, 2005). The debate on whether the many types of sex work in which women are engaged are consensual, entitled, or viable options for livelihood is beyond the scope of this book. This book is about the unwanted, coerced, forced sexual enslavement of women and girls worldwide and the conditions that create this servitude.

In order to try to separate the arguments of consensual and forced sexual slavery we offer the following criteria from the United Nations Commission on Human Rights:

Slavery should be understood as the status or condition of a person over whom any or all of the powers attaching to the right of ownership are exercised, including sexual access through rape or other forms of sexual abuse. Critical elements in the definition of slavery are limitations on autonomy and on the power to decide matters relating to one's sexual activity and bodily integrity. A claim of slavery does not require that a person be bought, sold or traded; physically abducted, held in detention, physically restrained or confined for any set or particular length of time; subjected to forced labour or forced sexual activity; or subjected to any physical or sexual violence although these are indicia of slavery. Further, a claim of slavery does not require any State action or nexus to armed conflict. And the mere ability to extricate oneself at substantial risk of personal harm from a condition of slavery does not in and of itself nullify a claim of slavery. (McDougall, 2000)

As we researched the sexual enslavement of women around the world, it became clear that particular practices occurred most frequently in certain world regions. It is also clear that reporting is heavily dependent on human rights organizations that are able to collect testimonies from survivors of the violence when other documentation is unavailable. For example, because there are many political and tribal conflicts occurring in Africa, the reports on sexual slavery during war have been heavily dependent on human rights reports from that continent. The human rights workers are some of the only people willing to enter war zones to report on local atrocities there. Even as we finished this manuscript, emerging human rights reports from Kenya suggested women are being targeted as a result of the political instability created by a recent election in which the results are disputed. Trafficking is a transnational problem and impacts multiple regions and countries. The United States, eastern Europe, and countries of the former Soviet Union stand out as major source and destination countries for this practice. Forced prostitution and sex tourism dominate the economies of Asian countries such as Thailand and Cambodia. Thus, while individual stories in this book may appear to concentrate on certain world regions, the stark truth is that women's sexual slavery occurs in many contexts throughout the world and is dependent on a host of social, economic, and political factors that may support one practice more than others. However, regardless of the context, women's sexual enslavement can be found in its many variations worldwide. While this is not a book on feminist theory, feminism drives our perspective on this issue and raises difficult questions regarding the power relations between men and women, particularly how they lead to the atrocities reported in this text.

Furthermore, we are aware of the diverse arguments about the role of cultural relativism. While it is our contention that sexual slavery of women is a result of universal patriarchal systems that must be challenged, we understand that certain cultural practices exist because they perform important functions in society. For example, the role of "fetish" shrines that enslave women has arguably been a legitimate system of justice in specific African cultures for centuries. We have to consider the role of cultural relativism when examining the practice. It is not our intention to condemn practices that have traditions and importance that we cannot fully realize as Western women. But to argue that something is right, in light of the physical or mental trauma it causes to women (sometimes even death), simply because of cultural tradition is not a worthy argument for us. We believe that there are certain universal truths that condemn women's sexual enslavement regardless of cultural explanations. To this end, we denounce the culturally sanctioned practices named in this book that, while originally accepted in certain regions, we find to be violent and threatening to women's well-being.

A book on violence against women would be limited in scope and understanding without examples of women's voices. We have included the words of women themselves in order to demonstrate the depth of trauma and violence but also to illustrate the remarkable strength of the human spirit. The following quotation explains our intentions: "statistics are people with their tears wiped dry" (Bertell, 2000).

Because of the overwhelming numbers of women who are sexually exploited on a daily basis, legislative changes are inevitably limited in their ability to significantly affect this global issue. Although we do give some attention to a few successful practices that have helped to address and eliminate some sexual slavery, there is no question that they fall short. For example, while the United States has applied a "sanctions" approach to evaluate countries' attempts to combat trafficking, in reality, the policies devised by the United States are inadequately outlined and inconsistently enforced (Chuang, 2005). Further, while the U.S. government reports that the laws are having an impact on trafficking, the sex industry appears unaffected as other governments simultaneously benefit from the practice.

Until there is a meaningful challenge to men's right to use women's bodies for profit and exploitive pleasure, attempts to address these practices will, at best, have only incremental effects. Simultaneously, the root causes of violence against women, such as racism, colonialism, economic deprivation, and global economies that exclude certain oppressed groups, support the continued subordination of women. An understanding of the complexities of and connections between exploitative practices must be clarified and examined. For example, the demand for pornography creates the demand for prostitution, which creates the demand for trafficking, and so on (MacKinnon, 2005).

Those interested in helping to stop women's sexual slavery must consider aspects of gender inequity in their own lives. While sexual slavery is one manifestation of women's lesser worth in this world, to begin a process of change, individuals must examine their own culpability in perpetuating a world of gender, social and racial disparity, and, most importantly, patriarchy.

This book is an overview of women's sexual enslavement. Each practice could merit a book by itself and requires greater in-depth analysis than is provided here. Our previous book, *Forsaken Females*, examined more broadly the many ways women suffer at the hands of men, both those known to them as well as strangers. As our discussions about women's enslavement progressed, we found ourselves wondering about the women who know or are married to men who enslave other women. Like the wives of *kommandants* of German concentration camps, who lived on the grounds and saw the smoke rising from the crematoriums, how do some women process and manage the knowledge that other women are suffering at the hands of men they know and love? An extension of this question is offered to all of us. Now that we know, what will we do?

Acknowledgments

We owe special thanks to several individuals who provided support and assistance in the preparation of this manuscript.

Debbie Chen, Preethi Nath, Lilly Robinson, and Sue Smith all helped in various ways with this project during the early stages of manuscript preparation.

J. C. Sheppard and Carrie Ost were invaluable in the development of the book, through research, editing, service as sounding boards, and the provision of feedback. We are extraordinarily grateful for their careful and detailed attention to this work.

Finally, we are most appreciative of the women quoted in this book whose voices and words helped us deeply understand male violence against women in ways that statistics alone cannot.

Abbreviations

AFRC	(Sierra Leone) Armed Forces Revolutionary Council
ASK	A legal aid and human rights center in Bangladesh
CEDAW	Convention on the Elimination of All Forms of Discrimination against Women
CFC 4	Christian Children's Fund
CRC	Convention on the Rights of the Child
CST	Child sex tourists
DEVAW	Declaration on the Elimination of Violence against Women
FAWE	Forum for African Women Educationalists
FBI (U.S.)	Federal Bureau of Investigation
INS (U.S.)	Immigration and Naturalization Service
I & I	Intercourse and Intoxication
ICPD	International Conference on Population and Development
ICTY	International Crime Tribunal for the former Yugoslavia
INTERIGHTS	An international human rights law center in London
FAWE	(Sierra Leone) Forum for African Women Educationalists
LRA	(Uganda) Lord's Resistance Army
NGO	Nongovernmental organization
PDF	(Sudan) Popular Defense Forces
R & R	Rest and Relaxation
RUF	(Sierra Leone) Revolutionary United Front
Rs	(India, Pakistan) rupees
UAE	United Arab Emirates
UN	United Nations
UNDP	United Nations Development Programme
UNESCO	United Nations Educational, Scientific and Cultural Organization
UNICEF	United Nations International Children's Emergency Fund

Part I

Sexual Slavery of Women in Context

1

The Scope of the Problem

> Your male and female slaves are to come from the nations around you; from them you may buy slaves. You may also buy some of the temporary residents living among you and members of their clans born in your country, and they will become your property. You can will them to your children as inherited property and can make them slaves for life. (Leviticus 25:44–46)

Violence against women is a global social epidemic. The magnitude of suffering is incalculable, as are the long-term effects of so many women being beaten, raped, battered, and tortured. This book examines one particular form of violence against women and girls: sexual slavery.

OVERVIEW

Sexual slavery emerges in many intersecting forms, influenced by shifting world politics, social practices, and interdependent global economies. Sexual slavery is often a subset of other manifestations of violence against women. For example, while rape is acknowledged as a weapon of war, there are circumstances in which women are kidnapped or held against their will by opposing forces while being dehumanized and repeatedly physically and sexually violated; sexual slavery within the context of rape is a weapon of war. An example of this are the atrocities committed against Korean, Filipina, and other women during World War II. As objects of sexual servitude, the women were known as "comfort women" and used by Japanese soldiers as sexual slaves.

Other forms of sexual slavery occur within the context of prostitution, sex tourism, ritualized devotion to a deity or temple (with sexual services an expectation), and other types of slavery, such as bonded labor, that demand sexual servitude. Sexual slavery within forced marriage is sometimes a lifelong misery when women are not permitted the opportunity to divorce; in some cultures, the right to divorce is the exclusive province of the male. Many of these forms of sexual slavery will be discussed in greater detail in later chapters.

There is little dispute that the primary cause of women's sexual exploitation is the gender-based social and economic inequality experienced by women worldwide. Women's vulnerability is key, but not exclusive, to their enslavement. Lack of economic resources, illiteracy, cultural expectations, family obligations, war and civil strife, and abuse within the home may force women to seek a better life or escape a torturous one, making them more vulnerable to forces that can exploit them.

Dawn (Canada)

I have often heard men say that I had a choice, and I did, it was either work as a prostitute or starve to death because it is illegal in Canada to work at 12, not to mention that no one will hire you if you have no address and are only 13 or 14.

After about a month or so I met the man with whom I would spend the next 10 years in a blur of drug addiction and crime. I did not immediately become a prostitute but almost immediately I began to use cocaine and any other drug I could get my hands on to kill the pain of knowing that no one loves you. My boyfriend and I slept on the street and lived by petty crime and panhandling. My life began to spiral out of control.

I got into prostitution at 16 when my girlfriend told me she could help me make enough money for a hotel room and living money. She had an older friend who liked to have "parties" with several young girls and I could come if I wanted to. I would make a few bucks. The "parties" involved several older men looking for sex with young girls. . . . at the first one I slept with 4 men and made $400.00 but I felt ashamed and remember crying while these men had sex with me. These "parties" continued for a long time.

Soon I was working about 16 hours a day, 7 days a week. During my life on the street as a prostitute I was raped in every possible way many times, thrown from a moving car, strangled to the point of unconsciousness, as well as assaulted and robbed. I have had 11 friends die while I was on the streets and since I have left, either through murder, suicide or drug addiction. I have tried suicide myself on 4 separate occasions. (Polaris Project, n.d., *Dawn*)

Cultures that express social preference for boys (e.g., Korea, China, India) have high rates of infanticide and feticide of girls, and the ratio of boys to girls has increased. In 2001, India's census showed 108 boys to every 100 girls. In 2005, China's ratio was 120 boys born to every 100 girls. In Vietnam the figure was 110 boys to 100 girls in 2006. There is speculation that this imbalance may contribute to women's sexual enslavement and trafficking as boys become men unable to find wives within their own cultures (Sang-Hun, 2007).

Open international borders, corruption, criminal organizations, and the possibility of high profit with low risk motivates those who may benefit from women's enslavement. In all cases, there is an overriding sense that women are expendable and replaceable. Women are manipulated, coerced, forced, kidnapped, sold or bought into slavery where parties benefit directly from their sexual enslavement, from money as a result of the enslavement, or both. Figure 1.1 illustrates how the many forms of sexual enslavement intersect, comprising a multidimensional problem.

Figure 1.1
Intersections of Factors Associated with Sexual Slavery

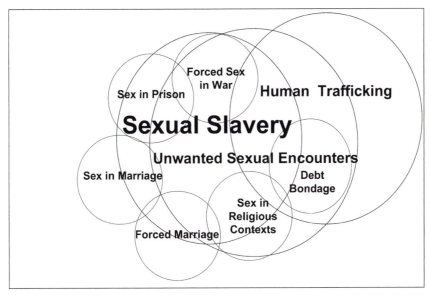

The types of sexual slavery identified in the figure above occur when there is repeated forced sexual contact, but this is not the case in all circumstances. For example, while sex in marriage is often desired, it can also be sexual servitude in some cases. The same is true for sex in prison. In the figure, where there is only partial overlap with unwanted sexual encounters, the issue of agency is the key factor.

HISTORICAL ROOTS

The historical roots of the sexual slavery of women can be traced back to the beginnings of prostitution and the control of women's sexuality. Lerner (1986) proposes that "sacred prostitution" was the earliest form, as a result of the ancient worship of fertility and goddesses. Ritual sexual slavery today (see chapter 5) can be traced to this idea of "sacred prostitution."

The worship of goddesses in ancient Mesopotamia and during the Neo-Babylonian period set the foundation for women to provide religious favors as a benefit to the temples. Once certain women provided this cultic sexual intercourse in the name of the goddesses, men often made a donation to the temple in return. Apart from the payment for sexual favors, food, oil, wine, and other valued commodities would have been offered to the goddesses in general to put the donor in good favor with the temple. It is speculated that these "donations" were eventually taken by individuals with self-interest and profit in mind. This may have developed into profiting from women's sexuality as well. In ancient cults, priests may have promoted the use of slave women and lower-class female servants as prostitutes to further benefit the temple, leading to the development of commercial prostitution (Lerner, 1986).

In addition to the associated sacred prostitution, militarism in the third millennium B.C. encouraged the enslavement of captured women. With slavery, sexual abuse became institutionalized. There are reports of masters creating brothels where their slaves were forced into prostitution (Lerner, 1986). Because a king's wealth and power was reflected in the numbers of servants and concubines he had, wealthy men and aristocrats followed suit by acquiring large numbers of slaves and women for sexual exploitation and sexual pleasure. Simultaneously, farmers and other poor society members found that children could be sold to repay debt (Lerner, 1986). All of these circumstances contributed to the creation of the use of women's and girls bodies for profit or personal benefit.

Poverty was and continues to be key in the development of sexual slavery. "[T]he prostitution of female family members for the benefit of the head of the family could easily develop. Women might end up as prostitutes because their parents had to sell them into slavery or because their impoverished husbands might so use them. By the middle of the second millennium B.C., prostitution was well established as a likely occupation for the daughters of the poor" (Lerner, 1986, p. 247).

It was Friedrich Engels who made the connection between the development of women's sexual enslavement and social class disparities, patriarchy, and profit motive: "Surrender for money was at first a religious act; it took place in the temple of the goddess of love and money originally went into the temple treasure. With the rise of the inequality of property...wage labor appears sporadically side by side with slave labor and at the same time as its necessary correlate, the professional prostitution of free women side by side with the forced surrender of the slave" (quoted in Lerner, 1986, p. 237). As the social order became increasingly dependent on male authority, first kings and rulers, followed by male family members with authority over women and children, from the second millennium B.C. onward, the sexual control of women has been a cornerstone of patriarchal power.

WOMEN'S SEXUAL ENSLAVEMENT WORLDWIDE

There are many contexts in which women are enslaved. The chapters that follow offer descriptions of some of the more predominant forms of sexual slavery. The challenges to estimating the numbers of women trapped in sexual slavery are multidimensional; there are varying definitions of what constitutes sexual slavery, and there is difficulty gathering information from survivors who fear that speaking out will further jeopardize them or their families. War zones or civil unrest often make it impossible to gather accurate data, where human rights workers may collect testimonies from individual survivors but are unable to do any kind of macroanalysis. Finally, cultural obstacles contribute to understanding why women's lives are sacrificed to this type of atrocity.

Some refer to trafficking for sexual exploitation as a "modern slave trade" (Hughes, 2000a), but estimating the numbers of slaves continues to be difficult. Because the very nature of the enslavement is secretive, there are debates about the actual scope of the activity. For example, in 2001, the U.S. FBI estimated that 700,000 women and children were trafficked worldwide, but in that same year the United Nations International Children's Emergency Fund (UNICEF) estimated this number to be higher, at 1.75 million. In 2001, the United Nations (UN) changed the estimate it had previously reported for 2000; the UN had reported that 4,000,000 were trafficked in 2000, but in 2001 it reduced the number to 1,000,000 (UNESCO Trafficking Project, 2003). Some reasons for the discrepancy are that statistics do not distinguish between illegal coerced trafficking to enslave women for sexual servitude and the illegal smuggling that is carried on with the consent of individuals who migrate to seek work in other countries. In certain circumstances, those who work in human trades establish ties with government officials who help to prepare false documents and ignore border and legal violations, most likely in return for bribes (Human Rights Watch, 2000). Furthermore, governments complicit in trafficking and sex tourism (see chapter 3) make information about the practices hard to understand or distinguish, which appears to minimize the scope of the problem.

Covert domestic trafficking is coordinated with ease. Typically, women are trafficked into the United States mainly along the Canadian and Mexican borders, as well as through the major international airports and harbors on both coasts. About one-third of the international women who are trafficked into the United States are also trafficked domestically once they arrive. Two-thirds of American women who are trafficked are moved domestically from one coast to the other. One study found that 1 in 5 women trafficked in the United States had an intimate relationship with their pimps, who took advantage of the women's emotional ties. Emotional and physical abuse, then, lures women into prostituting themselves.

There are 10,000 illegal immigrant women who have been forced into prostitution in Britain, mostly coming from eastern Europe (Gibb, 2003). In Southeast Asia, where sex industries have flourished, the trafficking of women and girls into China, Laos, Myanmar, Thailand, and Vietnam has increased dramatically in recent years.

Ying (Myanmar)

Ying was born into a poor family near the Burma/China border. When she was sixteen years old, a neighbor in her village contacted her parents to discuss taking Ying to Thailand to find domestic work. He told her parents that they would receive a big fee for Ying. Everyone agreed to this plan and Ying accompanied the neighbor to the border of Thailand. After they crossed into Thailand, the neighbor handed

Ying over to a new agent, a Thai national who told Ying she would stay overnight before going on to Bangkok. She was taken to his house with three other young Burmese girls. That night and for the following two nights, Ying and the other girls were forced to have sex with a series of Thai men. They had no choice. They were prisoners and couldn't escape.

After three days, Ying was shipped to Bangkok. When she arrived in Bangkok, she was taken, with 30 other girls, all under 18 years of age, to another house. In the morning, the girls were sent to a local massage parlor and forced to become prostitutes. One of the girls refused, and she was beaten, raped and confined to an unlit room for three days without food or water. This effectively broke the girls. All money from the sex acts went to the manager of the massage parlor. Thus, their conditions amounted to virtually a contemporary form of slavery. (iAbolish, 2008)

Other Asian countries also have experienced a sex industry expansion in recent years. In 1990, an estimated 1,500 women were working as prostitutes in Cambodia. By 1993, that number jumped to 20,000 and by 1996 an estimated 57,000 women and girls were working in the sex industry in Cambodia (Hughes, 2000b).

Marriages arranged by "fake" husbands or "marriage brokers" force women into commercial sexual exploitation or marriages to foreign men. Many of these men are part of international trafficking rings. Between 2004 and 2007, 20,000 Vietnamese women married Taiwanese men. From 2002 to 2007, there were 43,121 international marriages in South Korea. Of these, over 70 percent were South Korean men marrying non-Korean women, mostly from Southeast Asia and Mongolia, where known trafficking rings have a strong hold (U.S. Department of State, 2007c). In central Asia, "marriage agencies" are responsible for trafficking women, and it has been reported that these agencies are particularly active in the Kyrgyz Republic, Kazakhstan, and Uzbekistan.

Many suggest that the United States has been largely responsible for much of the growth of women's exploitation worldwide. Prostitution has markedly expanded in countries where there has been a large and prolonged U.S. military presence, as in Southeast Asia. More importantly, the United States is the center of the Internet industry. As a result, pornography, which has always been a highly profitable business, has taken hold online with over $9 billion spent on live sex shows, pornographic cable, magazines, and computer-generated images. For men who used to be secretive about their desires and demands, the Internet has provided private access to unlimited pornographic websites. In fact, the online sex industry is responsible for many of the Internet functions that support business today. "Privacy and security measures, fast payment transactions and web databases were developed by the online sex industry" (Hughes, 2000b, p. 7). Because of the profit-making ability and business competition, Web site creators incorporate ever-changing images to attract customers. Bondage, torture, bestiality, and child pornography are now easily within the grasp of any Internet user.

In 1999, an American named Dan Sandler who was living in Cambodia announced the start of a live bondage sex show on his Internet Web site. The site, which was called "Rape Camp," showed Asian women as sex slaves blindfolded, gagged, and tied during sex acts in "bondage, discipline and humiliation." The site asked viewers to "humiliate these Asian sex slaves to your hearts content" (Hughes, 2000b, p. 1). Sandler reported that his future plans included an interactive component where viewers, with access costing $15 per 15 minutes or $40 per 30 minute segments, could submit suggestions for torture that would immediately be implemented upon the women. The Cambodian minister of women's affairs became aware of the Web site, and Sandler was arrested for violating a Cambodian law that prohibits sexual exploitation and trafficking. Even after the arrest, however, the Web site remained intact because it was housed on a server in the United States (Hughes, 2000b).

Global sex tourism is on the rise where rampant poverty in the developing world is fueled by the international demand for a commercialized sex industry combined with easy Internet access and communication advancements (Protection Project, 2007; Farley et al., 2003). The transnational sex industry generates an estimated $57 billion a year (Hughes, 2000b). Children are also valued commodities in sex tourism and the demand is growing. It is estimated that 20 million U.S. dollars a year are spent on purchasing women and girls in Cambodia, and one-third of the girls in prostitution there are under 17, servicing 7–10 men per day. The age of those forced into prostitution has fallen due to men's belief that young girls are less likely to be infected with HIV (Hughes, 2000b). However, one report estimates that over half of the children forced into the sex industry in Cambodia are HIV positive (Independent Catholic News, 2008).

The methods of control used against women forced into sexual slavery vary. They include withholding money, isolation, and drug or alcohol dependence, which is most often used by women to cope with their lives although it is sometimes forced upon them. Women are often physically, mentally, and emotionally abused, and threats toward them or their family members may occur if they do not comply with the sexual demands. The financial enticement that is unavailable through more legitimate means can also be a powerful control.

Rei (Thailand)

Rei grew up in southern Thailand. She completed the twelfth grade in school and then got a job as a receptionist for five months. For the next four years, she took many different jobs, but didn't keep any of them for more than five months. During much of that time, Rei had no job at all. So, she said, "I heard about many women going to work in Japan, and I knew many agents in my neighborhood who could arrange for me to go. I knew I would have to be a prostitute, but the promise of a good salary was very appealing." (Human Rights Watch, 2000)

During war and civil unrest, all individuals are at risk, but women and children suffer disproportionately during armed conflict (Ward & March, 2006). Mass rape is not a new phenomenon but has recently garnered much media attention from the wars in Bosnia-Herzegovina, Congo, and Sudan. Sexual violence is used to control and dehumanize women, as well as demoralize the men in their lives. In many cases, women are abducted, kidnapped, or forced into circumstances in which repeated sexual violence can go on for years. Forced marriage to soldiers, forced prostitution to serve soldiers, and repeated rape by soldiers have all been reported and documented by human rights agencies.

Ajok Mawien Chan (Sudan)

They tied my hand together with a rope and led me away to the bush. They raped me in the bush, one after the other, all six of them. After that, I had to walk beyond the River Kiir with the other slaves. My hands were tied to a long rope. My sister was tied to it too. Along the way we were beaten and raped. We walked for four days. Then we reached a place where the soldiers divided us and the cows and goats amongst themselves.

I was given to Musa. My sister was given to a man named Ibrahim. Musa was a good friend of the leader of the raiders, Mahmoud Issa from Zeri (near Meiram). Musa had a body guard and was responsible for distributing slaves and cattle amongst the PDF [Popular Defense Forces]. This meant that he was away from home a lot. Musa took me to his home in Gos. I had to do housework for his wife. She is an Arab woman named Howah. She is a very bad woman. She always loved to hit me with a big stick, even when I was ill. She made me sleep outside in the courtyard. There was no shelter over my head. Only when it rained did she let me sleep in the covered cattle pen. Sometimes Musa would come to me at night, and take me to the cattle pen for sex. Whenever Howah discovered that her husband was missing at night, she would give me a good beating on the next day because her husband had come to me and not to her.

I had Musa's baby. He is now seven months old. Musa called him Ahmed, but I call him Thiop. Musa called me Howah, so he had two Howahs. The worst part about being with Musa and Howah were their threats to kill me. Whenever they told me to get water from a far place, or do some other hard labor, they would say that they would cut my throat if I didn't obey. Musa would threaten me like this when he wanted to have sex with me. My sister's throat was cut by her master. Howah's children told me they saw her body when they were going to the well. They said she had tried to escape, but was caught. (iAbolish, 1999)

Testimonies from women demonstrate that the violence does not necessarily stop once the conflict is over. After being "used" as sexual objects, many women cannot return home to their communities or they are ostracized by their families, husbands, and children. Survival after the conflict can be just as devastating as survival during it.

In some countries, girls and women are forced into sexual servitude or prostitution as a result of an obligation to a temple, priest, shrine, or goddess. The *devadasi* in India and "fetish" slaves in western Africa are the most prominent examples of the kinds of ritualized sexual slavery that girls endure, sometimes for a lifetime. An estimated 15,000 girls have been promised to the *devadasi* system in India, and there may be as many as 10,000 girls in western Africa who have been promised for sexual slavery to priests who run religious shrines. Chapter 5 examines these kinds of ritualized enslavement in more detail.

CONCLUSION

Although 105 countries have ratified the Rome Statute of the International Criminal Court, defining crimes against humanity (Article 7) as including "enslavement," "sexual slavery," "enforced prostitution," and "any other form of sexual violence of comparable gravity" (International Criminal Court, 2007), there is a good deal of work left to be done to ensure that the conditions leading to women's sexual enslavement are eradicated. The long history of violence and exploitation that has produced sexual slavery requires a multidimensional and transnational analysis to examine not only the conditions that lead to sexual slavery but the beliefs and values that support it. Sexual slavery is found on every continent, in a variety of contexts, which makes its elimination seem like an impossible task. Chapter 8 outlines many attempts to address the problem, but it will take not only an organized global effort but a universal paradigm shift addressing the gender inequities that justify sexual slavery.

2

Conditions Supporting Sexual Slavery

In this chapter the conditions that allow sexual slavery to flourish will be discussed, including social conditions, immigration status, regional conflicts and wars, political realities, and economic developments. Although these issues exist in many areas of the world, certain countries and regions will be highlighted in this chapter, including Laos, Sudan, Kosovo, the United States of America, China, Mexico, Korea, Japan, the European Union, Russia, the United Arab Emirates, India, the Democratic Republic of Congo, Uganda, Algeria, the Ukraine, and Bosnia. The unifying elements that support sexual slavery and trafficking of girls and women in these countries are generally the devaluation of females, patriarchal political systems, and political instability.

Inez (United States)

Before I came to the United States, I lived in a small town near Veracruz, Mexico. I helped support my family by working in the fields, harvesting lemons. Although I did not mind the work, I wished I could earn more money to help my family. Sometime in 1997, a woman named Maria Elena approached me and told me about opportunities for work in the United States. She told me she had worked there at a restaurant and had made good money. When I told my mother about the offer, she was skeptical. Since I was interested in helping my family out, I decided to learn more about this opportunity. Maria Elena set up a meeting with two men named Abel Cadena-Sosa and Patricio Sosa. At the meeting, the men confirmed that they had job openings for women like myself in American restaurants. They told me that they would take care of my immigration papers, and that I would be free to change jobs if I did not like working at the restaurants.

I decided to accept the offer. In 1997, I was brought into the United States through Brownsville, Texas. Maria Elena traveled with me. We were both transported to Houston, Texas, where a man named Rogerio Cadena picked us up and took us to a trailer in Avon Park, Florida. In Avon Park, I met a girl named Sue who lived in the trailer. She asked me if I knew why I had come to Avon Park. I said I was going to work in a restaurant. She told me that I was actually going to be selling my body to men. I looked at Maria Elena in utter horror, but she did not appear surprised. Maria Elena admitted that she had already worked in trailer brothels in the past. She said it would not do anybody any good to complain. I was going to have to do the work anyway, since I had a smuggling debt to pay off. Maria Elena also warned me, "If you escape, Abel Cadena will go after your family because you owe him money." Some of the other girls in the house also warned me that if I tried to escape, the men would find me and beat me up or abuse me. Rogerio Cadena said I had no place to run anyway, because my family was very far away and each trailer was located in a very isolated area. Rogerio then bought some tight clothes for me to wear when I worked and I was subsequently transported to a trailer in Ft. Pierce, Florida. A man named Jose Cuevas-Ataxca (known as "Lupito") told me he was in charge of selling "tickets" to customers so they could go into the sitting room and pick a girl to have sexual relations with. I learned that the tickets were condoms. I was told that each customer would pay around $22, and that, in turn, each girl would be paid about $3 per customer. The rest of the money would go to pay our smuggling fee, our rent, and water. I also learned that every 15 days, I would be transported to a different trailer to keep working. I did not understand what happened to me. There was no way out. I began "working" in the trailers. The work was demeaning and frightening. I never had a moment's rest. On the weekends, I would often have to see around 32 or 34 men, for $15 each. I would get myself drunk before the men arrived, so that I could stand the work. At the end of the shift, I would fill a bathtub with hot water and lay in it, drinking and crying. I would smoke one cigarette after another, and then go to bed drunk because it was the only way I could fall asleep.

—Inez, trafficked in the United States, originally from Mexico.
(Polaris Project, n.d., Inez)

OVERVIEW

Sexual slavery and its varying manifestations (forced marriage, sexual servitude, and sexual trafficking of girls and women) are all driven by social, cultural, political, and economic factors. The primary drivers differ depending on the specific situation, but education, religion, cultural values, family structure, socioeconomic status, traditional beliefs, myths, geography, economics, employment status, discrimination, patriarchal government policies, criminal statutes, political unrest, and natural disasters all affect sexual slavery and trafficking of women and girls. While these influences may operate as individual forces, they often combine to support a cultural ideology that perpetuates the violence and suppresses the forces that may oppose it. There is little debate that a belief in male superiority and the cultural male dominance that stems from it are at the core of the violence perpetrated against women worldwide (Parrot & Cummings, 2006, p. 23).

Many countries in which women are entrapped by sexual slavery experience political, social, and/or economic instability that often results in significantly high rates of unemployment. Unemployed women often become desperate and fall prey to criminals who promise fictitious jobs in other countries, which actually turn into sexual slavery. Trafficking victims are often subjected to conditions tantamount to sexual slavery, often resulting in serious physical abuse (Human Rights Watch, 1995b). La Strada International, the European Network against Trafficking Human Beings (2007), reports that increasingly restrictive immigration policies have made it more difficult for women to migrate to find work through legal channels, so they often rely on unscrupulous or illegal means to travel in order to make money to support themselves or their families. The lack of legal protection with regard to their migration puts women at risk of abuse or falling prey to traffickers. This chapter will examine in more detail some of the underlying factors that create an environment in which sexual slavery is supported.

SOCIAL CONDITIONS

As global stability fluctuates, changing family conditions appear to increase women's vulnerability. Political and social upheaval, changing environmental conditions, and exposure to changes in family roles may affect women's safety and standing in the home, aside from any preexisting culturally sanctioned practices.

The context in which women and girls are devalued as human beings is closely connected to changes within social, economic, and personal realms. These attitudes change as world circumstances change (Parrot & Cummings, 2006).

Because of the one-child policy in China, young women are sometimes kidnapped, trafficked, and sold into sexual slavery as "brides," being transported from one region of the vast country to another, as a result of the tremendous gender imbalance. The serious shortage of brides in China has created a market for women of marriageable age (Kurlantzick, 2007; Rosenthal, 2001).

Women and girls often end up as sex slaves or trafficked because they are socially disenfranchised, as in the case of homeless people or runaways.

Shahnara (United Arab Emirates)

I was twelve when my mother died. My father and my uncle had been using drugs for many years. Soon my father was imprisoned, I do not know for what offense. My uncle sold everything in our house to buy drugs. When I was 13 he forced me out to the street. I was living in the streets, sleeping under benches in the park. He told me to sell myself if I was not able to find money in another way. I went to the police and they sent me to Vartashen orphanage. Once my classmate told me that there was a woman in her neighbourhood helping young pretty girls to go to Germany to work for a fashion magazine. I could not believe it. I was so happy. Later the woman told me that after she had arranged documents for me and other persons. We would all travel together to Germany. After a short while the papers were ready and we could to start off. There were 14 of us, girls of different ages between 13 and 23. We went by taxi to Tbilisi, from there we travelled to Moscow and from Moscow to Dubai, as we found out later. The woman who had recruited me had 27 children employed mostly from orphanages, or from the streets. She deals in this business for 12 years already.

The hell I lived through at home continued in Dubai. They placed us in a hotel. They had special interest in young virgins. They were selling them at enormous prices to rich Arab sheikhs for one night, after which they were working with clients like other ordinary girls. We received only a fraction of what the sheikhs gave to the pimp. In some cases the girls received some special presents from the sheikhs.

My friend who was 13 was taken to a wealthy man. In the end the man asked her what she wanted from him as a present. The girl asked for two sacks of flour. Even the money given to the girls as a gift was confiscated by the pimps.

Two days later they took us to a night-club and explained the nature of our work and the amount that we should pay them every day. They explained that they had paid a lot of money for our passports and travel, in total US$6,000 for permission to fly and tickets. They were also paying for our room and food. Almost all the children were crying. They could not understand what was expected from them and how they were going to do it. The Arab partner of our pimp was getting angry when he was not getting the amount of money they were expecting us to provide. He was beating children with a belt and was very violent. I was also crying at the very beginning, but what could I do? Sometimes there were rich businessmen who hired us every time they came to Dubai. I was very happy when one businessman called me and said he was coming to Dubai. He spent his time only with me. He rented a room for me where I stayed and sometimes we went shopping together. The pimp also placed children with us when they were not able to earn enough money and requested the businessman to pay for them too, although at somewhat cheaper price.
                            —Shahnara, trafficked in UAE, originally from Armenia.
                                            (Polaris Project, n.d., *Shahnara*)

These young women often have no housing, no income, and no social support network, and their families do not know if they have been kidnapped or if they left of their own volition. In 2003, John Jamelske pled guilty to abducting and enslaving girls (some of whom were runaways) in Syracuse, New York, over a 15-year period, during which he imprisoned them in an underground bunker at his home for his sexual satisfaction (Fried, 2004). One of his victims was only 13 years old when he took her, and he held his victims for up to two years at a time. He purposely targeted runaways who were socially and economically disenfranchised and appeared to be "easy" targets for predators looking for sex slaves (Associated Press, 2003).

Sexual slavery is one result of migration gone wrong, poverty, and/or political and social instability (Feingold, 2005). Young women from medium-sized towns are more likely than girls from small villages (where much of the population lives below the poverty line, frequently as a result of political instability after war or civil unrest) to voluntarily move to cities in search of a "better life." Many victims are forced into sexual slavery within the same social class or country, although much trafficking takes place between poorer source countries and richer destination countries (Feingold, 2005).

Seema (India)

Seema had left the poverty of her home village to work in Kathmandu. She was barely twelve when a smooth-talking flesh trader lured her to Bombay with talk of a better job. She hoped to become a film star. Instead she was sold into a brothel. At first she resisted, screaming, crying and fighting off prospective customers, but the madam who ran the brothel would have none of it. She sent in a muscled toughie to hold the girl down while an old man raped her. The pain was so intense that Seema lost consciousness and had to be hospitalised for a week. After that it was back to the brothel where the other child prostitutes told her she could not win this battle. But Seema's spirit was not broken. Nine months later she escaped from the brothel and boarded a train, hoping to eventually get back home. A soft-spoken lady promised help. She lured the young girl to Calcutta and sold her. Seema had only escaped from one brothel into another. Now Seema appears resigned to her fate. She hits the streets of central Calcutta as soon as it gets dark and stands near a lamp-post soliciting customers. Her parents in Nepal have no idea where their daughter is. She does not have the courage to tell them, and anyway, they probably think she is dead. It is better that way.

—Seema, trafficked in India, originally from Nepal.
(Polaris Project, n.d., *Seema*)

Communities that maintain social norms in which women are subjugated and discriminated against provide the foundation for the commodification of females. Education, religion, cultural values, and policies establish normative ideologies through which members of a community are viewed, and which determine how they are treated. These practices become entrenched in a community (Parrot & Cummings, 2006).

Kala (India)

Kala grew up in West Bengal, and was married off by her family at the age of 12. Her new husband was twice her age. Within weeks she ran away to live with a great aunt, seeking refuge from her husband's sexual violence. She was forcibly returned to her husband, and suffered the drudgery of domestic servitude by day and sexual torture by night. Kala ran away again, six months pregnant, and found a "Good Samaritan" who sold her into prostitution for less than 25 US Dollars. Her new madam forced her to have an abortion and to serve customers at the brothel within days. Kala was rescued from the brothel and is now receiving care from an NGO.

—Kala, trafficked in India, originally from India.
(Polaris Project, n.d., *Kala*)

IMMIGRATION STATUS

Women frequently leave their home countries illegally to avoid religious, social, or political persecution or to find employment. Political refugees often end up in areas where, although they are accomplished and were gainfully employed in their native countries, they are not able to make a living because their degrees and/or licenses are not honored or recognized and they do not speak the language.

Patricia (China)

From her home in an impoverished village in rural Bolivia, the prospect of quick riches as an escort girl proved impossible to resist for 23-year-old Patricia Suarez. A neighbor working for a Hong Kong gang suggested the trip, promising the young mother an escape from part-time work as a domestic servant that paid only US $50 (HK $387) a week. Desperate for money, the former university student left her two-month old baby with her mother and six brothers and sisters—unaware that she was heading for a nightmare trapped in a sleazy underworld. Ms. Suarez speaks no English or Chinese. When she landed at Kai Tak airport last May she was met by another Bolivian woman who whisked her to a flat run by her pimp, known as Jacky. From there she was sent out to clients who had contacted the escort agency through adverts in pornographic magazines. At one point she became pregnant and an abortion was arranged by the gang.

> —Patricia, trafficked in China, originally from Bolivia.
> (Polaris Project, n.d., *Patricia*)

Women may seek employment through or with unscrupulous sources who trick them into situations that result in trafficking.

Tatyana (United Arab Emirates)

Tatyana is 20 years old. She is from a small town in Lugansk Oblast in eastern Ukraine. It was impossible for her to get a job there, because most industrial facilities in town were closed. A friend of her mother proposed that she take a housemaid job for a rich family in the United Arab Emirates. She was promised a $4,000 monthly income there, while at home she could not find a job that paid even a tiny fraction of that amount. However, when she arrived in the UAE, she was stripped of her passport, sold to a brothel and forced to receive clients in order to pay the fees she supposedly owed to the owner, who bought her for $7,000.

> —Tatyana, trafficked in the United Arab Emirates, originally from Ukraine.
> (Polaris Project, n.d., *Tatyana*)

If a woman is in a country illegally, she has few, if any, rights or protections. Women in these circumstances are especially vulnerable to traffickers because they are afraid to go to the police for fear of deportation or imprisonment because they have violated immigration laws.

According to Dr. Schurman-Kauflin of the Violent Crimes Institute, "Women and girls are trafficked from many countries in Europe, Asia, Africa, Latin America, and the Middle East" (2006). Mexico is the primary source for young female sex slaves in North America. Young women and girls are abducted, tricked, and sometimes sold by poor Mexican families into a caged life. When highly desired pre-teen girls sneak across the border into the United States, they are often abducted by Los Lenones (pimps) and "broken in." This "breaking in" process involves up to 30 men per day having brutal sex with the girls and women. They are beaten, drugged, and repeatedly raped until they are broken emotionally. The girls are then sold. Puerto Rico is another point of entry, as there are few U.S. border patrol agents on the island. Once girls and women enter Puerto Rico with forged documents, they can enter the U.S. mainland with less difficulty (Schurman-Kauflin, 2006). They are often forced into sexual slavery in the United States.

REGIONAL CONFLICTS/WARS

Reliable official statistics regarding the numbers of girls and women who have suffered sexual violence during war are impossible to obtain due to underreporting as a result of cultural expectations, fear of retaliation, a lack of faith in the criminal justice system, and a lack of resources focused on the issue (Human Rights Watch, 2001a). While women may know their perpetrators, it is rare that they file charges, for fear of reprisals against them and their families. Many of the conditions that lead to sexual slavery in peacetime also apply in war, but during war there are often several conditions in play that exacerbate each other (such as homelessness, poverty, economic instability, lack of resources, lack of police protection, and so forth).

The dehumanization of women during armed conflicts has been recorded throughout history. During World War II, the Japanese government kidnapped many young women, mostly from Korea, and forced them to serve as sex slaves for Japanese troops. These "comfort women" were held against their will for years and forced to sexually "service" many soldiers a day. The underlying theory was that the sexual release provided by the comfort women would enable the soldiers to act honorably in the field. Many of the women forced to serve as comfort women were seen as dispensable, and not deserving of basic human rights, because they were from among the enemy. Other manifestations of sexual slavery during war have been documented in recent armed conflicts including those in Rwanda, Bosnia, Sudan, and the Congo.

Abuk Deng Gau, Girl in Her Mid-Teens (Sudan)

I was captured in my home village Kur Awet near Warawar. It was early in 1997. We were suddenly surrounded by countless horsemen. A lot of my people were shot dead. The attackers who caught me were dressed in military uniforms. They raped me and many other girls. Our village was burned down completely. I lost my parents as well as my four brothers and two sisters in the attack. I don't know whether they are still alive. The attackers killed my uncle Alou Alou Deng right in front of me. We walked for about ten days, I had to carry a heavy load of sorghum grain. They had looted it from our stores. My master was Mahmoud Mahdi. I was mistreated terribly by him. I, together with 15 others, had to stay in an open pen near his house. He lived in Sidam. My master repeatedly raped me. Various other men who came at night also did this to me. (American Antislavery Group, 1999)

Natalia (Congo)

A rebel group in the Democratic Republic of the Congo recruited Natalia when she was 12: "One day, rebels attacked the village where I lived. I hid and watched as they killed my relatives and raped my mother and sisters. I thought if I joined their army, I would be safe. In the army I was trained to use a gun and I performed guard duty. I was often beaten and raped by the other soldiers. One day, a commander wanted me to become his wife, so I tried to escape. They caught me, whipped me and raped me every night for many days. When I was just 14, I had a baby. I don't even know who his father is. I ran away again but I have nowhere to go and no food for the baby. I am afraid to go home."

—Natalia, trafficked in the Democratic Republic of the Congo, originally from the Democratic Republic of the Congo. (Polaris Project, n.d., *Natalia*)

Ethnic cleansing of women occurred during the armed conflict between 1992 and 1995 when thousands of Muslim girls and women were repeatedly raped in detention camps in Bosnia and Herzegovina (Vandeberg, 2002). The motivation for the sexual enslavement of these women was to tarnish the "purity" of the ethnic stock of their offspring. They were raped repeatedly for months until they became pregnant with the offspring of their enemies. Following the conflict, many young girls were reportedly maintained as sex slaves and prostitutes to serve the sexual appetites of male United Nations peacekeepers. In 1995, 50,000 male UN peacekeepers descended upon Bosnia to help stabilize the area, and in some ways made the problems worse for women. Their presence resulted in an expansion of the sex industry. To meet the demand for sex workers, women were trafficked into Bosnia from Moldavia, Romania, and the Ukraine. The soldiers accounted for up to 90 percent of the customers (Wolte, 2004). Most of the local men were Muslim, and thus much less likely to seek the services of sex workers.

Economic instability in Afghanistan, due to war and the loss of males, has left many women unable to provide for their families. Social, religious, and political policies and realities result in women feeling too vulnerable to work outside of the home, and girls from attending school. Warring factions create unsafe streets. Thus, there has been an increase in girls being kidnapped into sexual slavery (McGirk, 2002). In addition the age of arranged marriage for girls in Afghanistan has become increasingly younger since many families have lost their livelihood due to the long years of political conflict. Female children are being offered as wives to much older men in return for monetary compensation in the form of a "bride price." These children often have no say in their future, and often face a lifetime of sexual servitude (UNICEF, 2005b).

During the Ugandan war of the 1990s and the first decade of the twenty-first century, many girls have been abducted in Uganda by the Lord's Resistance Army (LRA), and often forced into sexual slavery as "wives" of the commanders. Girls as young as 14 have been repeatedly raped, and suffered unwanted pregnancies and sometimes sexually transmitted diseases, including HIV/AIDS, through this sexual slavery (Wescott, 2003).

Angela (Uganda)

Angela was ten when she was abducted by the LRA. At age fifteen, she was forced to become a "wife" to an LRA commander. She gave birth to two children in the bush. The first, a boy, she named Komakech, which means, "I am unfortunate." The second, a girl, she named Can-Oroma, meaning "I have suffered a lot." (Human Rights Watch, 2003b)

In Algeria, women were forced into sexual slavery during a conflict that began in 1992, when the government suspended elections, and lasted more than a decade. The Islamists were expected to win. In response, armed Islamist forced women into sexual slavery in what were termed "temporary marriages" and killed women who opposed them (Human Rights Watch, 2001c).

POLITICAL INSTABILITY

Political instability creates conditions in which women's safety within communities is jeopardized because basic physical needs (such as those for food, water, and heat) and social needs (for education, communication, and so forth) are unmet. In these circumstances, women are sometimes compelled to venture into dangerous areas to provide for themselves and their children. For example, there have been reports of women and girls in Sudan who have been raped or kidnapped for sexual slavery while they were living in refugee camps. When women venture outside the camps to get firewood in order to boil water and thus make it drinkable, or to gather food, they are attacked (Human Rights Watch, 2005).

Child sex slavery involving international peacekeepers in southern Sudan has also been documented. Both peacekeeping personnel and civilian staff members have reportedly picked up young children and forced them to have sex (Walsh & Byrne, 2002). The UN has faced several scandals involving its troops in recent years, including child sexual abuse in the Congo and prostitution trafficking in Kosovo (BBC, 2006). Children as young as 11 have been subjected to rape and prostitution by UN peacekeepers in Haiti and Liberia, where peacekeepers have given food to teenagers in refugee camps in return for sex. UN staff have also been documented to have systematically raped women in Sierra Leone (Butcher, 2003).

Another example of the dire consequences for women as a result of political instability occurred in Afghanistan in 1999, when the Taliban set fire to homes in rural areas and kidnapped women. The Taliban invaded with guns and torches. Women ran out of the burning buildings without having time to put on their burqas, and the Taliban fighters were able to see their faces. The Taliban selected those who were beautiful, and took away more than 600 women in trucks and buses. Many of the women most likely ended up in Pakistan, sold to brothels or kept as sex slaves. These abductions are considered such a great dishonor that the victims' families almost never mention them (McGirk, 2002).

In southeastern Afghanistan, UN officials reported cases of kidnappings, rape, and forced marriages of girls and women to armed combatants. Soldiers would storm into houses, pick the girls and women they desired, and take them to be forcibly married. Families had to pay large sums of money to get their daughters back (Human Rights Watch, 2003c).

Political instability often follows war. This was the case in Rwanda, resulting in such difficult living conditions that some women are willing to take any opportunity to leave and start a new life. In one such case, a woman identified as Penny was trafficked from Rwanda to the United Kingdom, where she was kept as a sex slave for her trafficker for several weeks and then also forced to have sex with other men. She was told that she could have her freedom once she paid back the debt she had accrued as a result of her trip to the UK ($1,968 or 1,347 euros) (Holmes, 2008).

I. (Sierra Leone)

I. describes the 1995 rebel attack on her village when she was 13. She has the flat manner and voice of one who is severely depressed. Just once, tears slide down her cheeks, but she appears not to notice them. "It was late afternoon, I was washing dishes at the river with six other girls. We tried to run, but they caught us. Three girls resisted. To punish them, the rebels cut off their ears. They knifed out their eyes. Then they killed them. I was so afraid, I couldn't move. They said if we struggled, they would kill us too. They raped us. They held me down. It was the first time I had sex." Over the next four days, the tall, graceful girl, now 16, was gang-raped repeatedly by rebel soldiers. It was two weeks before she could walk again. Later, at the rebel base, the assaults went on. "Each night we were tied by the ankles to the girl next to us. The rebels had sex with us in the presence of everyone. It was always different men. Every time, they hurt me. If I cried, they beat me. I prayed all the time I would not become pregnant." (Polaris Project, n.d., I)

ECONOMIC INSTABILITY

Many economically unstable nations become source countries for the trafficking of women, sexual debt bondage, or prostitution. Human trafficking and the sexual enslavement of women for sexual exploitation are highly lucrative, second only to drug trafficking (Pallen, 2003). An estimated 700,000 women are trafficked each year for sexual purposes, and about a quarter of them come from eastern European countries in which there is political and economic instability (United Nations Development Programme [UNDP], 2005). Organized crime has been linked to the trafficking of girls and women because it is such a lucrative enterprise with few serious consequences (Miller, 2006).

When social services fail to provide necessary programs and resources, and governments fall, leaving citizens without economic or social safety nets, women are disproportionately affected by the instability and poverty that ensues. Rises in cost of living, declines in real wages, cuts in public spending, the erosion of social benefits, and the privatization of social services all contribute to women's need to seek alternate ways of feeding and supporting themselves and their children (UNDP, 2005).

Elena (Montenegro)

Elena was a naive 19-year-old when a man started flirting with her in the market place of her home town in Moldova. She and her mother were near destitute after her father had left home and she believed the handsome stranger when he offered her a job as a waitress at a coastal resort in Montenegro. Instead, she was taken to the Serbian town of Novi Sad, where she was drugged, beaten and repeatedly raped.

After a couple of weeks of relentless abuse, stupefied by drink and drugs, she was taken to northern Montenegro, where she was sold as a sex slave. (Polaris Project, n.d., *Elena*)

After the fall of the Soviet Union, the sexually charged atmosphere and the economic instability, combined with a new independence, a lack of international travel experience, and a desire for adventure, made many women (especially from Russia and the Ukraine) targets for traffickers (Schuckman, 2006). Low wages, the declining value of local currencies, porous borders, and ambiguous visa categories all helped to make border guards amenable to bribery, providing an easy way to transport women into neighboring countries (Schuckman, 2006). But women were not only kidnapped or taken against their will. Unwittingly, they often signed fraudulent contracts to become mail order brides, nannies, or waitresses, for example, in the West. Only when they reached their destinations did they discover that they had been sold into sexual slavery or debt bondage.

Another economic change that led to an increase in sexual slavery occurred in Laos over the past decade (United Nations, 2006). The U.S. government spearheaded a campaign, with the support of the European Union, to eliminate the opium poppy trade there. When international forces went to work to reduce the production and sale of poppies in rural villages across the mountains of northern Laos, much of the income generated by poppy sales, which had supported the villages, dried up. The campaign almost eliminated the opium poppy trade across the mountains of northern Laos. As a result of the eradication of poppy production, an estimated 65,000 hill tribe people became impoverished or displaced, resulting in food shortages, malaria, and other social and medical problems (Fawthrop, 2005). Furthermore, since there were no other easily obtainable sources of income, many girls were either trafficked or left the village in search of employment and then fell victim to unsafe migration practices that resulted in sexual slavery and prostitution (Fawthrop, 2005).

CONCLUSION

One of the realities for girls and women who have been trafficked into sexual slavery is that if they try to escape or succeed in escaping, their families are often at risk. Because the traffickers often know where the sex slaves came from, the women are often told that their younger sisters will be taken to replace them if they escape, or their family members will be killed. In addition, they are told that there will be retaliation against their family members if they ever testify against the traffickers. These threats often prevent the women from trying to escape, or from providing testimony.

Maria (Mexico)

The Bosses carried weapons. They scared me. The brothels were often in isolated areas. I never knew where I was. It was all so strange to me. We were not allowed to go outside of the brothels. I knew if I tried to escape I would not get far because everything was so unfamiliar. The Bosses told me that if I escaped, INS (United States Immigration and Naturalization Service) would catch me, beat me and tie me up. This frightened me. I did know of one girl who escaped. The Bosses searched for her and said they were going to get the money she owed them from her family. They said they would get their money one way or another. I know of another girl that escaped and was hunted down. The Bosses found her and beat her severely. The Bosses would show the girl that they meant business by beating and raping her brutally. All I could do is stand there and watch. I was too afraid to try to escape. I also did not want my family put in danger. I was enslaved for several months, other women were enslaved for up to a year. Our enslavement finally ended when the INS, FBI, and local law enforcement raided the brothels and rescued us. We weren't sure what was happening on the day of the raids. Our captors had told us over and over never to tell the police of our conditions. They told us that if we told we would find ourselves in prison for the rest of our lives. They told us that the INS would rape us and kill us. But we learned to trust the INS and FBI and assisted them in the prosecution of our enslavers. Unfortunately, this was difficult. After the INS and FBI freed us from the brothels we were put in a detention center for many months. Our captors were correct. We thought we would be imprisoned for the rest of our lives. Later, our attorneys were able to get us released to a women's domestic violence center where we received comprehensive medical attention, including gynecological exams, and mental health counseling. Thanks to the United States government some of our captors were brought to justice and were sent to prison. Unfortunately, not all. Some of them are living in Mexico in our hometown of Veracruz. They have threatened some of our families. They have even threatened to bring our younger sisters to the United States and force them to work in brothels as well.

—Maria, trafficked in Florida, originally from Mexico; Testimony before U.S.
Senate Foreign Relations Committee, 2000.
(Polaris Project, n.d., *Maria*)

Governments and the international community need to react more quickly and competently to stabilize regions in political turmoil. Peacekeeping forces must be trained to work toward eliminating problems instead of exacerbating them. Source countries, transit countries, and destination countries all experience circumstances and issues that contribute to these problems. Understanding the reality of the political issues, sociocultural circumstances, and factors driving these countries' contributions to the problems will lead to more effective prevention strategies and legislative efforts.

Nongovernmental organizations (NGOs), national governments, and the international community each have a critical role in eliminating sexual slavery. Successful approaches to eliminating sexual slavery must acknowledge the realities of the factors that created the environment in which the sexual slavery is condoned. Effective approaches must be multidimensional.

No single strategy, by itself, will eliminate sexual slavery and trafficking of girls and women. Removing migration restrictions, reducing poverty, eliminating discrimination, and supporting sustainable development are all pieces of a very complex solution (UNDP, 2005). Improving or reversing the social, political, and economic conditions that support sexual slavery and trafficking is critical, but it is not enough. Control measures, effective legislation, and appropriate legal approaches are also necessary. All of these measures need to take into consideration the sociocultural realities of specific countries. There are effective prevention models in place in some parts of the world, and they will be discussed in chapter 8. Some components of those programs may be effective in other places, or could be modified to meet the needs of different regions and populations.

More funding is necessary to enable social service agencies to provide the programs and resources that are needed to keep women from being trapped in trafficking and sexual slavery. There must also be funding for programs that rescue sex slaves or buy women and girls out of their contracts.

More research funding must be allocated and more research needs to be conducted to determine the incidence, prevalence, and circumstances of trafficking and sexual slavery in the sociocultural context of the various regions of the world.

Part II
Types of Sexual Slavery

3

Trafficking

This chapter highlights sexual slavery as one aspect of human trafficking. An extensive literature on the many varieties of trafficking is available for those seeking a more in-depth understanding of the issue and its worldwide impact.

OVERVIEW

According to the June 2005 *Trafficking in Persons Report* by the U.S. Department of State (2006), trafficking is a modern form of slavery that threatens the lives of millions of women and children. The specific numbers of women trafficked internationally are difficult to estimate because "the trade is secretive, the women are silenced, the traffickers are dangerous and not many agencies are counting" (Hughes, 2000a, p. 627). Furthermore, definitions of trafficked persons vary from country to country and few governments collect data that distinguishes between "trafficking, smuggling and illegal migration" (Gozdiak & Collett, 2005). For example, some reports include statistics that combine undocumented noncitizens crossing national borders with women who are moved for the sole purpose of sexual slavery.

Today, the most profitable aspect of trafficking involves the sexual slavery of millions of women and girls. One report's best estimate is that as many as 800,000 individuals are trafficked internationally each year (Lederer, 2007), and approximately 80 percent are women and girls with the vast majority of these females trafficked into commercial sexual exploitation. The term "trafficking" does not adequately describe its central feature: the denial of freedom to an individual. The term implies some kind of movement rather than the loss of liberty and agency for the women used for sexual exploitation (Chuang, 2005). The unpunished violence, probability of death, loss of freedom of movement, and transfer between owners/masters for money or goods without informed consent certainly meet the criteria for slavery (Kempadoo & Doezema, 1998). Quite simply, trafficking turns human beings into commodities.

The sexual exploitation and slavery often begin before there is actual trafficking involved as women are coerced into sex industries in their home countries before then being trafficked internationally.

Anna (Poland)

When Anna was 17 years old, she answered an advertisement in her home town of Szecin, Poland, and took a domestic job at the cottage of an acquaintance, Piotr Ruso. There she met Dzem, a Turk, and his Polish girlfriend, Olympia, who tempted her away with the offer of similar work at their home in Berlin. When the three arrived in Berlin, Dzem and Olympia said they were going to visit a friend and told Anna to put on an elegant dress and some make-up. They drove her to an old house and Dzem announced that this was to be Anna's first house-visit as a prostitute.

Shocked and dumbfounded, Anna thought of running away, but the door was locked behind her and she was left with a man of about 60, who stank and seemed quite drunk. Frightened, she submitted to a 90-minute sex ordeal, until Dzem and Olympia came back to pick her up.

Anna protested vehemently that she wanted to return home, but the couple beat her severely and took away her identity card. Kept under constant guard and terrified of further violence, she was forced to prostitute herself, serving five or six clients per night. Dzem and Olympia sold Anna and eventually she ended up in a Swiss brothel near Zurich. A client she confided in took pity on her and alerted the police, who raided the brothel and arrested the owners. After a month of police interrogation, she was deported back to Poland. Police later arrested Piotr Ruso, suspected of having trafficked at least 71 Polish women to agencies abroad. (United Nations, 2000b, February)

The reasons for trafficking are solely economic. Trafficking is a by-product of "supply and demand" where devalued, marginalized women and girls are used for profit by men and for men. "With the exception of the dynamic of former victims becoming recruiters, . . . women do not traffic themselves or organize themselves en masse to travel internationally to enter prostitution. Women do not voluntarily put themselves in situations where they are exploited, beaten, raped and enslaved" (Hughes, 2000a, p. 644).

Penny, from Rwanda, wanted to emigrate but did not understand the conditions of her escape. She was told she would be provided with employment and a place to live.

"I ended up going with him to his place," she said. "I stayed with him that day. After four days he came on to me and started demanding sex. I refused. I didn't think that was the kind of deal I had with him. He forced himself on me, started raping me. From that day, for about two weeks, it would just be daily." Soon he brought men with him and Penny was forced to have sex with them too. (Holmes, 2008)

It is the most vulnerable women in society who get trapped into being trafficked and forced into sexual slavery. They are exploited "because they can be" (Brown, 2001, p. 3). While transnational attempts to stem the tide of trafficking are often highlighted in the media, the reality is that the crime thrives on conditions that leave women in the lowest ranks of society, with the least opportunity for social mobility.

The United States is a key destination country for sex traffickers. San Francisco in particular is a highly valued destination city for international sex traffickers due to its coastal location, its large immigrant population, its tradition of arresting prostitutes instead of the pimps or the "johns" who frequent massage parlors and other commercial sex trade institutions, and its tolerant sexual atmosphere. The majority of women trafficked into San Francisco are from Southeast Asia, the former Soviet Union, and South America. Many women are also smuggled into the United States from Mexico and then moved domestically to various states.

Maria (Mexico)

Once over the border, I was kept at a safe house. Then, I was transported to Florida. Once in Florida, Abel Cadena, one of the ring leaders, told me I would be working at a brothel as a prostitute. I told him he was mistaken and that I was going to be working in a restaurant not a brothel. He then ordered me to work in a brothel. He said I owed him a smuggling debt of approximately $2200 and the sooner I paid it off the sooner I could leave. I was eighteen years old and had never been far from home and had no money or way to get home.

Next, I was given tight clothes to wear and was told what I must do. There would be armed men selling tickets to customers in the trailer. Tickets were condoms. Each ticket would be sold for $22 to $25 each. The client would then point at the girl he wanted and the girl would take him to one of the bedrooms. At the end of the night, I turned in the condom wrappers. Each wrapper represented a supposed deduction to my smuggling fee. We tried to keep our own records, but the Bosses would destroy them. We were never sure what we owed.

There were up to four girls kept at each brothel. We were constantly guarded and abused. If anyone refused to be with a customer, we were beaten. If we adamantly refused, the Bosses would show us a lesson by raping us brutally. They told us if we refused, again it would be even worse the next time. We were transported every fifteen days to another trailer in a nearby city. This was to give the customers a variety of girls and so we never knew where we were in case we tried to escape. I could not believe this was happening to me.

We worked six days a week and twelve-hour days. We mostly had to serve 32–35 clients a day. Weekends were worse. Our bodies were utterly sore and swollen. The bosses did not care. We worked no matter what. This included during menstruation. Clients would become enraged if they found out. The Bosses instructed us to place a piece of clothing over the lamps to darken the room. This, however, did not protect us from client beatings. Also, at the end of the night our work did not end. It was now the Bosses' turn with us. (Polaris Project, n.d. *Maria*)

The recent reports on trafficking of women and girls for sexual exploitation speculate that the problem is on the increase. One half a million central and eastern European women are estimated to be living in the European Union as prostitutes (Hughes, 2000a), many having been trafficked to their present locations, and in the Netherlands, non-European women reportedly comprise 30–60 percent of the prostituted women.

Mass migration due to economic destabilization in many countries contributes to the trafficking trade. Because women are often forced to migrate from rural towns to cities in order to survive, traffickers have an endless supply of vulnerable women and girls. In addition, certain countries, such as those in the European Union, are relaxing or decreasing border security. Traffickers are finding alternate routes into countries by land, sea, or air. They are increasingly able to deceive women into believing jobs in other countries will not be sex-industry related. In short, the trafficking of women for purposes of sexual exploitation has become easier for those intent on profiting from women's bodies.

Eleni (Bosnia)

Eleni, 25, didn't know the friend who wrote inviting her to work as a waitress was now a prostitute. Once at the Bosnian restaurant her new owner told her she had been bought for 900 DEM and had to repay him by having sex with his customers. When she refused she was beaten until she couldn't walk for days but was still forced to have sex. She said: "My owner told me 'You are lying down anyway so you can still work for me.'" After two months she was sold on to a man who held a pistol to her head when she threatened to go to police. Eleni was moved to a remote house after corrupt police tipped off her owner that Interpol was looking for her. He raped her several times then passed her to a third owner as she had become "too dangerous." She said: "I was a slave. I was no more than a piece of meat." She fled one night and made it to police. Amna Saric, who is now protecting the girls, said: "These are just two of thousands being lured and tricked into prostitution." (Polaris Project, n.d., *Eleni*)

The United Nations has analyzed the regional flow of trafficking from countries of origin to destination countries and compiled listings that range from very high to very low reported incidence.

The UN list includes 127 origin countries that provide trafficked humans to 137 countries. Examples of transit countries (those that facilitate the movement and can be destination countries) that rated high or very high on the UN list included Albania, Poland, Thailand, Bulgaria, Italy, Greece, Bosnia/Herzegovina, Ukraine, and Myanmar. Examples of destination countries that rated high or very high included the United States, Israel, China, France, India, Saudi Arabia, and Canada. The examples named here give a picture of the broad sweep of trafficking worldwide (United Nations, 2006).

Trafficking of women and girls in Africa provides a good example of the transnational nature of this problem. Trafficking into and out of the continent has increased dramatically with women often trafficked from sub-Saharan Africa to other African nations. However, women are also trafficked out of the region to European countries and the Middle East. Women from conflict areas such as Sierra Leone are forced into prostitution where reports of young girls being kidnapped from conflict areas and sold to serve as sex slaves either to rebel commanders or to wealthy men in other countries have surfaced. It has been reported that young girls from Kenya are trafficked out to Europe by Japanese organized crime groups, while girls from India and South Asia are trafficked into Kenya for the local sex industry (Adepoju, 2005).

The sex industry, fueled by transnational trafficking, encompasses many "services": strippers, go-go dancers, erotic dancers, street walkers, massage parlors, escort services, sex tourism, and brothels. The industry forces young girls to stay in it against their will, as they are subjected to extreme forms of violence without recourse, either from those who patronize them or those for whom they work. They may be trafficked across borders, with no passport or knowledge of the local language and law. They are often forced to work long hours in inhumane conditions (with no food, water, light, or fresh air) for the sole purpose of financial gain for those who control them. Once in the "receiving" country, trafficked women may be subject to arrest as criminals or illegal immigrants.

Jo (Thailand)

Jo, who traveled to Japan in 1990 at age twenty-three after seven years of sex work in Thailand, confided, "I never knew the law in Japan or even in Thailand. When I arrived in Japan I knew that I had come illegally, so I was afraid of being arrested. They [her bosses at the snack bar] said that if you meet police or immigration officers you have to run away from them. Everybody said that we stayed illegally, but nobody explained what was legal or illegal." (Human Rights Watch, 2000)

FROM HUMANS TO COMMODITIES

Large-scale commercial trafficking in Asia began with Chinese women being sold to brothels in Malaysia, Singapore, and Thailand to satisfy male Chinese migrant workers. In the 1880s, poor Japanese girls known as *karayuki san* were exported to Southeast Asia for exploitation. Asia's sex industry grew due to economic development, which started with colonialism and increased especially after World War II. Now that Japan is the second largest economy in the world, it has reversed the flow and now imports poor women from other countries to satisfy Japanese male clients.

In Japan today, there are brothels euphemistically referred to as "snack bars." Snack bars (often referred to as "snacks") are frequented by the Japanese as places in which to enjoy conversation with others and relax. There are many different types of snack bars, and they may all appear similar to an outsider. However, "a *baishun*—or prostitution—snack bar is one which involves sexual exchanges and is almost exclusively patronized by men" (Human Rights Watch, 2000).

Industrialization in Asia moved more people into cities for work, which allowed men making more money to buy women on a whim. Military prostitution flourished as brothels took root outside of forts and military bases. During the Korean and Vietnam wars, American troops headed to Thailand for R & R (Rest and

Relaxation: a common military term) or what the soldiers referred to as I and I (Intercourse and Intoxication) (Brown, 2001, p. 3).

Reports from Thailand describe inhumane conditions for girls trafficked into the sex industry. Girls and women trafficked to Thailand may end up in brothels "surrounded by a wall with iron gates meeting the street. Within the wall is a dusty yard, a concrete picnic table and the ubiquitous spirit house, a small shrine that stands outside all Thai buildings. A low door leads into a windowless concrete room that is thick with the smell of cigarettes, stale beer, vomit and sweat. This is the 'selection' room (hong du). On the side of the room are stained and collapsing tables and booths; on the other side is a narrow elevated platform with a bench that runs the length of the room. Spotlights pick out this bench and at night the girls and women sit here under the glare while the men at the tables drink and choose the one they want" (Bales, 2004, pp. 34–35).

The dissolution of many communist cultures in eastern Europe has created organized crime organizations that traffic women from Russia, Poland, the Ukraine, Bulgaria, the former Yugoslavia, and the Czech and Slovak Republics (Jeffreys, 1999). Because Russian women are so prevalent in some countries (for example, Israel and Turkey), the prostitutes there are called "Natashas" (Hughes, 2000). Because of Russia's economic breakdown, desperate Russian women turn to prostitution and the production of graphic pornography. "Some appear, for instance, on bestiality pornography sites. On one such site, several Russian speaking women are sexually abused in a video entitled Gorilla Wives. The passage describes these women being sexually penetrated by a gorilla and a chimpanzee. The only English word they use is 'daddy,' addressed to the gorilla" (Jeffreys, 1999). Only the most vulnerable and desperate of women can be manipulated, abused, and exploited in this way.

As cited in Corrin (2005), a UNICEF report on trafficking in southeastern Europe explains that

> At the same time, as in other Central and Eastern European countries with economies in transition, the social and political situation of women is deteriorating. Violence against women, the contradiction between their lowly position in the family and their responsibility for the family well being, their lack of influence in public/political life and their exclusion from decision-making processes, are increasing trends. (Corrin, 2005, p. 544)

Today, it is difficult to enforce laws related to trafficking and there are few successes. In 2005, three men were convicted of 27 counts of forcing young women from Mexico to work in brothels in the New York City area. The three men admitted to over a decade's worth of smuggling Mexican women into the United States. They also admitted to using physical brutality, threats, and physical restraint in order to force the women to engage in prostitution. While this was an important breakthrough case, even the United Nations admits that the laws in place are not adequately addressing the size of the problem they were meant to contain (Holmes, 2008).

As the following quote demonstrates, most traffickers operate freely within regions and boundaries, expanding operations when possible:

These are good escorts but if you taking [sic] a playboy scale they are only about 5–7. They are attractive but they are escorts, not models but my bigger concern is logistics of bringing them to Alaska. All of those jobs will pay off only if they get visa. We need to control them. We may be better off controlling models [than] escorts, but escorts are better at sales and communication. I rely on you as far as Alaska market goes. I have seen girls that [are] just about as good as the ones you seen making good money in Atlanta and Mexico. (quoted in Kandathil, 2005)

In April, 2008, Cambodia took a unique approach to stop the trafficking of women. The government suspended marriages between Cambodian women and foreigners in response to a perception of an increase of marriage brokers operating within the country. The ban was a result of an International Organisation for Migration report on the increasing number of poor, uneducated women in brokered marriages to South Korean men. The suspension is temporary until the government can develop a strategic plan to address foreign marriages. Some argue this is a "knee-jerk" reaction to marriages that often provide a more comfortable lifestyle for women than may be available in Cambodia. Others applaud the unusual effort that will help to determine whether brokered marriages are a cover-up for mass sexual exploitation (Expressindia, 2008).

THE EFFECTS OF FORCED PROSTITUTION THROUGH TRAFFICKING

For women and children who are trafficked into the sex industry, there are devastating consequences including lifelong physical and psychological trauma, exposure to diseases including HIV, drug addiction, malnutrition that can lead to physical and emotional damage, and unsanitary and inhumane living conditions.

Escape from the life determined by the traffickers is usually impossible. The women and girls who are forced into prostitution are rarely able to keep any of the pay offered for their services. If they are provided monetary compensation, it often goes toward an alleged debt, supposedly incurred due to travel or living expenses. This keeps women in debt for as long as they are being used. Aside from being financially enslaved, they may be locked into brothels and not allowed time outside. Some women are chained to beds, reportedly even having to provide sexual services while shackled. It is reported that some children in Bombay are kept in cage-like cubicles in brothels (P. Williams, 1999) where the girls are purchased by an average of six men per day, who pay US$1.10–2.00 per sex act (Friedman, 1996).

Neela (Nepal)

When "Neela" was 14, her stepfather took her from their Nepalese village to a suburb of Kathmandu, where one of his friends got her a job in a carpet factory.

A few months later, a young male co-worker suggested they leave for another town where working conditions were better. She agreed and her stepfather, his friend and the young man took her out of the factory. After a six-day bus trip, they arrived in Bombay. There, she was taken to a temple and introduced to two women who took her to a house where 16 or 17 girls were sleeping on the floor. She was taken to a separate "training" room where she was kept for three months and then told she had been sold for $500 and would have to work there as a prostitute until she paid her debt. As the youngest, Neela was never beaten, but she saw others, who had tried to escape, thrashed so severely that "blood came from their mouths." After about a year in the brothel, Neela was picked up in a police raid and taken to a children's shelter. There she tested positive for HIV. Because she was ashamed, she decided not to find her family and remained in the shelter. (United Nations, 2000b)

There is a paucity of studies of the health consequences for women and girls who have been forced into prostitution through trafficking. However, in one study of over 800 people with current or former experience in prostitution, 71 percent reported having have been physically assaulted during their time as prostitutes, 63 percent had been raped, 75 percent had been homeless, and 67 percent had post-traumatic stress disorder. Almost 90 percent of those still in prostitution wanted to leave the business but had no other options for survival (Farley et al., 2003).

Another study found that girls younger than 18 years of age reportedly comprise at least 20 percent of Bombay's brothel population, and it is estimated that at least 50 percent of them are infected with HIV (Jeffreys, 1999). Banerjee reported that 45 percent of all trafficked women in India are HIV positive (2008).

A 2007 study that looked at women who had been trafficked for sexual exploitation from Nepal to India and then repatriated found that 38 percent were HIV positive. Over 60 percent of the girls who had been forced into prostitution before age 15 were also HIV positive. The researchers argue that today, HIV infection is the most serious health consequence for women who are trafficked (Harvard School of Public Health, 2007).

CONCLUSION

Women and girls are forced into sexual slavery when there are social and political frameworks that make it impossible for them to live in a humane context. The feminization of poverty, familial obligations, sexual abuse, homelessness, political turmoil, economic downturns, civil unrest, war, and natural disasters all create circumstances that enable those intent on profit making to use women and girls as sexual objects.

The public health costs of trafficking are enormous. Victims of trafficking experience inhumane living conditions, physical and sexual trauma (which some define as torture), exposure to disease and sexually transmitted infections, including HIV, and mental health consequences as a result of trauma and enslavement.

As trafficking is a transnational human rights concern, there are global efforts to address the movement of women and girls from continent to continent for sexual purposes. The extent of success of these efforts has yet to be determined, with questions directed at the effectiveness of policies, the enforceable consequences for those responsible, and the prioritization of trafficking of women as a global human rights concern.

It is not enough to simply police the trafficking industry. Cultural norms and customs that devalue women must concurrently be examined and altered. In a world in which women and girls are dispensable due to patriarchal power dynamics that measure a woman's worth in currency, trafficking is fueled by women's role as commodities rather than human beings.

While some governments, especially the U.S. government, claim that transnational efforts to impose laws against trafficking are making a difference, some governments passing the laws simultaneously profit from the practices. Laws alone will do little to stop the highly profitable forms of prostitution that many Third World governments now rely on, as will be seen in the section on sex tourism in chapter 7. These practices will come to an end only through efforts that regard trafficking as a human rights concern, that give comprehensive attention to the conditions that support trafficking (such as women's poverty), and that criminalize the purchasing of sexual services.

As long as there are men who objectify women and prefer to buy sex rather than engage in it in a mutually satisfying reciprocal relationship, as long as there are pedophiles intent on sexual gratification, and as long as there are individuals for whom financial gain is the only concern, women and children will continue to be kidnapped and enslaved.

4

War-Induced Sexual Slavery

"Our combatants don't get paid. Therefore they can't use prostitutes. If we politely ask women to come with us, they are not going to accept. So, we have to make them obey us so we can get what we want." A soldier during the Congolese conflict. (Ward & Marsh, 2006, p. 5)

Rape during armed conflict is not a new phenomenon. What changed in the latter part of the twentieth century was the media coverage of sexual atrocities committed during war, and public condemnation of the incidents. As a result, there is more awareness of the sexual violence that disproportionately affects women and girls during armed conflict. This chapter will describe incidents of sexual slavery associated with the sexual crimes committed during war.

OVERVIEW

We know considerably more now about the contexts in which sexual violence occurs during armed conflict than ever before. There are few documents attesting to rape or sexual slavery during past conflicts. For example, there is little that records the sexual violence and forced marriage of women that took place during the Armenian genocide from 1915 to 1917, although it did occur (Derdian, 2005). But media reports from wars and periods of political unrest in the second half of the twentieth century, especially in Bosnia-Herzegovina, Rwanda, the Congo, and Sierra Leone, have highlighted the sexual violence perpetrated against women. The awareness of war-induced sexual violence may also be due to reports surfacing from the increased numbers of racial, religious, or ethnic civil wars, which appear to have replaced conflicts between national armies. Civilian populations are affected on a much greater scale when the conflicts rage in neighborhoods and communities, rather than on battlefields. It is estimated that in these situations, civilian casualties may be as high as 75 percent compared to the estimated 5 percent of civilians who have been killed during national wars (Ward & Marsh, 2006).

The threat of rape during war has always operated as a form of terrorism. It is used against individuals within communities, against entire female populations, and against detainees and political prisoners. "It breaks the spirit, humiliates, tames, produces a docile, deferential, obedient soul. Its immediate message to women and girls is that we will have in our own bodies only the control that we are granted by men and thereby in general only that control in our environments that we are granted by men" (Card, 1996, p. 2). Furthermore, the primary purpose of rape in war is to destroy individuals (both the vulnerable women and the men to whom they are related) while terrorizing and humiliating entire communities.

According to Card (1996), one of the features of rape during war is that as a practice, it has unwritten rules. For example, in most cases the sexual violence is carried out against women (although that is not entirely true in some conflicts), the age of the victims is irrelevant, the soldiers and insurgents who rape enemy women are not reported, and there are no consequences. Not only are there no negative consequences for those who perpetrate sexual violence, but sometimes soldiers who are pressured to participate in such violence fear retaliation and humiliation if they do not. In some cases, the rape of enemy women has been encouraged and justified by commanding officers (Card, 1996; McDougall, 2000). The United Nations Commission on Human Rights reported that in 1999, in Sierra Leone, a rebel commander ordered all virgin girls to be physically examined. Once their virginity was confirmed, the girls were forced to make themselves available to the rebel soldiers each night so they could be raped (MacDougall, 2000). During the Bosnian war, a soldier from Sarajevo admitted to raping and shooting three women. However, he reported that had he not, his superiors would have ordered retribution: he was threatened with having to serve at the front lines, with jail, or with displacement from his home (Card, 1996).

In some wars, women who belong to particular ethnic groups are targeted, as was the case in Bosnia and Rwanda. In other cases, women are attacked and held indiscriminately. Some of the sexual violence occurs in private settings, while some is intentionally performed in public, as community members and/or family members are forced to witness the atrocities. In some cases, women are abducted and repeatedly forced to serve enemy soldiers as sexual objects, sometimes in "rape camps." Women who are kept as prisoners sometimes become targets of repeated rape and sexual humiliation. Some are forced into prostitution, serving multiple men or groups of men daily. Some women are forced into marriage with combatants. The following examples of sexual slavery describe the contexts in which vulnerable women have been forced into sexual servitude during war.

WORLD WAR II

Reports of Soviet soldiers holding German women in 1945 revealed a pattern of sexual violence perpetrated against all females older than 12 or 13. It is estimated that in a one-month period during World War II, thousands of women and girls were attacked, often raped by many men, sometimes in front of family or neighbors. The Soviet soldiers sometimes held women for days, during which time they were subjected to sexual torture. It is difficult to determine how many women were victimized. One report estimates that approximately 100,000 women were raped as the Soviet army moved through Germany. This form of terrorism was reportedly justified by indirect propaganda that encouraged the Soviet soldiers to take "revenge for everything" (Wood, 2006). Additionally, German soldiers reportedly forced many Soviet women and girls into prostitution. It is estimated that 50,000 Soviet women were held in German military brothels, as well as in brothels in labor and concentration camps.

Other forms of sexual slavery and violence that are now known to have occurred during the period preceding and during World War II include the rape and killing of an estimated 20,000 to 80,000 women during the Japanese occupation of Nanjing in 1937.

> Never have I heard or read of such brutality. Rape! Rape! Rape! We estimate at least 1,000 cases a night, and many by day. In case of resistance.... there is a bayonet stab or a bullet. We could write up hundreds of cases a day.
>   —From the diary of an American missionary in Nanjing, China, 1937.
>   (Neill, 2000)

As a direct result of these events, more than 200,000 women, mostly Korean, were forced to serve as prostitutes in "comfort stations" for Japanese soldiers. This organized system of military-sponsored brothels was thought to help prevent the indiscriminate rape of women such as had occurred in Nanjing. Most of the "comfort women" were 14–18 years old and it is estimated that up to one-third of them died during the war. Chapter 7 provides more details of this type of sexual slavery.

WARS OF THE MIDDLE TO LATE TWENTIETH CENTURY

Asia

The rape of Vietnamese women by American soldiers during the 16 years (1959–1975) in which the United States was involved in the Vietnam war experience has been confirmed. Women were abused by soldiers as individuals, as well as during mass rapes such as occurred during the My Lai massacre in 1968.

Further, it has been charged that the American military was involved in the commercial sex business with the purpose of encouraging soldier morale while fighting the unpopular Vietnam war. Neill (2000) asserts that the Pentagon knowingly promoted brothels in U.S. base camps throughout Vietnam. He also reports that the U.S. military was involved in providing "sex tours" for troops on leave in Thailand, the Philippines, and Taiwan. Providing women to soldiers is not unique to the Vietnam experience, but it does support the idea that a good soldier needs a woman for sexual gratification. It is not hard to understand how this philosophical foundation contributes to the atrocities committed during wartime.

Eastern Europe

It is estimated that 20,000 women and girls were raped during the war in Bosnia in the 1990s, mostly Muslim women raped by Bosnian Serbs (Wood, 2006; Parrot & Cummings, 2006). Many of the women were assaulted when they were being held in "detention" centers, set up for the purpose of providing sexual servitude, where Serb men would choose from the group, and then rape them there or somewhere nearby. Gang rape was not uncommon, nor were public rapes in front of villagers and neighbors (Wood, 2006; Stiglmayer, 1994). Women reported rape camps where hundreds of women were held, repeatedly raped many times per day, and deliberately impregnated (Stiglmayer, 1994). The forced impregnation of Muslim women by Serb men was an effort to "taint" the Muslim population. There were reports of pregnant women being held captive until late in the pregnancy to prevent them from attempting to abort the fetus (Ward & Marsh, 2006).

Kadira (Bosnia)

Women who got pregnant, they had to stay there for seven or eight months so they could give birth to a Serbian kid. They had their gynecologists there to examine the women. The pregnant ones were separated off from us and had special privileges; they got meals, they were better off, they were protected. Only when a woman's in her seventh month, when she can't do anything about it anymore, then she's released. Then they usually take these women to Serbia. (Stiglmayer, 1994)

What was distinct about the Bosnian rape context was that soldiers reportedly were commanded to sexually assault women in order to humiliate the women and their families and ensure that they would leave the area.

Amela was raped by at least 15 Serbian soldiers and recalls why she was taken:

"Because I am a Muslim," the married, red-haired woman says simply. "Their aim was to humiliate me, to make me lose my honor, to prove that they're the masters and they can rape and kill you just as they please. We are like their slaves." Now she feels her life, quite literally, is ruined. It is only the thought of her two-year-old son that stops Amela from killing herself.

"I try to be brave, but without even thinking about it, I just feel a physical urge to throw myself in front of a car or a tram." Amela—a pseudonym selected by the former factory worker—was rounded up last August [1993] along with all other residents of her husband's small Muslim village in northwestern Bosnia, between Banja Luka and Duboj. The men were separated and, she believes, shot, and their bodies burned on the spot. Her husband, whom she hasn't heard from since last July, was not among them because he was off fighting for the Bosnian defense forces. Sixty women, girls and children were taken to a lumber factory in Kotor Varos, where, after nightfall, the gang rapes began.

Selecting their victims by the light of matches, the Serb irregulars led Amela off with a knife to her throat. She thinks the men were under orders to rape because, when she begged to be let go, her Serb tormentor replied: "I can't. I have to." She was raped twice, let go briefly, then led back into a pitch-black room where she was brutally raped for hours on a cement floor. She estimates at least 20 other women were gang-raped during the night, including a 15-year-old and a woman already nine months pregnant. (McKinsey, 1993)

The targeted ethnic "cleansing" gained the attention of the international human rights agencies. The United Nations commission that investigated the war in the former Yugoslavia found there was a systematic approach to the raping of Muslim women, suggesting that the sexual violence was a planned campaign against the Muslim culture, not simply a consequence of the war conditions (Wood, 2006). As a result, the International Criminal Tribunal for the former Yugoslavia (ICTY) investigated the matter and convicted three members of the Bosnian Serb Army of rape, torture, and enslavement. The trial lasted eight months with testimony from 63 witnesses. Sixteen survivors described their ordeals of sexual enslavement. They had been held for months during which they were repeatedly raped by the three defendants as well as others. The convicted men received sentences ranging from 121 to 28 years in prison.

This was the first time in history that an international tribunal brought charges for crimes of sexual violence against women specifically, determining that rape and sexual enslavement are crimes against humanity. The decision set a precedent, as a result of which the sexual enslavement of women could finally be deemed a crime against humanity, providing a legal standard with which to press for future prosecutions in other wars (Human Rights Watch, 2001a).

Africa

In 1991, armed conflict broke out in Sierra Leone when the Revolutionary United Front (RUF) staged an uprising against the military leader of the country. The brutality of the war soon became evident, with beheadings, reports of torture, and the displacement of millions of people fleeing the violence. The conflict lasted almost 10 years and reportedly ended in 2002.

The extent and degree of the sexual atrocities perpetrated against the women of Sierra Leone is almost unimaginable. A mental health worker in Freetown stated that "being raped is like being bitten by a mosquito, it's that frequent" (Shanks, Ford, Schull, & de Jong, 2001, p. 304). One survivor described a young woman who was raped to death by six men (Human Rights Watch, 2003f).

A hallmark of the atrocities was the abduction of thousands of women and girls by RUF rebels. The women were often kept as sexual slaves or were "given" to a rebel as a wife, forced into both sexual and physical servitude. The rebels often marked the women they abducted by carving "RUF" or "AFRC" somewhere on their bodies, often on their chests.

Early on, the RUF became known for hit-and-run raids, returning to base camps with stolen merchandise and abducted women. Because more than one rebel faction was formed during the conflict, some women reported escaping and being revictimized. One 13-year-old reported that she was abducted from Koinadugu by one group, gang raped, and then forced out of the camp when it was attacked by another rebel group. She was then found and taken by a second group of men, and subsequently raped by two child soldiers (Human Rights Watch, 2003f).

A survey conducted by Physicians for Human Rights in Sierra Leone found that of the interviewees who reported war-related sexual violence, 15 percent had been subjected to sexual slavery and 9 percent had been forced to marry a rebel (Human Rights Watch, 2003f; Wood, 2006). Because it is not uncommon in Sierra Leone for men to be polygamous, many rebels had polygamous "marriages," including those with kidnapped women who were forced to "marry" them. Because the more brutal combatants often physically abused as well as raped their "wives," they tired of individual women who were too injured or sick to provide the sexual services demanded. Many times women were raped by others when their "husbands" were out on patrol or away from the camps (Human Rights Watch, 2003f).

The brutal conditions in these camps spawned the most unlikely alliances. Women combatants, who knew how vulnerable they were regardless of who they were "married" to, often became complicit in crimes for their own survival. According to the Forum for African Women Educationalists (FAWE), women who were already married to rebels who abducted other women often killed the new "wives" if their husbands showed a preference for the newcomers. One 14-year-old reported:

> I was put under the control of Commander Patrick, a Liberian. He was married to a woman called Neneh who was very jealous of me. Once, after the commanders had gone to the war front, Neneh told one of our guards to open up the cage where I was being held and take me out. She said, "My husband is interested in you. If you accept him to have sex with you, I'll kill you, so be forewarned." Neneh and Patrick have one child. She told me she'd joined the rebels voluntarily. She said, "You are just a captive. Do you think I was abducted? I was not abducted. I joined voluntarily. So you have no right to fall in love with my husband." (Human Rights Watch, 2003f)

Some women managed to escape the slavery but other women, particularly if they had children with the rebels, found it more difficult to leave. For many, the rapes were their first "sexual" experience. It is speculated that many fell prey to the "Stockholm Syndrome," a condition in which the person held in slavery comes to associate herself with those who are keeping her enslaved. Many women reported that they adjusted to the violence because it became a "normal" way of life for them and they knew what they had to do to survive. Others were afraid to leave because they were told that they would be blamed for their sexual servitude and ostracized by their families if they tried to return home. There is no way to estimate how many women remain with their rebel husbands or how many attempted to return to their homes and families of origin (Human Rights Watch, 2003f).

While the conflict in the Darfur region of Sudan that began in 2003 has received a good deal of worldwide media attention, civil unrest in Sudan is not new. The first civil war in Sudan began in 1953 and the country has been in conflict ever since. But the government-sponsored groups known as "Janjawid" (armed men on horses) or the "Arab militia" that became dominant in 2003 have conducted sweeping human rights atrocities against women and girls, atrocities unsurpassed in many other conflicts. Although a peace accord was signed in 2005, there are still concerns about the abuses in the Darfur region, especially those targeting women and girls.

It is estimated that as many as 10,000 young girls have been kidnapped and given to militia leaders as "wives" (McDougall, 2000). Some women and girls kidnapped during attacks by the Janjawid were forced to stay in military camps. Survivors who spoke to Amnesty International reported sexual slavery and torture.

> They took K.M., who is 12 years old in the open air. Her father was killed by the Janjawid in Um Baru, the rest of the family ran away and she was captured by the Janjawid who were on horse back. More than six people used her as a wife; she stayed with the Janjawid and the military more than 10 days. K, another woman who is married, aged 18, ran away but was captured by the Janjawid who slept with her in the open place, all of them slept with her. She is still with them. A, a teacher, told me that they broke her leg after raping her. (Amnesty International, 2004)

According to Human Rights Watch, there is a considerable stigma attached to rape in the Sudanese culture. Therefore, many women hesitate to describe what has happened to them. They continue to live with the experience, telling no one and not getting the medical care they may need in order to heal from the trauma (Human Rights Watch, 2004a).

Civil war in Northern Uganda has lasted two decades, and there are reports of the rebel army having abducted over 20,000 children. The Lord's Resistance Army (LRA) has been accused of war crimes including large-scale abductions, forced recruitment of adults and children, and rape of girls whom it assigns as "wives" or sex slaves to its commanders. When boys are abducted they are trained to be soldiers, but girls are given to commanders as sex slaves (Human Rights Watch, 2008). One girl reported that she was given to a commander twice her age when she was 13 and he would beat her if she refused to provide sexual favors.

During the 1994 genocide in Rwanda, reports of Hutu military groups perpetrating sexual violence against Tutsi women were deemed crimes against humanity. Rape was widespread and committed by individuals and gangs and often followed by torture and/or sexual slavery. As in Bosnia, there were reports that the militia leaders sanctioned the attacks on women and children and told the soldiers to spare no one (Human Rights Watch, 1996a). Although

Hutu women were also victimized in this way, the majority of reports of sexual violence were from Tutsi victims. It is impossible to estimate the numbers of women victimized during the 1994 genocide (Human Rights Watch, 1996b). A third of Rwandan women surveyed in 1999 reported being raped and 75 percent of those surveyed said they knew someone who had been raped. One survivor described her ordeal:

> The Interahamwe shared women. Each one took a woman or a girl. The Interahamwe chased young girls and women. Most were taken by two militia. I was taken by one who kept me for two weeks in Mid-May. He told me he would kill me after two weeks. Then he got tired of me and kicked me out.

After she escaped, this same woman was found by another militia and raped:

> I was taken by force—They were like wild animals. You knew it was your last days but I fought back anyway. (Human Rights Watch, 1996a)

As war continues to rage in the Congo, there are reports that as many as 90 percent of the women in some villages have been raped. A result of the aftermath of the Rwandan genocide, the Congo war is a struggle for land and power between the Congolese Army and rival ethnic groups and insurgents. It has generated more casualties in the Congo than were generated during World War II (CBS News, 2008). A tactic common in this conflict is the attempt to destroy communities using rape as the primary weapon. In addition to being raped, women are often brutalized in unspeakable ways to send a message to their families and villages. As in other recent conflicts, many of the victims are raped in front of relatives and neighbors. The goal is to maximize the terror, fear, and humiliation in order to induce feelings of helplessness. As a result, the women are often doubly victimized through rejection by their husbands and families, which leaves them homeless and isolated (Kimani, 2007; CBS News, 2008).

Ombeni (Congo)

Abducted two years ago when she was 16, Ombeni was kept as a concubine in the forests of eastern Congo. She became pregnant and at nearly nine months gestation, her captors cut her vagina with a machete, leaving the baby dead and abandoning the teenager in the forest. "I laid there for one week," Ombeni said. "Until insects came out of my body." Ombeni was eventually rescued by a woman who was foraging for food and made her way to a clinic for rape victims. (CBS News, 2005)

As a result of the attacks, millions of women face lifelong consequences. According to Dr. Mukwege, who has treated thousands of rape victims in Congo's Panzi hospital, "it's not just physical pain. It's psychological pain that you can see. Here in the hospital, we've seen women who have stopped living" (CBS News, 2008).

Générose (Congo)

I was on the road from Kalonge to Mudaka. I had money that my fiancé gave me to buy a wedding dress. A soldier attacked me on the road. He said things in Kinyarwanda. [Later she said he was Hutu.] He took me away to a place in the forest where there were three other soldiers. They roughed me up.

This was August 8 [2001] and they kept me until August 25 and each one of them raped me every day.

There wasn't a house as such but a shelter under some plastic sheeting. I ate the things that they stole from time to time—pâte [a kind of cassava dough] made from stolen flour and sometimes meat. I found out that they had another woman there before me and I was sleeping where she slept, and then later they would get another woman after me. I wore the same clothes all the time.

If I tried to speak, they hit me. They were all the same-horrible men.

They finally just sent me away when they were tired of me. They took away the clothes I was wearing and gave me rags.

I went to a health center that treats rape victims and got medicine. The Lord is the only one who can help me. He saved me from being killed; there is nowhere else to turn. (Human Rights Watch, 2002)

The children, husbands, and other family members who witnessed the rape of their loved ones suffer from trauma as well (Kimani, 2007). There are few resources available to help the millions who have been displaced, much less to address the trauma experienced as a result of the country-wide atrocities.

REFUGEE VICTIMIZATION

Women who flee their homelands do not always find shelter from the violence that erupted in their native communities. Being refugees may increase women's vulnerability, making them targets for sexual violence, harassment, and physical attacks. Displaced from their communities, without social or legal support networks, women may find themselves exposed to dangerous conditions. Refugee camps may provide some safety from civil unrest or political turmoil, but there have also been cases of rapes and sexual violence perpetrated against women and girls living there. Concerns about gender-based violence in refugee camps have surfaced in recent years. Some of the violence was at the hands of other refugees, but other reports from refugees emerged of sexual violence perpetrated by those who were charged to protect them.

In 2001, it was reported that humanitarian aid workers in Ghana and Sierra Leone demanded sex in exchange for food for refugees. The men distributing the aid reportedly demanded sex mostly from girls (but also from some boys) in order for the basic supplies to be delivered. In November 2002, a report documented 18 cases of sexual exploitation, including rape, perpetrated by aid workers against Bhutanese girls and women in a Nepal refugee camp. After the tsunami in 2004 devastated Asia, girls in Sri Lankan refugee camps reported being attacked by other refugees when they ventured out in search of firewood or food (Parrot & Cummings, 2006). While war conditions may increase women's vulnerability to sexual slavery, those who flee war areas may still be exposed to sexual attacks as defenseless refugees.

Other reports have accused peacekeeping troops of exploiting women who were already enslaved.

> On buses and cars—and crossing borders on foot—Natasha followed a path to sex slavery trodden by thousands of other hapless women, passing, under the watchful eyes of a gang of Balkans thugs, through Romania, Serbia and Kosovo before ending up in the former Yugoslav republic of Macedonia.
>
> In Velesta, a key transit town in the sex trade where women are beaten and raped into submission, Natasha was bought by Meti, an ethnic Albanian pimp wanted by the Macedonian police on smuggling and prostitution charges.
>
> "Meti beat me if he heard that I didn't want to go with a client, or if I disobeyed him," Natasha said.
>
> Clients by the dozens would come to the bars where Meti made her work, the Bela Dona and Club 69. Natasha estimates she was forced to sleep with more than 1,000 men during her nine months in Velesta. Besides the Albanians and Macedonians, there were men from "France, Germany and the United States," Natasha said, referring to soldiers from the NATO peacekeeping mission in Macedonia and nearby Kosovo.
>
> "They were as bad as the rest," Natasha said. "They did anything they wanted to us. And besides, if Meti heard me asking them for help, he would have killed me." (Mendenhall, 2002)

These reports raise serious concerns about soldiers who, while not actively engaged in warfare, may perpetrate violence against the very women they have been sent to protect.

CONCLUSION

Conditions of civil unrest and war may lead to attacks on those left most vulnerable amidst regional chaos. Although men are also brutalized and tortured, women and children suffer disproportionately during armed conflict. Women, however, are often targeted as the means to achieve genocide, revenge, or the humiliation and obedience of the enemy party. Unfortunately, the sexual exploitation often does not stop with the end of armed conflict.

> One young girl in Sierra Leone who previously had been abducted by rebels voluntarily became a prostitute after she was released by her captors. She reportedly considered herself fortunate that she was now being paid. (Ward & Marsh, 2006, p. 9)

Women remain vulnerable due to lapses of security, shattered economies, inadequate reconstruction efforts, and residual patriarchal laws that do little to provide women with the necessary basic needs after war. Trafficking expanded in the Balkans after the war in Yugoslavia, as criminal gangs and mobs took advantage of the economic and political instability to continue to sexually exploit women (Ward & Marsh, 2006).

After armed conflict, struggling infrastructures usually do not support the medical or emotional care that is necessary for women to heal. Instead, lack of services contributes to the ongoing physical and mental trauma experienced by women and girls. Pregnancies as a result of rapes can increase a community's trauma. After the Rwandan genocide, it was reported that 5,000 babies, known as *enfants mauvais souvenir* (children of bad memories) were born and some were reportedly abandoned or killed (Shanks et al., 2001).

For some women who have been raped during armed conflict, the social consequences prolong the trauma. Many women cannot talk about their experiences for fear of being ostracized. In some cultures, husbands will divorce their wives once they learn that the wives have been victimized by rape. For unmarried women, the social stigma prevents them from finding men who are interested in future relationships. When women do choose to speak out about the atrocities, other women often feel threatened and will separate themselves from or ostracize those who report the crimes (McDougall, 2000).

As is often the case, when the perpetrators of the crimes are members of the military or civilian authorities in control of the area, women as well as their families are at great risk if they talk publicly about their rape. Members of non-governmental organizations (NGOs) and medical and religious personnel who have disclosed mass rape or talked about their concerns, especially when their comments are perceived as critical of local authorities, have been threatened. This continues to help silence those who witnessed the atrocities and diminishes the likelihood that survivors will get the help and care they need and deserve.

Rape victims are often stigmatized by the rest of the community and even by their own family members. Speaking about the crime may expose survivors to rejection. Family members may share the concerns of the survivors about security and standing in the community and may urge them to keep silent. Moreover, victims who recount the circumstances of the crime may suffer from renewed or intensified psychological and physical stress reactions that are characteristic of post-traumatic stress syndrome.

There are circumstances of armed conflict, however, in which sexual violence does not occur. Wood reports that there has been little evidence of sexual violence during the ongoing Palestinian/Israeli conflict, although the killing of unarmed civilians has been condemned by critics. Wood speculates that the ongoing examination and reporting of this particular conflict may actually act to deter sexual violence (2006).

When rape is used as a weapon of war it is often a calculated, systematic expression of hostility toward the enemy. But rape during war raises an even larger question about the meaning of the defilement. If each rape exploits women, how can these acts be a manifestation of cultures that condone the abuse of women? "When men are set apart from women and issued a rifle, as in war, are women abused sexually because they are representatives of the enemy, or—questions

(Susan) Brownmiller—because women are specifically women and therefore the enemy? As such, sexual aggression becomes an instrument of contempt against women and not necessarily a part of the activity of war" (Neill, 2000).

Whatever the motivation, sexual slavery and rape are no longer viewed as unintended consequences but are now recognized as inherent parts of the atrocities that happen during war.

5

Ritual Sexual Slavery

In certain contexts, religion justifies the sexual exploitation of women and girls as being due to their assumed inferiority, the overriding needs of the family or community, a general cultural ignorance of the impact the experience will have, or the need to control females. This chapter describes some of the situations that force women into sexual servitude through ritualized justifications.

OVERVIEW

Ritual sexual slavery occurs when girls and women are forced into sexual servitude, forced into prostitution, or bound to a ritualized environment that obligates them to provide sexual favors under the guise of religious devotion. The *devadasi* in India and "fetish" slaves in western Africa offer examples of the kinds of enslavement that young girls endure in the name of religion. Sometimes families volunteer their daughters for ritual sexual slavery, neither fully aware of the horrors that await them nor anticipating that sexual servitude is a part of the sacred cultural obligation. In some cases, religious beliefs obligate women to endure sexual servitude out of fear that they will be cursed if they do not submit or that they will be ostracized by a religious hierarchy. Regardless of the context, manipulation and control in the name of religious justification have been documented as imposing sexual servitude on thousands of women around the world.

DEVADASI: SACRED PROSTITUTION

> My life is finished because of this. I never thought I would become a Devadasi. I never thought I would be a prostitute. (Kirloskar & Cameroon-Moore, 1997, p. 28)

In southern India, *devadasi* is a centuries-old tradition of dedicating young girls to temples where sexual servitude is expected (Narula, 1999; Power, 2000). The system began as a system of piety and dedication to the temple. The term *devadasi* translates as "female servant of a deity." Originally, the tasks expected of the dedicated young women were sacred functions including preparation of the temples, lighting lamps, dancing to serve the deities, and providing sexual contact for the priests. However, more recently, *devadasi* has become associated with a system close to prostitution or sex work, where women engage in sexual relations with men who can afford to pay. *Devadasi* are not permitted to marry an earthly man because commitment to temple service represents a marriage to God (Shankar, 1990). Because *devadasi* are not allowed to marry, the payments offered amount to a kind of "marital" support from the perspective of proponents of the institution and to paid prostitution from the perspective of critics.

In medieval times, women servants of the deities were known as expert artists in music and dance. However, through the centuries, the *devadasi* became exploited by the upper classes. Their servitude was transferred from the gods to kings, priests, and lords, and finally to the wealthy men of society. Because the use of women's bodies is sanctioned by religious expression, the practice is considered socially permissible (Parrot & Cummings, 2006).

Although there have been attempts to eliminate the *devadasi* system (it was outlawed in 1982) it is estimated that 15,000 girls still become *devadasi* annually (Power, 2000). Many of the girls sacrificed to this service are Dalit ("untouchables"), those of the lowest status in India. Sister Bridget Pailey reports that "Only in this aspect do 'Untouchables' suddenly become touchable. The upper castes wouldn't drink from the same glass as a devadasi but they make use of her body" (Power, 2000, p. 1).

Once parents hand their daughters to the local temples as human offerings, the girls are symbolically married to God. After their first menstrual period, the girls are expected to become sexual servants to upper-caste men in their villages (Power, 2000). While some men keep their *devadasi* as personal servants, others make them available to other men, cost-free. Grey argues that "temple prostitution, practiced by Dalits on their women and girls, is violence sanctioned by religion" (2005, p. 139).

There are a variety of reasons why a girl may be dedicated to the temples. A family may be unable to support its many children and this is seen as a way to legitimately relieve the financial burden. In other cases, a girl may be promised before she is born, by parents desperate to have children but willing to sacrifice one should they ultimately be able to produce offspring. Dedicating a girl to a temple may provide some financial stability to the family. Some families believe in superstitious signs, such as "matted hair," as an indication that a girl must serve. Dedicating a girl to service may also be an opportunity for lower-caste parents to raise themselves in the caste system if their daughter is connected to an upper-caste man (Grey, 2005; Parrot & Cummings, 2006).

Some girls become *devadasi* after recovery from illness. "Due to lack of medical services, people go to Mathamma temples believing that the goddess has healing powers when the Dalit girl is sick. She is taken to the temple and left there, till her sickness is cured.... Once the child is cured, the child is named after Mathamma, and married to the goddess with the 'pottu Thali' (wedlock). After[ward] she becomes a dancer and belongs to the temple. During temple festivals she dances and earns her livelihood. She is not treated with respect and is publicly humiliated by men who harass her sexually.... Once the girl is married to Mathamma, she cannot marry others to lead a family life. Men take her as a partner, exploit her and leave her with a child" (Grey, 2005, p. 140). In many of these cases, girls are committed to a temple against their will and forced to engage in sexual relations with wealthy men who seek the *devadasi* service (Halli, Ramesh, O'Neil, Moses, and Blanchard, 2006).

Girls are not always happy about their parents' abandonment of them to the temple. The anger is rarely conveyed to the parents but instead manifests itself as aggression or depression.

Talema (India)

Talema was dedicated by her mother after her father died. "I find it very difficult to stomach," she says. At her dedication ceremony, she had no idea what being a devadasi meant. "When the high-caste man came to me," she remembers, "I began to wonder why my mother did this." (Power, 2000, p. 2)

Imla

"My parents didn't have any sons, so there was nobody to earn the family a living," says Imla. "Instead they turned me into a whore. I don't even remember when I started because I was so young. My parents thought at least they'd get some money from me." (Grammaticas, 2007)

Other *devadasi* argue that they voluntarily choose to enter into this kind of sex work. A quick search on the Internet can turn up information about *devadasi* in many contexts, including examples of voluntary sex work outside of India. A young woman named Kama, who lives on the outskirts of London, advertises herself on her website as follows: "I am devadasi. I believe intimacy with men is divine and draws me closer to my Gods." Her site offers photos of herself and field reports from two men who have visited her and paid for her services as well as descriptions of the kinds of sexually pleasing "positions" that might cost extra (see http://www.princesskama.com/home.html).

Despite *devadasi* like Kama, who claim to voluntarily become devadasi, most argue that the system should be culturally condemned because girls are forced into living a life that, though initially based on religious duties, displays all the hallmarks of cheap prostitution (Shankar, 1990). And once girls are dedicated, they cannot be freed.

Shoba

"I can't get out of the system, even if I say I'm not a devadasi any more nobody will come forward to marry me," she says. "I keep telling other people not to make their daughters devadasis, you are abused, it's a horrible life." (Grammaticas, 2007)

TROKOSI: "FETISH" SLAVERY

In sections of West Africa including Ghana, Benin, Togo, and parts of Nigeria, some girls continue to be committed by their parents at a young age to a ritualized life that amounts to sexual slavery. A system that has its origins in the Ewe practices of Ghana, the *trokosi* system is practiced in shrines that are dedicated to the god *troxovi*, the god of transformation, suggesting a system that exists for the good of the people. There are specific rituals associated with Troxovi, who is there to protect the people. The roots of this system are hundreds of years old and deeply established in some African communities. "Until the police force was introduced, fetish was the policeman, the judge, and the god of goodness" (Boaten, 2001).

Tradition dictates that in order to atone for the sins of a family member who may have offended the gods, young girls, usually before puberty, are sacrificed to the fetish shrine. Under the pretext of justice, these girls are held as slaves, often raped by the priests, and forced to work without pay or compensation. Denied education and health care, they are required to live as "wives of the gods." If the girl dies, is shunned, or becomes ill, the family must replace her with another female until the "debt" is paid.

In Ghana, these slaves are known as *trokosi*. Although the practice has been banned since 1998 when Parliament passed a law forbidding all forms of ritualized forced labor (Women's International Network, 2002), and it is illegal according to the Ghanaian constitution, the laws are often ignored and as many as 10,000 girls may currently be held at shrines.

One girl describes her experience as a *trokosi* slave:

> We were living like slaves. We were made to suffer hunger. We had no soap for our bath. We did farm work under severe pressure. In the nights the priests just ordered any one of us to sleep and have sexual intercourse with him. If you felt sick, it was the responsibility of your people to give you medication. In fact, it was terrible for a human being to live in such a condition. (quoted in Boaten, 2001, p. 95)

Priests may require the girls who have been dedicated to the shrine to work more than 12 hours a day, under severe conditions, with little food or rest. There is no compensation for their labor. Any income from farming or petty trade that the girls may earn is immediately turned over to the priests. A man in this culture gains status from the number of children he fathers, so many of the slaves become pregnant at a young age and bear many children.

The shrine owners are generally elder members of the clan and they too benefit from the economic profits that result from the slave girls' labor. The *trokosi* system in Ghana provides goods and money highly valued by the priests and the owners (Aird, 2000). Often, visitors to the shrine must bring some kind of offering with them, such as alcohol, cash, or food, in order to be allowed visitation rights.

Depending on the severity of her relative's crime, the length of time a girl is expected to serve can range from a few years to a lifetime. On average, a *trokosi* slave will be kept in servitude for over 10 years (Aird, 2000). If she is compensating for a murder, a longer penalty will be exacted. If necessary, the family of the accused will be expected to provide generations of virgin daughters in order to atone for the incident (Parrot & Cummings, 2006).

Families are often afraid that a disaster or catastrophe will befall them if they do not sacrifice their daughters to the shrine. In some cases, the sin was committed so far in the past that the girls cannot identify the crime committed or the person in their family who was responsible for the offense. Some individual women serve what amounts to a lifetime to pay for the crime of an ancestor. A father described his decision to commit his daughter to the shrine:

> "They will keep her forever," says Abla's father Patrick (real name...withheld). "They [the priests] said that if she is a student, after performing the rites for them they will allow her to come home to continue her education. But I don't know whether it is true." While Patrick would like to refuse the demands of the priest, his family is so afraid of deaths occurring in the family (to date, nine of Patrick's brothers have died, and the priests say the deaths are a result of the grandfather's crime) that he feels pushed to comply. "If you refuse bringing what they need, they make sure that the one who is refusing will die, or another person will die," Patrick explains. "We were told, if we don't do the rituals that they are demanding, another person will die." (Ocansey & Hayhoe, 2004)

Juliana Dogbadzi was taken to a shrine in 1981 at age seven to atone for her grandfather's sin against the community. She spent 17 years at the shrine, bearing two children. After escaping from the shrine, she spoke out about her experience.

> My grandfather, they said, had stolen two dollars. When he was suspected of the crime and asked to return the money, he defended his innocence. The woman who had accused him of the crime went to the shrine and cursed my grandfather's family, at which point members of my family began to die. In order to stop the deaths, a soothsayer told us that my grandfather would have to report to the Trokosi shrine. The priest told my family that it must bring a young girl to the shrine to appease the gods. A sister was sent to the shrine at Kebenu some six hundred miles away, but she died a few years later. Since I had been born just after my grandfather's death, I became her replacement.
>
> I lived and worked in the priest's fields and kept the compound clean. While doing so, I was raped repeatedly by the priest on torn mats on the cold floor of windowless huts. The other female slaves and I received neither food nor medical care. We had to find time after working on the priest's farm to burn charcoal or to sell firewood in the nearest town in order to make enough money to buy food. There were times we lived on raw peppers or palm kernel nuts to stay alive.
>
> Because I was just a kid, I didn't know what to do. There was an elder woman who was a slave and took care of me. She couldn't help me much because she had so many kids as a consequence of being raped by the priest. She said, "Look, little girl, take care of yourself or you will die." There used to be a hundred women slaves in my shrine, but the priest sent about ninety of them to work on his farms in other villages. Collectively, they had about sixty-five children and would have to work to look after the children.

Twelve of us, four women and eight children, lived in a one-room, thatched-roof house. It was built of mud and lacked both windows and doors. The rain got in. The snakes got in. The room was twenty feet long and twelve feet wide. The ceiling was low, just shy of our heads, and we all slept together on a mat on the floor. This is not everything that I can remember, but saying it brings back pains of old and it's difficult to go back through all those experiences.

You see, in the shrine you have no right to put on shoes or a hat to protect yourself against the hot sun. If it is raining or cold, you have only a small piece of cloth around yourself. A typical day in the shrine was as follows: you wake up at five o'clock in the morning, go to the stream about five kilometers away to get water for the compound, sweep, prepare meals for the priest (not eating any yourself), go to the farm, work until six o'clock, and return to sleep without food or to scrounge for leftovers. At night, the priest would call one of us to his room and would rape us. I was about twelve when I was first raped.

There was favoritism even in slavery. The priest liked girls who would readily give in to his sexual demands and hated those who would always put up a fight. Consequently, these girls were beaten. The ones he liked always said they were being wise because they wanted to avoid being beaten, while some of us maintained that they were foolish and were enjoying sex with a man they didn't love. When I saw people who came to the village to buy food wearing nice dresses, I started to think that I had to do something for myself. I had to get freedom. (Polaris Project, n.d., *Juliana Dogbadzi*)

Unlike many *trokosi*, Dogbadzi has managed to build a new life with her two children away from the shrine. She has dedicated her time to freeing other *trokosi* slaves. She continues to work for women's rights and due to her accomplishments, she has received international recognition.

Some argue that Trokosi slaves serve a greater purpose within the communities where the fetish system is practiced, establishing systems of justice acknowledged as preferable by those who live there. However, this cultural-relativist argument accepts the idea that girls, unlike boys, are valued at such a low level as to support their being handed over for life, without any concern for their well-being. Alternative means of securing justice within the community need not jeopardize the health and well-being of girls, unless, of course, girls are considered dispensable and unworthy of independent, free lives. This is the point worth challenging.

VOODOO

In some parts of the world, where witchcraft, animistic religious practices, and other such rituals are prevalent, the use of these rituals has pressured some women into being trafficked or kidnapped for use in sex industries. A study of Nigerian women reported that women were obligated to swear an oath of allegiance before being trafficked. Personal substances such as pubic hair and blood were kept by the traffickers to ensure that the women complied with the obligation imposed on them to provide sexual services (Cole, 2006). The significance of bodily substances to those who adhere to animistic religious practices was known to the traffickers, who initiated the rituals to assure the full compliance of the women.

Occult fears used to assist in the trafficking of Nigerian girls to the Netherlands were documented by van Dijk (2001). In the mid-1990s, organizations that tracked prostitutes in Amsterdam, Rotterdam, and The Hague began to notice a marked increase in the numbers of very young African girls in the red light districts. In an effort to examine the increase in under-age girls linked to prostitution, Dutch police uncovered an intricate web of traffickers, "madams," and brothels that had been involved in the exploitation and enslavement of young girls through the use of voodoo-like practices. The police noticed extreme anxiety and fear among the girls they interviewed in brothels. With some probing, the police found that the girls had engaged in certain rituals before they left Nigeria and when they arrived in the Netherlands. The police observed that the girls were in possession of small parcels wrapped in cloth. The parcels contained an assortment of objects; finger- and toenail clippings, hair, underwear that appeared to have been stained with menstrual blood, nuts, metal, and soaps or powders. These packets, coupled with the girls' extreme anxieties led the police to the discovery that occult threats were the driving force behind the exploitation of these young girls in sex work. During interviews, the girls admitted that if they did not comply with the "voodoo oaths," certain spirits would kill them or hurt or murder their families back in Nigeria. Part of the threat involved the huge debt that the girls had incurred in order to travel to the Netherlands. Like the obligations that are incurred in debt bondage, the rituals conducted before they left Nigeria tied them to the debt, which could be as great as US$20,000. Furthermore, once established in a brothel in the Netherlands, the girls would be obligated by the rituals to pay the madam for their upkeep, which could add an additional US$25,000 to their debt. The enslavement of girls through ritual obligations was initially effective and was then reinforced by physical violence and threats from those who controlled them (madams and pimps) once in the Netherlands (van Dijk, 2001).

The enslavement of African girls using occult threats proved to be a complex issue for the Dutch authorities to investigate. It was complicated by different cultural expectations, misunderstandings of "voodoo," legal snags that affected immigration policies, and a political quagmire that resulted in African ambassadors having to answer questions from Dutch politicians about embassy involvement in the trade.

OTHER RELIGIOUS CIRCUMSTANCES

Buddhism

In Thailand, prostitution is illegal, yet thousands of girls and women are traded, bought and sold into sexual slavery each year. The dominant religious beliefs in most of Thailand confirm the inferiority of girls, who have always been obligated to help pay family debts. If there is a crop failure, or the death or disability of the father, which compromises family income, or general unending family debt, daughters (never sons) may be sold as slaves or servants. The sales have two benefits: removing or easing the family debt and supplying workers, maids, servants, and prostitutes for the Thai community (Bales, 2004). These sales are not uncommon among people in poverty, and are not necessarily judged as tragic. According to Bales (2004), girls are viewed as expendable in part because of the type of Buddhism practiced in Thailand (Theravada); it is often believed that only men can attain "enlightenment" (although there are different interpretations arguing that Buddha believed both women and men were capable of enlightenment). Certain Buddhist writings are believed to sanction prostitution: "the *vihaya*, or rules for monks, lists ten kinds of wives, the first three of which are 'those bought for money, those living together voluntarily, those to be enjoyed or used occasionally'" (Bales, 2004, p. 38). Furthermore, Thai Buddhism is grounded in resignation and acceptance of life's burdens because the tragedies that befall an individual are the individual's own fault, or destiny due to past errors or sins. Thus, even a child forced into prostitution must learn to accept her destiny.

> When Siri wakes, it is about noon. In the instant of waking she knows exactly who and what she has become.... Siri is fifteen years old. Sold by her parents a year ago, her resistance and her desire to escape the brothel are breaking down and acceptance and resignation are taking their place. (Bales, 2004, p. 34)

A girl's resignation to the violent life that has been forced upon her provides a coping mechanism. It is a way to make sense of the atrocities she has been forced to endure.

Catholicism

In 1998, a report entitled "The Problem of the Sexual Abuse of African Religious in Africa and Rome" detailed allegations that nuns and other religious young women had been forced into sexual relations with priests and bishops in 23 countries, but primarily in Africa (National Catholic Reporter, 2001; Kennedy, 2001). The report claimed that some Catholic clergymen exploited their power and authority by forcing religious women to provide sexual favors, sometimes in exchange for work in a diocese. The allegations date back to 1995 when Sister Maura O'Donohue briefed Cardinal Eduardo Martinez, prefect of the Vatican congregation for religious life. In her briefing she described "widespread abuses of African nuns. Nuns who became pregnant were forced out of their orders. The priests were routinely transferred to new assignments" (Berry, 2001, p. 9).

Because Africa suffers disproportionately from the HIV/AIDs epidemic, it was speculated that young nuns and religious women were considered particularly safe targets for sexual activity, compared to prostitutes who might have been exposed to HIV and could transmit the virus to the priests who were in search of sexual activity. In a number of cases, reports allege rape as well as the impregnation of nuns, who were then forced to have abortions (Allen & Schaeffer, 2001). There is one report of a priest who presided over the funeral for a nun who died from a botched abortion, having been impregnated by the very same priest (Berry, 2001).

The women who were reportedly abused in this way were unable to refuse, due to both religious and cultural constructs that emphasized men's power over women. Use of the Church's established authority in the region helped these priests manipulate and gain sexual access to religious women when they might not have been able to do so otherwise. The response from the Vatican to these allegations was, as Berry described it, curious. A Vatican spokesperson noted that "Work is being done both on the training of people and the resolution of individual cases. A few negative situations cannot make one forget the often heroic faith of the great majority of monks, nuns and priests" (quoted in Berry, 2001). Regardless of how religious hierarchies perceived and investigated allegations such as those discussed above, the abuse women suffered from those within the hierarchy was, at the very least, an abuse of power within a religious setting.

CONCLUSION

Due to the identification of sexual coercion and servitude as a type of religious doctrine, in many cultures women and girls find themselves without recourse or any ability to end the abuse and rape they experience. The power of certain religious beliefs imposes a double bind on these women: not only are they abused by a system that dismisses their autonomy and worth, but they are chained by the system because it also manipulates their families and communities into believing there is some justification for what they suffer. Efforts to change the social beliefs in parts of Ghana in order to release *trokosi* slaves have had some success (see chapter 8) by replacing the human sacrifice with objects that have value to the shrine (such as farm animals and cash). This is an example of the remedies that are possible. But the ritualization of abuse sanctioned by religious beliefs presents an acute obstacle to preventing a particular form of enslavement of women and girls.

6

Forced Marriage

In this chapter, forced marriage using a variety of different mechanisms will be examined: child marriages, forced arranged marriages, and bride kidnapping. Although these types of sexual slavery occur in many countries, Kyrgyzstan, Uzbekistan, the United States of America, Bangladesh, India, Pakistan, and the United Kingdom provide the examples that will be examined in depth here.

OVERVIEW

Forced marriage is one means of curtailing women's autonomy and controlling their sexuality. It can occur through or result in coercion, mental abuse, emotional blackmail, intense social pressure, physical violence, abduction, detention, rape, sexual abuse, and/or murder (Bangladesh National Women Lawyers Association, 2001; Hossain & Turner, 2001; INTERIGHTS, ASK, & Shirkat Gah, 2000). Forced marriage takes place against one's will, or with the coerced consent of both parties. Although both women and men may be forced into marriage, most reported cases involve young females. The girl's father, mother, or siblings are usually the ones responsible for arranging the marriage (INTERIGHTS et al., 2000). However, not all arranged marriages are forced. This chapter will examine marriages created against the woman's will and without her consent, where forcible compulsion is present.

Migration sometimes plays a role in forced marriage. Some people from cultures in which forced marriage is common move to different countries, where arranged or forced marriage is not part of the culture. Several human rights organizations (including INTERIGHTS, an international human rights law in London; Ain o Salish Kendra [ASK], a legal aid and human rights center in Dhaka, Bangladesh; and Shirkat Gah, a women's resource center in Lahore, Pakistan) have been monitoring forced marriage in the United Kingdom, among the Hindu, Muslim, and Sikh women in Bangladeshi, Indian, and Pakistani communities (Hossain & Turner, 2001).

Forced marriage takes several forms. If the woman has no agency, cannot leave, cannot refuse, and is often obligated to have sex on demand, it is a form of sexual slavery. The types of forced marriage to be discussed at length in this chapter are child marriages, forced arranged marriages, and bride kidnapping.

CHILD MARRIAGES

Child marriages, by definition, are a form of forced marriage because children are unable to understand the nature of marital relationships and what is expected of them. There are varied motivations for marrying children. Children are given or promised in marriage to guarantee virginity at the time of the contract, to create family or political alliances, to pay off a debt, to earn money through bride price, to avoid pregnancy before marriage, to ease an economic burden, to ensure obedience, and/or to maximize the number of children a woman can produce. Regardless of the motivation, conjugal obligations are required, and often forced upon the child throughout her development into adulthood.

Cultures and traditions on almost every continent justify or support the provision of children for sex, or the facilitation of sex with minors through early marriage, sometimes to old men who provide compensation (Group for the Convention on the Rights of the Child and EPCAT, 2001).

Tabatha (United States)

In Horse Creek, Kentucky, United States...a "tall, skinny girl hides her face behind the baby in her arms like a child might do with its doll. She shoos away the chickens that roam at her feet. It is only this protective movement that gives any suggestion the baby could actually be hers. She looks too young but, in fact, it is her second child. Like several girls who live in her tiny community, Tabatha was 12 years old when she married. Her cousin, Alice, who appears at the makeshift front door of the same shack, also married when she was 12. Her husband is 74.... There is no running water inside the squalid shack, no toilet, and a family of eight share the two tiny rooms." Although in Kentucky the legal age of marriage is 16, local communities accept and even encourage the marriage of younger girls. According to Tabatha's school principal "This is the Bible Belt, there's a tradition of getting married early here because, not so long ago, life expectancy was short due to poor medical care. If you were going to die young, there was an urgency to get married." (Group for the Convention on the Rights of the Child and EPCAT, 2001)

The families of child brides rarely permit the girls to refuse to marry. Community norms (social, economic, and religious) often make it nearly impossible for the girls either to avoid an early marriage or to leave the marriage at a later date (UNICEF, 2005). According to the United Nations, child marriages are not uncommon in rural areas of Egypt, Afghanistan, Bangladesh, Ethiopia, Pakistan, India, and the Middle East. Young girls in these societies are rarely allowed out of their homes unless it is to work in the fields or to get married; this is in order to maintain their virginity, thereby protecting the family's "honor." Girls are often married as young as 11 years of age, although some are as young as 7. In Afghanistan, approximately 60 to 80 percent of marriages are forced (UNICEF, 2005). The legal age for marriage in Egypt is 16, and in India and Ethiopia, the age is 18. However, these laws are frequently ignored, especially in rural areas where child marriages are considered socially acceptable. As migration from countries where child marriage is widespread increases, female children are being married in secret illegal ceremonies in countries, like England and the United States, where such marriage is not the norm (UNICEF, 2005).

In Pakistan, women and girls of any age, even babies, are given away in marriage as compensation for crimes committed by the men in their families. This practice, called *swara,* is intended to prevent bloodshed. Daughters and sisters are given away to resolve conflicts. Informal tribal councils often employ this approach as an accepted dispute resolution mechanism (Ebrahim, 2006). For example, "In May 2006, in Murad Satthar village of Shikarpur, Sindh, a tribal council ordered Mohammad Ramza, to give his 9 and 1 year old daughters in payment for three buffaloes because the father did not have the money to pay for them. The father consented" (Ebrahim, 2006). Furthermore, if a family does not have girls to be used as compensation, the family sometimes purchases girls from another poor family. "Afsar Ali bought 13-year-old Bibi Jan in a marketplace in Peshawar, for Rs 53,000 (US$1 = Pak Rs 57.46 at the time). He used her to settle his debt because he did not have a close female relative to hand over. Bibi Jan was rejected by the recipient family claiming that she was mentally challenged" (Ebrahim, 2006).

Traditional wisdom in some parts of Pakistan holds that when girls are brought in from an enemy's family, any children born to such girls will belong to both families, which will put an end to feuds. However, this does not always happen. "'I'll taunt and humiliate her for she's the price paid for my son's death,' says a villager elder. He will accept her as part of the tribal council's decision and he will feed and clothe her, but she is not considered part of the family and cannot partake in any rituals or festivities" (Ebrahim, 2006). Not everybody in the culture condones *swara.* According to Justice Fida Mohammad Khan of the Federal Sharia Court, "Islam prescribes that a punishment should be punitive, retributive, reformative and act as a deterrent. Swara doesn't have any of these features. The criminal goes free, and an innocent girl pays the price" (Ebrahim, 2006).

Some child brides have attempted to refuse to honor their marriages.

Amna (Pakistan)

In November 2005, Amna Niazi, 22, a masters student, her two sisters and two cousins refused to honor the marriage vows that took place in 1996, when they were between six and 13. Niazi's uncle had shot a man, and the jirga [tribal council] had ordered that the five girls be handed over as swara. When they refused to comply, the jirga ordered that they be abducted, raped or killed. The father has since paid the blood money and refused to hand over his daughters "like goats to illiterate men." (Ebrahim, 2006)

There have been some instances in which laws against child marriage have actually been enforced. In 2006, "an imam who had conducted nikah (marriage) of a one-month-old girl *swara* was arrested. In Mardan, local police arrested jirga members who had allowed the rival party to take an 11-year-old *swara* victim with them to a tribal area" (Ebrahim, 2006). Though such arrests occur, they are uncommon, and most child brides are forced to remain with their husbands for their entire lives.

Girls who are married under these circumstances often suffer severe consequences as a result. Young brides are often denied educational opportunities, resulting in illiteracy, which can lead to a lifetime of poverty. Physical abuse is common.

Nasreen (India)

Thirteen-year-old Nasreen, hailing from a small village of Punjab and now living in a shelter home here, has experienced far more harsh realities of life than girls her age generally do. "Three years ago my father, Rana Bashir, married me off to an old man, Mohammad Shafee, in return for Rs 60,000. I didn't know what was happening. They took my thumb impression on a paper and later I learnt that I had been married to a man who appeared older than even my father, most of the teeth in his mouth were also missing." Her husband regularly beat her up, claiming that he was well within his rights to do so because he had purchased her. He said that he had also given Rs 10,000 to the person who had arranged the match. "He used to hurl threats at me, saying that he would sell me to his brothers for more money." "He would also sharpen his dagger and brandished it in front of me menacingly," she added. "My weeping would often become another excuse for my further thrashing."…[H]er husband sold sugarcane juice. "About six months back, he took me to a shrine called Abdullah Shah Ghazi's tomb. There I decided to run away."… Her husband was aged between 55 and 60. She doesn't know the proper address of her father's house. She only remembers the name of her village as "Mochiwala" in Punjab. (Hassan, 2007)

If girls are able to leave the marriage or if they are widowed, they often have trouble earning enough to support themselves and their children (Stritof & Stritof, 2008). Many child brides give birth when they are quite young, often resulting in severe health problems, such as fistulas (tears between the birth canal and the rectum or the urethra, resulting in constant leaking of fecal material or urine from the vagina), maternal mortality, or HIV/AIDS (Salopek, 2004). The health consequences cause lifelong suffering and often social isolation, and in some cases premature death.

FORCED ARRANGED MARRIAGES

Forced arranged marriages are perpetrated for motives similar to those involved in child marriages: to maintain family honor, as reparation for a crime, and/or to satisfy tradition or cultural norms. Forced marriages differ from other arranged marriages, which are common in some cultures. The difference is in the issue of consent: a woman may consent to an arranged marriage but does *not* consent to a forced marriage (INTERIGHTS et al., 2000). Forced arranged marriages take place both in countries where such marriages are the cultural norm and among diasporic members of a culture who have relocated to another country where they are not common.

Approximately 1,000 women per year are taken from the UK to their country of origin to be forced into marriage. Most of these are Muslim, Hindu, and Sikh women from the Pakistani, Indian, and Bangladeshi diasporic communities in Britain (Hossain & Turner, 2001). Some cases of forced marriage involve the abduction of a woman and her transfer from one country to another, as when a Bangladeshi or Pakistani woman who lives in the UK is forced to get married in her native country. Typically, in these cases, a teenage woman is induced or forced by her immediate family members to travel to Bangladesh or Pakistan, ostensibly for a holiday or to visit an ailing relative. Upon arrival in the destination country, she is taken to her family's home, often in a remote, rural, and conservative area. The arrangements for her marriage take place without her consent. She is often kept under "house arrest" by her family, and has no way to communicate with the outside world. In some cases she does not even know the customs or the language of the country. Her passport may be taken from her. If she is being held in an area where women rarely travel alone, she risks serious violence if she leaves. Her family may even inflict physical and mental abuse upon her if she fails to comply with the marriage arrangements (Hossain & Turner, 2001). When she fails to return to school or work in Britain, she loses contact with friends, classmates, and colleagues. In some cases, she reappears, months or years later, with her new husband. In other cases, she seems to vanish (Hossain & Turner, 2001).

Women reporting a threat of abduction and forced marriage to the police, social services, or teachers sometimes face indifference or inaction by these authorities. Such inaction may be due to ignorance of the practice or unfamiliarity with it, or to a lack of knowledge of appropriate responses. Sometimes families bribe the authorities to allow the abduction. In other cases, the authorities fail to act due to ingrained gender and cultural biases, such as the assumption that forced marriage is a "family matter" and a legitimate religious or cultural practice, and therefore does not require external intervention (Hossain & Turner, 2001).

If the alleged abduction has already occurred, family members or boyfriends in the UK seeking the recovery of the woman concerned may find it difficult to obtain relevant information or advice from the authorities in countries in which forced marriages are common. In some primarily Muslim countries, the laws on abduction and other criminal offenses relevant to forced marriage are usually based not on Muslim law but on colonial penal codes, which in turn are based on common law. In some Muslim countries, religious leaders have no formal role within political or legal systems. Religious or community leaders, however, are likely to uphold the status quo and highly conservative viewpoints that support the control of women rather than the promotion of women's rights

(Hossain & Turner, 2001). Even when an abduction is reported to the police, the response may be inaction. In cases where the police have evidence regarding the abduction, detention, and threatened forced marriage of a woman, they may not be able to act without a witness statement from the victim (Hossain & Turner, 2001). If an allegation of abduction and forced marriage is made to the UK police, they may in turn seek the cooperation of the local police in the destination country. Police in either country may fail to uncover false documentation provided by the woman's family. Failure of the authorities in either country to interview the woman in private or to guarantee her confidentiality often results in false statements (Hossain & Turner, 2001).

Salma (Bangladesh)

Salma, eighteen years old, was persuaded by her family to go on holiday to Sylhet. While in Sylhet, she became aware of her parents' plans to marry her off against her will. As plans for the forced marriage developed, Salma eloped with a Bangladeshi man, whom she married in defiance of her family's wishes. Their families purported to attempt to resolve the situation through mediation. As part of the agreement reached through this process, Salma and her husband surrendered to the police. Salma then discovered that her parents had brought charges of kidnapping against her husband. He was arrested and remanded into custody. Salma herself was also held in jail, in so called "safe custody" as a putative victim of a kidnapping. Despite documentary evidence of Salma's age, and her own repeated statements of the circumstances in which she was being held, the Court relied on medical reports and found that she was aged 16. It then directed that she be placed in her father's custody. Salma refused to do so and insisted that she would prefer to remain in prison. (INTERIGHTS et al., 2000)

Forced arranged marriages take place in many places in the world; the countries highlighted above are but a few. In almost all such cases, the women or girls are not consulted because their opinions are considered irrelevant by those arranging the marriages. Girls and women are forced into these marriages because they are considered to be the property of the men in their families. In most of these cases, the marriages are political alliances between two families. Although we have presented cases of arranged marriages that are forced upon the woman concerned, it is necessary to point out that some arranged marriages are agreed to by both bride and groom, and can have very positive outcomes.

BRIDE KIDNAPPING

The countries in which bride kidnapping is most common today are Kyrgyzstan, Kazakhstan, Uzbekistan, Ethiopia, India, Pakistan, and Bangladesh. Bride kidnapping may be resorted to in order to obtain a bride without having to pay a bride price, because the woman or her family are not in agreement with the marriage, or to honor tradition. The practice is illegal and often results in a dismal existence for the bride, involving years of sexual slavery and physical abuse and even sometimes suicide or murder. However, since cultural norms condone or accept the practice, the abductors are very rarely ever arrested, convicted, or even reported.

Kyrgyzstan

Ala kachuu (meaning "to take and run away" in Kyrgys) is the act of abducting a woman for purposes of marriage in Kyrgyzstan. Nonconsensual bride kidnapping in Kyrgyzstan typically involves a young man and his friends taking a young woman by deception or force to the home of the young man's parents or a near relative. The young woman is held in a room until the young man's female relatives convince her to put on the marriage scarf. If she does not agree, she is kept overnight and sometimes raped, and is thus threatened by the shame of no longer being a pure woman (a virgin).

Feruza (Kyrgyzstan)

He forced me to have sex with him the first night. A woman came to say that they'd prepare my bed; I thought I'd be alone. I lay down to sleep, then he came in and he forced himself on me and raped me. I was saying no and he still did it. I cried and screamed. I still have psychological problems because of that incident. There were other times too when he raped me. I didn't want to ever go to sleep. I'd fight him off and try to sleep and he'd fight with me and hit me and force me. He especially hit me at night. I didn't want to have sex with him, but he forced me. I told my mother-in-law that I didn't want to live with him, but she just said I needed to stay, she said, "It happened to me also and I lived through it and so should you."

I was there for a year-and-a-half. I saw my parents only two times.... I told them I was unhappy and that he was treating me badly and was not a good man. My mother said she wanted to take me home, but my mother-in-law promised to tell my husband not to beat me. My mother believed them and left me there. Later, I told my parents I would die from it. Then my father said to wait a few more months and he would write a letter and ask me to come home for an urgent visit. [When the letter came] I told my mother-in-law, so they let me go and I got home. I was ill, psychologically, and had heart problems. I was not able to sleep. My parents took me to the doctor, who gave me medicine. When my mother-in-law came for me, they refused to give me to her. She yelled at my parents. She said I was lying about the way he treated me.... I am still afraid; afraid that it will happen again. I won't talk to any men. I am afraid of everything now. I don't talk to anyone.... I was seventeen years old when they took me.

—Feruza F. (Human Rights Watch, 2006d)

The "marital sex" during the many years of marriage that follow a forced bride kidnapping is a form of sexual slavery. Approximately 35 to 45 percent of married ethnic Kyrgyz women were married against their will as a result of bride kidnapping (Amsler & Kleinbach, 1999; Kleinbach, Ablezova, & Aitieva, 2005).

Some women are kidnapped by strangers. In cases of abduction by an acquaintance, deception is often used to gain the woman's trust. She may be invited to a party or offered a ride home from school, but she will be taken to the home of her abductor instead.

Nargiza (Kyrgyzstan)

When I was 18 years old I was kidnapped....This guy liked me and decided to steal me. He is the brother of one of my friends whom I studied with. She told me that her brother liked me, and so she introduced us. When I first saw him I didn't like the way he looked, and I said that I didn't want to date him. But then I went on one date with him, but I still didn't like him. On the second date he proposed to me. I said no. He argued a bit, but then he seemed to give in and said, "OK. I won't date you, I won't try to convince you." But he said that he wanted to give me a ride home. I said no, but he insisted. So I got in his car but instead of taking me to my house he took me to his family's house.... The night that my husband kidnapped me, he took me home to his house at about 6 p.m. They put me in a room in the corner with the curtain for the bride. I cried, I resisted, I asked them not to force me, because I was still so young. This resistance went on until five the next morning. And all that time they couldn't get me to calm down. There were numerous female relatives from my husband's family: his mother's brothers' wives, and his father's best friends' wives. They were all older, all around fifty-five. They sat with me, trying to convince me. They said, "He's a good boy, he doesn't smoke, doesn't drink, won't beat you, he is very gentle. If you go now, you don't know who you'll eventually marry."

I begged them to give me the telephone so that I could call my parents but they wouldn't let me call. They feared that my parents would come and take me. There is a tradition that the bride should write a letter that she "willingly agrees" to the marriage and this letter will be given to the bride's parents. They pressured me to do this. I didn't want to do it, but in the end, I did. I thought that if my parents came they would still take me home with them, even if I wrote this letter. I just wanted my parents to come. My mom's best friend came to the house to convince me to stay. We have this belief that once a girl has crossed the threshold, she can't turn back, or else she will have trouble all of her life. She told me that everyone she knows who left a marriage after kidnapping was unhappy. She said that I won't be happy, I won't get married, I won't have children. So I told her, "If you think I should stay, then tell me to stay, and I'll stay." But she didn't want to take this responsibility on herself. So she called my uncle. He is my friend, we are close. He was the one who convinced me. He said, "You'll get used to it all. This is a good home." So, in the end, I agreed. I figured, I'll have to get married anyway one day. The moldo [local cleric] came and performed the marriage ceremony.

—Nargiza N. (Human Rights Watch, 2006d).

Forced marriage is often violent and traumatic. It's a serious crime, but the police tend to treat is as a harmless version of a cultural practice. Although Kyrgyzstan has progressive laws on violence against women, the authorities fail to enforce them because they do not view such acts as crimes (Human Rights Watch, 2006c). Women have been kicked, strangled, beaten, stabbed, and sexually assaulted by their "husbands." Instead of attaining safety and access to justice if they try to escape, they are often encouraged to seek reconciliation with their abusers.

Uzbekistan

In Uzbekistan wife-stealing cases, there are many reports of the future husband raping the abducted woman as a way of making the marriage irreversible. The victim will then have little chance of marrying anyone else in tightly knit communities where everyone is aware of neighbors' activities.

Kidnapping of brides was traditional before Soviet rule, because it saved a man, especially from a poor family, from paying the high bride price that is customarily required. The woman or her family would sometimes acquiesce, because the arrangement was convenient and saved face all round. The poor man could acquire a wife in the "traditional way" without having to pay a bride price, and if the woman's family was poor its daughter could be married without the expense of a wedding feast.

The Soviet period in both Uzbekistan and Kyrgyzstan ushered in an ideology of gender equality and secular, rational freedom from traditions such as arranged marriage, bride price, and payment of dowry. Moscow frowned on kidnapping of brides and did its best to stamp it out. Nonconsensual kidnapping for marriage was not, however, uncommon during the Soviet period, and it has been on the increase since Uzbekistan became independent in 1991 (Handrahan, 2000a, 2000b; Kuehnast, 1998). Local nongovernmental organizations report that in recent years one in five brides in Karakalpakstan has been abducted before marriage, and one in 20 has never previously met her future husband (Aminova, 2004). This practice is illegal, and it is a distorted version of the traditional custom since it now frequently involves coercion and rape.

CONCLUSION

Early marriages and forced marriages of all types violate basic human rights. Forced marriage and the resultant sexual slavery condemns women to a life of isolation, sexual service, health problems, and abuse. Early marriage also denies women education and autonomy (UNICEF, 2006). Because marriage under the age of 18 threatens a child's basic rights (education, good health, freedom of expression, and freedom from discrimination), the best way to ensure the protection of children's rights is to set a minimum age limit of 18 for marriage (UNICEF, 2006).

Laws and policies on the local, national, and international levels need to make early marriage and bride kidnapping illegal, and these laws must be enforced. Penalties for those who violate these laws must be severe and consistent. One way to ensure that girls are not married when they are younger than the legal marriage age is to require registration of births (UNICEF, 2006). Those working against early or forced marriages need to be supported socially, culturally, and financially (Salopek, 2004).

7

Sexual Servitude

Several forms and examples of sexual servitude will be addressed in this chapter: "comfort women" during World War II, girls and women in bonded labor, "customary marriages," and girls and women being used in sex tourism. Although sexual servitude of girls and women occurs in many countries, those that will be highlighted in this chapter include China, the Philippines, Japan, Cambodia, Uganda, Thailand, Vietnam, Mexico, and Palau (in the South Pacific). There are many differences in the circumstances surrounding these situations, but they all have one thing in common: girls and women are forced to provide repeated sexual acts as a result of being claimed by another person.

OVERVIEW

Although some of the types of sexual slavery described in this chapter exist much as they did hundreds and thousands of years ago (bonded labor, for example), other forms (such as sexual tourism) have changed quite markedly in response to social and technological advances. Sex tourism did not exist in the past to the extent that it does today and was not of the type we see today. People now use the Internet to find the best locations for the type of sex tourism they desire. While sexual servitude during war has existed since time immemorial, it has also changed considerably since World War II. The sexual servitude that comfort women endured during that war will be addressed in this chapter. Sexual slavery during recent wars is discussed at length in chapter 4.

THE SEXUAL SERVITUDE OF COMFORT WOMEN

The rape of women is one consequence of war. Women are often raped during war by the conquering army. However, for some women the rape continues as they are used as sex slaves in rape camps, as was the case during conflicts in Bosnia, Rwanda, and the Congo, and has also been documented during countless other wars. In the not-so-distant past, the Japanese government forced many thousands of women into sexual servitude during World War II. These women were euphemistically called comfort women, and many of them were kidnapped, tricked, or taken by force to "comfort stations" or rape camps to be used as sex slaves for the Japanese soldiers.

Comfort Women

These sex slaves were mostly from Korea, but some were from other countries, including China, Indonesia, the Philippines, and Taiwan (Robinson, 2007). The rape camps were established by the Japanese government to satisfy soldiers' needs/desires, increase troop morale, prevent soldiers from raping enemy women, control sexually transmissible diseases (STDs), and keep military secrets secure (Robinson, 2007). The women were held as sex slaves during the war, and if they survived, they were released after the war ended to resume their previous lives. Many of them found this impossible. A small number of these women are still alive. In the following stories gathered by Amnesty International, women tell about their abduction and sexual slavery.

Lee Doo-soon (China)

When she was 17, Lee Doo-soon believed that she was going to work in a factory in China:

> Instead we were taken to a "comfort station." I was kept there for six years. Sometimes I was beaten by drunken soldiers. We were put to work the day after we arrived. It was beyond description. When I came back home, I just told my parents I had been working in China. I stayed at home for a while, but wasn't very comfortable. I moved to Pusan to make money working as a dishwasher. I have three children, I was just abused by men, there was no love or feelings involved.... I registered in 1992 as a "comfort woman" at the suggestion of my local authority. One of my sons looks after me. I did not expect that I would ever be able to marry properly. I could not love anyone, any man. (Amnesty International, 2007b)

Hwang Keum-joo (China)

When she was 19 years old, Hwang Keum-joo was forced by the Japanese army to leave her family after graduating from high school. She was informed that she was to work in a military hospital as a translator. She was transported to China with many other girls. Although she was housed near the hospital, she was forced to work as a sex slave in a comfort station for six years.

> They said I couldn't go home until my country became free. I was bruised and battered. I still feel pain in my womb and have back pain as they hit me with guns. My lower backbone was broken. My body is weak. Korea doesn't know how Korean girls were treated by the Japanese military. I was raped by doctors and high ranking officers, between four and 15 times every day. On the day of emancipation, I was told to leave the place quickly, otherwise the Chinese would get me. I walked; it took four months to get to Seoul. I begged for food and slept on the streets. It was a very painful time. When I returned, I learned my father had passed away. I had no desire

to go home, I didn't try to find my family. I couldn't tell anyone what happened as I was so ashamed, but when I saw Kim Hak-soon's interview [Kim Hak-soon was the first comfort women who came out], I decided to come out too. (Amnesty International, 2007b)

Lola (Philippines)

When Lola was 15 years old, she and her mother were dragged by Japanese soldiers into their garrison. The women were kept locked inside a room for three months. They managed to escape in October 1944 when the door to the room they were in was left unlocked.

> I can't remember the number of soldiers that raped me; I just closed my eyes and sometimes lost consciousness. After the incident in San Ildefonso and the Red House we [she and her mother] never talked about it. What happened to us was very shameful, it was a very difficult time. I have no more tears left. About 10 years ago my sister was watching TV and she saw Lola Rosa Hensen [the first Filipina survivor to publicly speak out] and said "what happened to you and mother also happened to other women—you can get justice. You should also speak out." If Lola Rosa had not spoken out we'd have never have talked about it. I've now been to many places to campaign about this issue: Tokyo, Hong Kong, the Netherlands. Children should never go through what we went through, there's nothing more painful and difficult than what we went through. It should never happen to other women especially to younger women. It should never be repeated. (Amnesty International, 2007b)

Kang Soon-ae (Palau, South Pacific)

When Kang Soon-ae was lining up for food one day she was selected by Japanese military officers to be sent to Hiroshima and then later to Palau in the South Pacific where she was taken to an army camp.

> A few days later, American ships surrounded the island. There were so many bombings, it was really intense. The Japanese soldiers went mad, when girls didn't obey, they took them into caves and cut their breasts and genitalia. That's when I was raped. I was so small and they were so big. I was only 14. I was just too young, I knew nothing. I was seriously hurt and bleeding. I was kept in a house made from palm trees and raped from then until the 1945 liberation. I was 19 then. Now I can't feel any pain, my flesh is all dead. My life was ruined, totally ruined. I was so ashamed. I feel tired, I feel really tired. Nobody knows my pain. The Japanese government should see me and realise what they did. They have to admit what they did. You will never know what I went through. I can never describe what happened. I don't know when it will pass away. (Amnesty International, 2007b)

Although some of the comfort women have come forward recently to describe their ordeal as sex slaves, they have done so at tremendous emotional and personal cost. Many harbor great shame as a result of their experiences. The Japanese government has been reluctant to acknowledge its role in forcing these women into sexual slavery. Under international pressure it has reluctantly offered to financially compensate them for their years as comfort women. However, some of the women have refused the money, explaining that if they accepted it their experience would then become prostitution, rather than slavery. Many of the women are still demanding a formal apology by the Japanese government.

SEXUAL SERVITUDE THROUGH "CUSTOMARY MARRIAGE"

The term "customary marriage" is used in many contexts, depending on the culture involved, but it generally refers to marriage that is other than traditional but is accepted by a culture. In the Middle East, customary marriage takes place when wealthy men from Gulf countries (notably Saudi Arabia and Qatar) marry young women from poorer Islamic countries (such as Egypt) or from Islamic groups in Asian countries (such as India). According to Islam, a man may have as many as four wives. Men, in consort with the girl's family, often obtain false certificates from doctors indicating that the new bride is old enough to marry legally. These certificates are necessary if the original date of birth was never recorded and the girl's actual age is unknown, or if the girl is under marriageable age. The brides are taken to their new homes, often in a different country, where they are divorced and forced to perform unpaid labor or sold or trafficked to be "married" to another man (Calandruccio, 2005). This was not the original intention of customary marriage, but this practice has been corrupted like so many other social practices related to sexual slavery.

Bopha (Cambodia)

Bopha lived in a rural village and married at 17. Her husband immediately took her to a hotel in another village and left her. Bopha discovered the hotel was a brothel and tried to escape, but she was forcibly detained and told she must pay off the price the hotel owner had paid for her. Bopha's debt kept increasing due to charges for her food, clothing, and other necessities. Bopha could not leave. Ravaged by HIV/AIDS, she was thrown out on the street and finally found her way to an NGO shelter in Phnom Penh. She has been there for two years receiving treatment; it is not known how much longer Bopha will live.

—Bopha, trafficked in Cambodia, originally from Cambodia.
(Polaris Project, n.d., *Bopha*)

A customary marriage contract sometimes involves the giving of a young girl (usually by her father), as payment for the father's debt, in situations where men view their wives and children as their property. In Uganda, Sara became a wife through the payment of bride price to her father, which, her husband believed, gave him the right to have sex with her at any time.

Sara (Uganda)

My husband would beat me often....He used to beat me when I refused to sleep with him....He wouldn't use a condom. He said "when we are man and woman married, how can we use a condom?"...It's a wife's duty to have sex with her husband because that is the main reason you come together. But there should be love....When I knew about his girlfriends, I feared that I would get infected with HIV. But he didn't listen to me. I tried to insist on using a condom but he refused. So I gave in because I really feared [him]. (Human Rights Watch, 2003b)

Forced marriage, either as in bride kidnapping (as is the custom in Kyrgyzstan and Uzbekistan) or during war (commonly engaged in during many civil conflicts including Sierra Leone's civil war) has been referred to as customary marriage (Belair, 2006). However, both these terms, "forced marriage" or "customary marriage," are a "complete misrepresentation and distortion of the [girls'] experience" (Alfredson, 2001). These girls are forced into sexual servitude or sexual slavery.

BONDED LABOR

Bonded labor—or debt bondage—is one of the least known forms of slavery today, even though it is the most common method of enslaving people. People in need of cash for daily survival are forced to sell their labor, or their children's labor, in exchange for a loan. A person becomes a bonded laborer when his or her labor is demanded as a means of repayment for a loan. The person is tricked or trapped into working for very little or no pay, often for seven days a week. The value of this prolonged work is likely much greater than the original amount of money borrowed or expended on behalf of the laborer, but most of the people in this situation are educationally, socially, and economically disenfranchised. The work can be in a factory, in a home as a domestic, in the fields, or in sexual servitude, but because we are focusing on sexual servitude, the other types of work will not be addressed here.

People enter debt bondage in a variety of ways. Labor may be required as a means of repayment of a loan or an advance. Employers may pay up to $5,000 for a worker to the holder of the original debt. This amount is added to any earlier debt, and then deducted by the employer from the worker's salary until the employer is reimbursed, which often takes years (Calandruccio, 2005). In the event that the worker requires medical treatment as a consequence of the sexual servitude, such as an abortion (possibly forced) or medication for a sexually related disease, this amount is added to the debt, prolonging the length of service. Failure to work off the debt can have dire consequences (Human Rights Watch, 2000).

Chan (Japan)

Chan had been working in debt bondage for three months when a client left her to take a taxi back to her apartment alone. Instead, she took the taxi to Tokyo and asked how to get to immigration. Immigration officials were not very helpful. "My mama's husband had followed me to the Japanese immigration office, but neither the Thai translator nor the immigration staff would help me hide from him."

Finally, the Thai translator called a travel agent to help arrange Chan's trip back to Thailand, and the travel agent referred her to a nearby guesthouse for the night. The next day, Chan went to the Thai Embassy and, after spending one night there, she was sent to stay at a women's shelter until she was deported later that month, in February 1994. After Chan was deported, an agent followed her to her home in Korat asking for the rest of the debt. "I was afraid, so I left my family's home and came to Bangkok. I am still afraid they are following me even though it is one year later. I am afraid that if they catch up with me they will kill me. When I was in Japan, I heard that that is what they do to those who don't repay their debt. That is why very few women dare to escape. Everyone I knew stayed and finished their debt." (Human Rights Watch, 2000)

These workers often lack the skill set to effectively advocate for themselves or demand their rights. As a result, many remain in debt bondage long after their "loan" is repaid. Children are often sold by their families or kidnapped as a result of debt bondage. In some cases, children are sold by their families for as little as $75. More commonly, bonded laborers or their employers trade their children in exchange for monthly payments of a few hundred dollars for one or two years of service. Traffickers often get as much as $5,000 for each child (Calandruccio, 2005). Female children who are traded to "pay off" a debt often work off the debt in sexual servitude.

As a mechanism of sexual slavery, bonded labor has existed for many centuries. It became common in South Asia because of the poverty of people in low castes and remains common in the global south today. Bonded laborers are routinely threatened with physical and sexual violence and endure it repeatedly (Anti-Slavery International, 1999).

Poverty and the exploitation of the desperation of others are the foundations of this practice. People involved are often illiterate and lack the skills to support themselves or their families. Bonded labor is illegal in most countries where it is commonly practiced. However, governments rarely enforce the law or attempt to punish those who exploit others in this way. Millions of people are currently in bonded labor worldwide (Anti Slavery International, 1999).

Sometimes women agree to bonded labor believing that they will be taken to another country to work as a nanny or waitress, only to discover that they are expected to provide sexual services once they reach their destination either instead of the duties they expected or as part of these duties.

Soi (Thailand)

Soi was born in Chiang Rai province and was a seamstress in Bangkok. She was making 3000 baht (US$120) a month. Soi was twenty-four years old when she was recruited in 1990. A Thai friend whom she had known for two years asked her if she would be interested in going to Japan. As Soi recalled, "[My friend] didn't tell me what kind of work there was, but said I could make a lot of money. I was interested." (Human Rights Watch, 1994; Human Rights Watch, 2000)

Such women are told that they are free to go once they pay back the considerable transportation expenses they have accrued, as well as their living expenses during their employment. The sum they are expected to repay often greatly exceeds the actual sum they should owe.

Faa (Japan)

Faa, who worked at a sewing shop in Udon Thani province before going to Japan, explained to Human Rights Watch that she knew she was going to work as a sex worker, but not that she would have to work off a debt. At nineteen, she arrived in Japan to find that she had to work every day for the next five months without compensation as she struggled to pay the money she "owed." (Human Rights Watch, 2000)

In central and western Africa alone, an estimated 200,000 children are traded each year (International Labour Conference, 1998). Landlords can bond a child worker for as little as US$1.50, and family debts are manipulated so that there is no hope of repayment.

Phan (Japan)

The Thai man who recruited Phan to work in Japan told her that she would have to pay off a debt of 100,000 baht (US$4,000) and that it would take her about two or three months to do so. "I said I wanted to go, but I didn't have any documents. They said, 'no problem,' they could arrange all the documents. I saw so many other girls going to Japan, so I agreed." Later, when Phan arrived in Japan, she found that her debt was more than seven times the amount to which she had agreed. (Human Rights Watch, 2000)

The commercial sexual exploitation of children is increasing, and organized networks can be found in Latin America, Asia, Africa, and, most recently, eastern Europe. Ironically, as prostitutes, the children often fall victim to the legal system that should be protecting them, when they are arrested for prostitution rather than being treated as victims and given the help they deserve (Scanlon, 2002).

Nuch (Japan)

Nuch was arrested in 1993 when police officers raided the snack bar where she was being forced to work off a debt of 380 bai (3.8 million yen; US$34,000). According to Nuch, the police came at 9:00 A.M. before anyone had gotten up, and, when the mama's [Madam's] daughter opened the door, she was faced with numerous police officers and police cars. The officers included three Japanese women who spoke Thai. Nuch recalled, "they asked me and the others in Thai whether we wanted to go home, and said if so, to get our clothes. Only myself and one other woman got our clothes, but everyone was arrested: the mama, her husband, his two Taiwanese friends, and the seven Thai women [who worked in the snack bar (place of prostitution)]. One Thai woman had just finished paying off her debt after two years and was about to be paid for the first time for twenty clients. She was especially upset.

We were all taken to the police station in the town. There we were asked for all of the details about what had happened to us." (Human Rights Watch, 1995a)

Nuch was then detained in three different jails over the next few months before being transferred to an immigration detention center, and finally returning to Thailand (Human Rights Watch, 2000).

SEX TOURISM

An estimated 1 million children in Asia are victims of the sex trade, much of it focused around sex tourism (United Nations High Commissioner for Human Rights, 1996).

> "They're not like prostitutes. They stay with you all day. They rub in the sun tan oil, bring us the towel. She even washes your feet. What English tart would do that? The problem is getting rid of them. Once you've bought them they stick to you. They even fight with each other over you. It's wicked." English sex tourist in the Dominican Republic. (Williams & Stein, 2002)

All one needs to do is search "adult travel" on the Internet and a host of websites advertising everything from sex tours to sex with teens or sex in groups will appear. There are individual women who display their personal pictures and bios, and time with them can be "booked" ahead. There are also links to hotels and restaurants, which make sex tourism on the Internet a one-stop shopping process.

"Sex tourism" is simply a euphemism for "prostitution tourism," which better describes the circumstances that women and girls experience (Farley et al., 2003). "Tourism" suggests fun and entertainment, but that is not how it is seen from the perspective of the person providing the "service." However, prostitutes who are involved with sex tourism are not "sex slaves" per se. Although children are sold in the sex tourism industry to service pedophiles, the majority of individuals serving the tourism are adult prostitutes, some of whom chose to be there.

> "I've had sex with a 14 year-old girl in Mexico and a 15 year-old in Colombia. I'm helping them financially. If they don't have sex with me, they may not have enough food. If someone has a problem with me doing this, let UNICEF feed them." Retired U.S. Schoolteacher. (U.S. Department of Justice, 2007)

The U.S. military presence in Asia, particularly in Vietnam, Thailand, and the Philippines, paved the way for sex tourism in that part of the world. In bars in the Philippines, women were often described as "three-holers," suggesting that they are inanimate objects with three "holes" that can be penetrated sexually. One woman reported that an American "wanted to do things to me that I didn't like, such as three holes." Another described her experience with an American: "I didn't know about blow jobs and three holes.... It was anal sex that made me cry" (Jeffreys, 1999, p. 190).

In 1998, the International Labour Organization reported that 2 to 14 percent of the gross domestic product of Indonesia, Malaysia, the Philippines, and Thailand was derived from sex tourism (Jeffreys, 1999). In addition, while Asian countries, including Thailand, India, and the Philippines, have long been prime destinations for child-sex tourists (CSTs), in recent years, tourists have increasingly been traveling to Mexico and Central America for their sexual exploits as well. Burmese girls as young as 13 are illegally trafficked out of Burma into Thailand by recruiters and sold to brothel owners (U.S. Department of Justice, 2007).

Thailand provides a good example of sex tourism as a motivation for trafficking women and girls. During the 1960s, prostitution was made illegal in Thailand. However, another law, the Service Establishments Law then made certain forms of "entertainment" legal. Women in entertainment were expected to provide special sexual services. The owners of brothels became "entertainment providers" and brothels became "service establishments." American soldiers on leave from the Vietnam War fueled this burgeoning sex tourism, but the war ended and the soldiers left. The Thai government encouraged sex tourism to make up for this loss. Thailand's interior minister was a proponent of the sex tourism trade. "International tourist arrivals jumped from 2 million in 1981, to 4 million in 1988 to over 11 million in 2003" (Bales, 2004, p. 75). Two-thirds of the "tourists" visiting Thailand are single men (Hamlyn, Peer, & Easterbrook, 2007).

Like adult forced prostitution, child sex tourism is often protected by inadequate law enforcement, criminal gang activity and corruption, the Internet (which facilitates contacts and can protect anonymity), today's ease of travel, and the endless poverty that leaves no hope for a better life for children. The people who buy sex from these girls come from all socioeconomic backgrounds and may hold positions of trust and esteem. Previous cases of child sex tourism involving U.S. citizens have featured a pediatrician, a retired army sergeant, a dentist, and a university professor. Child pornography is frequently involved in these cases; drugs may also be used to solicit or control the minors. Tourists engaging in CST often travel to developing countries looking for anonymity and the availability of children in prostitution.

Publicity materials lead sex tourists to believe that the women involved in sex tourism do not live in the same conditions of slavery as do young girls indebted to pimps and brothels: they expect cooperative, elegant young women. Two examples from sex tourism brochures illustrate the fantasy aimed at individuals interested in sex vacations:

Slim, sunburnt and sweet, they love the white man in an erotic and devoted way. They are masters of the art of making love by nature, an art that we Europeans do not know. (Life Travel, Switzerland, quoted in Bales, 2004, p. 76)

Many girls from the sex world come from the poor north-eastern region of the country and from the slums of Bangkok. It has become a custom that one of the nice looking daughters goes into the business in order to earn money for the poor

family.... you can get the feeling that taking a girl here is as easy as buying a package
of cigarettes... little slaves who give real Thai warmth.
    —Kanita Kamha Travel, the Netherlands. (quoted in Bates, 2004, p. 77)

The reality is that most children who are integrated into the sex tourism trade
are young teenage girls who are "used by situational abusers, i.e. men who neither
know nor care how young the girls are" (Jeffreys, 1999, p. 179).

CONCLUSION

People enter sexual servitude in many ways. They may be sold, kidnapped,
tricked, abducted, or manipulated, or they may even offer themselves for labor
through debt bondage. Some of the terms of sexual servitude are finite, while others are indeterminate and often unending. Because of the nature of sexual slavery
or sexual servitude, many individuals (most often girls and women) never live
to the end of their term of servitude because the vast number of them contract
AIDS or are abandoned due to aging, injury, pregnancy, or abuse.

Part III

Attempts to Reduce or Eliminate Sexual Slavery

8

Solutions: Success Stories and Legislation

While comprehensive policies or success stories do not exist for all of the practices discussed in this book, there is a very limited number of examples that show a great deal of promise or have already made a difference in reducing the impact or incidence of sexual slavery. Attempts to reduce, eliminate, or mitigate the effects of sexual slavery fall into several categories: community sensitivity and awareness-raising programs, life skills education programs, social marketing/edutainment (International Center for Research on Women [ICRW], 2007), law enforcement efforts, and legislative efforts. In some cases national or international agencies or organizations have identified best practices, but in other cases these programs have yet to be evaluated. In the latter cases, while an organization's practices might appear to represent good ideas, there are no data to confirm that they actually work. This chapter will highlight some of the most successful practices in the effort to eradicate sexual slavery on the part of individuals and NGOs, and collaborative and national efforts from many different countries, including Israel, Ghana, Niger, Romania, Uzbekistan, Australia, Nepal, Kenya, Bosnia and Herzegovina, the United States, the United Kingdom, and Sweden.

OVERVIEW

There are a few isolated successes worldwide when it comes to reducing sex trafficking and the sexual slavery of girls and women. In many parts of the world where these practices flourish, greed, a sense of male entitlement, patriarchy, illiteracy, devaluation of females, poverty, and cultural norms support them. As a result, trying to reduce or eliminate these practices seems close to impossible. But there have been a few "shining stars" in the darkness that have made a difference. These stars are individuals, NGOs, or lawmakers who are outraged by the injustices and who commit their efforts to stop them, often at extreme personal sacrifice. This is not a matter for one particular country or region alone. Because sexual slavery and human trafficking are often not only national but multinational or even global problems, the efforts originate from around the globe, as they must if they are to yield success.

In this chapter we provide examples of success on the micro as well as macro levels, representing programs from many continents. While there are several exciting examples below, as a whole they are insufficient, and many more initiatives are needed to impact the growing transnational problems.

SUCCESSFUL INDIVIDUALS

Israel (Anti-Trafficking Services Coordinator)

Rahel Gershuni is the Anti-Trafficking Coordinator for the Government of Israel. She started out doing this work in a voluntary capacity, but was officially appointed by the government to continue this work in 2006. She has tirelessly led the Israeli effort to fight sex trafficking. She became committed to this problem while helping one victim navigate the government bureaucracy. Since then she has not only continued to help individual victims, but she also began a reform movement within the Israeli government, working to develop policies that recognize trafficked women and children as the victims rather than the criminals of human trafficking. As a result of her efforts in the past few years, she has changed the attitudes of others, created or revised policies, and saved lives. Rachel Gershuni demonstrates that one person really can make a difference with enough drive, energy, and commitment. (U.S. Department of State, 2006).

Ghana (Escaped *Trokosi* Sex Slave)

At the age of seven Juliana Dogbadzi was taken to the shrine of the local Fetish Priest and made a *Trokosi* slave. She, like many other *Trokosi*, was given to atone for the sin of a male relative. Julie's parents gave her to the shrine to compensate for a petty theft committed by her grandfather, a man she never knew. Julie endured many years of slavery, sexual and otherwise. When she escaped, rather than trying to hide her shame and avoid recapture, she spoke out about her experience to increase public awareness of the practice and to work toward the release of all of the thousands of remaining Trokosi sex slaves. While a number of religious groups and NGOs have been helpful in freeing Trokosi sex slaves, two are highlighted here. International Needs Ghana partnered with International Needs Australia to buy as many Trokosi sex slaves out of sexual servitude as possible and provide them with shelter literacy and job training skills. Through the efforts of these groups, thousands of Trokosi and their children have been liberated from the shrines. As of 2007, International Needs Ghana has freed over 3,500 Trokosi slaves, but there are an estimated 2,000 still bonded along with their 8,000 children, who are subject to the same conditions as their mothers. (IN Network, 2007).

Without social services, literacy and job skills training, and safe and secure places to live, many liberated Trokosi slaves go back because of the stigmatization they face once freed, and because they lack alternatives. (United Nations Population Fund [UNFPA], 2007)

Juliana Dogbadzi is still living in Ghana, where she is waging a campaign to help end Trokosi, practiced in seven of Ghana's 110 districts. Through her efforts and those of International Needs, government groups and NGOs, thousands of women have been freed. Dogbadzi received a Reebok Human Rights Award in New York in 1999.

I visit the shrines and meet with the women personally. I explain to them that there's a need for this practice to change, and there's a need for them to be strong and get out of the shrine. Some see me on TV, they hear me on the radio and they hear that I've been to places in the cities to advocate for their release. So I serve as a role model, and this helps the cause. I'd like to start my own business. But for now, I'm still thinking about the women in bondage. My duty is to get them out of slavery. Then I can think about myself" [Dogar, 1999]. "What I do is dangerous, but I am prepared to die for a good cause. People send threats by letter and others confront me openly. Thank God that those I work with are very strong and give me encouragement. At the moment, eight girls have joined me in my work with the organization. My next step to disbanding Trokosi is to ensure enforcement of the law and to get allied organizations in the Republics of Togo and Benin to stop this practice in their respective countries. I do believe I have a calling because it is strange to be alive and sane and working after going through what I went through. The help that I have received from International Needs and my own confidence have made all the difference. I have totally forgiven my parents because I know that what they did to me was done through ignorance and fear. I don't want them to feel guilty so I avoid telling them about my experiences. I don't, however, see them often. I am glad to say that I am now happily married and have just had my first planned baby with the man I love. My life today is like the life of any other young woman. (Polaris Project, n.d., *Juliana Dogbadzi*)

Niger (Hadijatou Mani—Former Sex Slave)

Hadijatou Mani is suing Niger for failing to enforce laws that they had passed in 2003 to outlaw slavery. She contends that the government didn't protect her from being sold into sexual slavery and servitude when she was 12 for just £250. She says she was bargained over like a goat. "I have not had a day off in my life, and I want the suffering of so many women to stop. This situation must end, so I am very pleased I have been able to tell the judges about my case." She is claiming compensation of about £40,000 hoping that a judgment in her favor will strengthen legislation in Niger, where anti-slavery laws appear to have made little impact since being introduced...For ten years, Ms Mani was forced to carry out unpaid domestic and agricultural work, and was later abused as a sexual slave by her owner, who had four wives and seven other such slaves. When Niger outlawed slavery, Ms Mani was released officially and given a "liberation certificate." Her "master" refused to let her go, claiming that she was his wife, but a local tribunal allowed her to leave. However, when she married another man, she was found guilty of bigamy and was forced to spend three months in jail...Ms Mani, who is thought to be 24, is the first former slave to bring an action against a state. In the past, members of slave castes in countries such as India have mounted legal challenges against individuals or former employers. Her lawyers argue that slavery is still accepted in customary law, despite being outlawed by Niger's criminal code and constitution.

About 43,000 people are thought to be enslaved in the impoverished desert nation of Niger...If successful, her case—tried in the Community Court of Justice of the Economic Community of West African States—could pave the way for similar claims from the hidden population of slaves living in their hundreds of thousands across the region." (Bannerman, 2008)

NGOs THAT HAVE MADE A DIFFERENCE

The first two NGOs discussed below were highlighted in the 2006 *Trafficking in Persons* report as representing "International Best Practices." While they both provide shelter for women who were victims of sex trafficking, each of the programs has some additional noteworthy element. Each of these programs (from Romania and Uzbekistan) provides direct assistance to survivors of trafficking and sexual slavery, but each program offers some additional unique services that greatly increase its effectiveness. The last three NGOs discussed in this section (from Australia, Nepal, and Kenya) focus on work with children, child sex tourism, child prostitution, and child marriage.

Romania

The Reaching Out program's specialty is assisting survivors with employment. It includes a one-year recovery and assistance program that provides victims with shelter, health care, legal aid, and the opportunity to complete their education and to learn new skills that enable them to enter the workforce. The program assists survivors in finding jobs so they can support themselves and their families and will not have to return to prostitution as the only means of making money. Reaching Out also conducts information-awareness campaigns targeting potential victims, and maintains an active dialogue with local officials. Police now routinely refer victims to Reaching Out's shelter.

Uzbekistan

The Istiqbolli Avlod program now operates a shelter for survivors of trafficking and sexual slavery who have returned to Uzbekistan. Before the shelter existed, however, the staff took these survivors home to live with them, or they rented apartments for them. As a result of the program's work, 10 trafficking hotlines have been established; these took in over 13,000 calls in 2005. Istiqbolli Avlod has created a good working relationship with the Uzbek consul in the United Arab Emirates, and this has facilitated the repatriation of many Uzbek women.

Australia

The NGO Child Wise combats child sex tourism. Working with the government of Australia, it sponsored a regional education campaign to combat child sex tourism that was adopted in 2006. The program aims to heighten awareness of child sex trafficking/tourism among airline personnel, travel agents, immigration and visa officials, and the general public. It urges target audiences to call a local hotline to report suspicious activities. The program is especially valuable for local law enforcement agencies' efforts to detect and prosecute pedophiles and child sex offenders. The 18th Global Task Force to Protect Children from Sexual Exploitation in Tourism invited Child Wise to present its campaign model at the task force's March 10, 2006 conference in Berlin, Germany. Australia has begun numerous child sex tourism investigations and prosecuted 17 people under this legislation. (US Department of State, 2006)

Nepal

Maiti Nepal's mission is to protect Nepali girls and women from domestic violence, sexual trafficking, child prostitution, child labor and exploitation, and torture. A group of socially committed professionals formed Maiti Nepal in 1993. Their primary foci are preventing sex trafficking and rescuing and rehabilitating sexual slavery survivors. They are also dedicated to finding justice for survivors of sexual slavery by engaging in criminal investigations and legal battles against abductors. Maiti Nepal advocates from the local to the national and international levels (Maiti Nepal, 2006).

Among repatriated Nepalese sex-trafficked girls and women, more than one-third are HIV positive. Compared with those trafficked at 18 years or older, girls trafficked prior to age 15 years were detained in multiple brothels and were at greatly increased risk for HIV infection. Additional factors associated with being HIV positive include being trafficked, and longer duration of forced prostitution. Because of the high rate of HIV and AIDS among rescued girls, Maiti Nepal has established an AIDS hospice for these girls (Silverman et al., 2007). The hospice services include rehabilitation, shelter, care, and medical treatment (Maiti Nepal, 2006). Jeena was taken to Maiti Nepal's hospice.

Jeena (Nepal)

16-year-old Jeena Shrestha...was just 7 when she was sold into prostitution. "My baby teeth started falling out after I had been in the brothel for eight months," she says. She was diagnosed as HIV-positive at age 9, and she didn't even reach puberty until a year after she arrived at the hospice....she has full-blown AIDS. Jeena tried several times to escape. Each time, she was severely beaten and nearly starved as punishment. "The gharwali told me if I kept running away, she would grind hot chilies and put it in my private parts. She said this was a torture that would make me scream. After that, I just gave up. I was 7; I couldn't fight these people." Four months later, Jeena was sold to another brothel, where she lived and worked in a cage. Then, one day, she woke up with no feeling in her legs. Doctors discovered that she had suffered spinal-nerve and disk injuries from being raped by men considerably larger than she. They also tested her for HIV. She was positive, and also infected with multiple STDs. Jeena was 11 when she came to hospice. (Goodwin, 2003)

Kenya

In 1999 the Christian Children's Fund (CCF) started a program to prevent child marriage among the Maasai of Kenya. In the Maasai culture, girls are promised in marriage when they are babies or even before birth. This practice is called "booking." The CCF has instituted a new practice of booking girls into schools instead. This program, called Naning'oi, functions within the current dowry system, as the girl is promised to the school, rather than to a husband, and the girl's father is given gifts in return for this promise. As of 2007, 350 girls were enrolled in school, and at least 500 more are booked and will begin school when they are older (ICRW, 2007).

NATIONAL EFFORTS

Sometimes successes result from programs that are administered by a branch of a federal government or that represent a combined effort by many initiatives within a country, both public and private in nature. It is rare that national legislation is developed as a result of a comprehensive understanding of the complex issues that contribute to sexual slavery and the trafficking of girls and women. In this section, we present examples of the few outstanding multiagency successes, as well as effective legislation.

Bosnia and Herzegovina

The Anti-Trafficking Strike Force in Bosnia and Herzegovina conducted raids in 2005 and 2006, during which 26 victims were rescued and 14 traffickers were arrested. These arrests and rescues were a result of coordination between government agencies, prosecutors, and police (U.S. Department of State, 2006). In just one year, the Office of the State Anti-Trafficking Coordinator registered 43 new trafficking victims, assisted 59 victims, and was able to repatriate 12. Most of these women trafficked into Bosnia had come from Serbia, Ukraine, Moldova, Romania, and Russia. Almost half of the rescued victims were minors (U.S. Department of State, 2007a). The governments of Bosnia and Herzegovina implemented a victim referral network including several NGOs that operated shelters for trafficking victims. Shelters and safe houses that offered services to these victims existed in Sarajevo, Doboj, Banja Luka, Mostar, and Bijeljina. In addition to providing shelter, they also offered medical care, counseling, psychological and legal assistance, repatriation assistance, and some vocational training. The staff of the U.N. High Commissioner for Human Rights also trained attorneys in the country to assist trafficking victims who needed help with criminal and civil cases, involving victims' immigration status and legal rights (U.S. Department of State, 2007a).

United States

The Polaris Project is like a modern day Underground Railroad to combat sexual slavery. It has not only worked against human trafficking but has also developed effective partnerships between NGOs and the government, including the DC Office of the Deputy Mayor of Public Safety and Justice, the Peace Development Fund, the DC Task Force on Trafficking in Persons, the criminal and civil rights divisions of the Department of Justice, the U.S. Attorney's Office, the FBI and local police, child welfare and community organizations, and victim-support groups.

Polaris operates in Washington, DC, New Jersey, Denver, and Tokyo, and relies heavily on volunteer help from many countries. In addition to providing direct services, emergency shelter, and referrals for human trafficking victims, it also conducts workshops and outreach for girls in juvenile detention centers who might be trafficking victims, and conducts similar programs for women in the DC jail. One of its programs assists judges and law clerks to identify victims in trafficking-related cases. Polaris also trains building code inspectors to identify signs of trafficking in any buildings they inspect for building code violations. In one case, a police officer trained by Polaris encountered two potential trafficking victims who had been brought to Washington from the Midwest for sexual slavery. The women did not know in which city they were living, but the police officer had them call the Polaris hotline to get help (USINFO, 2007).

LEGISLATION

Legislation by itself is often unsuccessful in reducing sexual slavery. However, in the past few years some countries have thought about these issues creatively, and have managed to reduce the incidence of sexual slavery or practices that support it within their borders.

United Kingdom

Every year, approximately 100 school-aged children in the United Kingdom are forced to wed, oftentimes in arranged marriages in their countries of origin (such as Bangladesh and Pakistan). Some of these children are in their early teens. In response to this problem, some schools in the UK have instituted an electronic system to monitor truancy. If a child is missing for extended, unauthorized periods, the system notifies the authorities (Brettingham, 2007). Although this may not prevent parents from taking their children out of the country for a forced marriage, it can serve as an early warning system to allow the authorities to mobilize in the hope of stopping the forced marriage of a child.

Sweden

Sweden's formal stand on prostitution is that it is male violence against and exploitation of women and children. The Swedish government passed legislation to criminalize the buying of sex, while decriminalizing its sale, in 1999 (De Santis, 2005). Now, if men rob or beat a sex worker they have paid for sex, they are likely to be arrested and convicted. Sex workers are now considered victims rather than criminals (BBC News, 2007). An essential element of Sweden's prostitution legislation provides for comprehensive social service funds to help prostitutes desiring to change professions, and additional resources to raise public awareness.

The Swedish government funds police and prosecutors to work toward the elimination of human trafficking and provides intensive training that demonstrates that trafficking will not be tolerated in Sweden. As a result of this initiative, Sweden has dramatically reduced the number of women in prostitution. There are some major Swedish cities from which street prostitution, massage parlors, and brothels have almost disappeared. There were almost no foreign women trafficked into Sweden for sexual exploitation in 2007. The Swedish government estimates that between 2002 and 2007 only 200 to 400 women and girls have been annually sex trafficked into Sweden, compared to 15,000 to 17,000 females yearly sex trafficked into neighboring Finland (BBC News, 2007).

CONCLUSION

One person who is passionate about an issue can move mountains, sometimes from within the system, and other times working from without. Some of these people are religious, some are survivors of sexual slavery or trafficking, some are family members of victims. Individuals can make a difference by turning tragedy into hope. Success can occur in the local, national, or international arenas. The funding can come from private individuals or governments.

Some countries, notably South Korea, Taiwan, and Thailand, have virtually eliminated child marriages within the last decade (ICRW, 2005). These successes are not the result of one initiative, but rather the result of several that combine to create a multifaceted approach. There is no one perfect formula for all countries, since the issues and needs of countries vary. The best and most efficient way to achieve success is to truly understand the culture, the problem, and the socioeconomic and cultural issues that drive the problem. Recent successes have occurred as a result of increased educational initiatives, economic opportunities and growth, improvements in nutrition and in health and welfare access and services, and amendments to national laws (ICRW, 2005). The functions of practices such as child marriage must be understood within the culture, and if they are to be eliminated, a substitute may have to be found.

The best success strategies are often creative, consider the problem from a new vantage point, and are designed to work over time (rather than being expected to produce immediate results). Programs that have shown long-term sustainability, from the point of view of the survivors and the community, tend to include an educational component for women, girls, and the general community.

What is clear is that laws alone are not enough. In 2007, the Afghan Supreme Court passed legislation with the intent of stopping child and forced marriages in the country. The Afghan Independent Human Rights Commission estimates that up to 80 percent of current marriages in Afghanistan are forced. The legal age for marriage is 16 for girls and 18 for boys, but thousands of Afghan girls are forced to marry at a younger age each year (Empowering Women and Girls, 2007). According to the United Nations Children's Fund (UNICEF), 57 percent of marriages in Afghanistan involve girls below the legal age. The new marriage law is intended to ensure that brides are at least 16. One way the law attempts to ensure this is for couples to apply for a marriage certificate on which the girl's age is verified and approved. Yet, some girls in Afghanistan do not have birth certificates. They may have been born at home and no certificate was ever issued, or their families may have lost their papers while fleeing from political unrest. Even if the girl does have a birth certificate, many who marry do not apply for a formal marriage license. In Afghanistan, only a third of the people who marry actually apply for the formal marriage certificate (Empowering Girls and Women, 2007). Thus, many people circumvent the law by not requesting a marriage certificate in the first place.

Where laws do not have a significant penalty component or comprehensive approach, and are not enforced, people ignore the laws. Laws must be informed by the importance and place of the behaviors within a culture, and alternatives must be found. A critical mass of progressive female policymakers is also important, so that women can introduce policies and legislation from a female vantage point, rather than feeling they have to prove that they are just like men in order to be respected by their colleagues (Parrot, 2008).

Effective strategies require "buy in" from a majority of the stakeholders impacted by the practice. When a practice is taken away, it must be replaced with a suitable alternative, as in the case of *trokosi* sex slaves being traded for other items of value, such as cattle. Although cattle are not comparable in value to women, owning them does raise their owner's status, and they produce food and fuel (dried cow dung) that is valued in the community (Parrot and Cummings, 2006).

If an NGO or partner from outside the community is involved in sponsoring an alternative practice, it should not be the lead agency, and should provide technical support and funding rather than creating programs (Parrot, 2008). Grassroots strategies are often most effective because people from the affected culture not only understand the complexities of the problem but are also impacted by the change strategy, and therefore stand to benefit the most if it is successful. Therefore change agents and NGOs from within the community are often the most effective in creating meaningful and lasting change. What is clear is that there is no "one size fits all" program. Because cultures, countries, and regions differ in their circumstances, the program to combat the problem must be tailored to the specific set of circumstances and personalities involved. What all of the successful programs have in common is the presence of one or more person who cares passionately and will work tirelessly to end sexual slavery and/or trafficking of girls and women.

Because the trafficking of girls and women for sexual servitude and slavery are often cross-national problems, the solutions must address the realities in both the source countries and the destination countries. They must also address the underlying ideologies that drive the practices, such as patriarchy, greed, the devaluation of women and girls, illiteracy, and poverty. Laws or programs that work in just one country or region will not stop the trafficking and sexual slavery: they will merely reallocate the problem.

9

Consequences of Sexual Slavery and Trafficking of Girls and Women

This chapter will address the consequences of sexual slavery through religious justification, sexual servitude, forced marriage, and trafficking on girls and women worldwide. These include health (both physical and mental) and social consequences. Examples of victimization resulting in health or social consequences are provided from Thailand, the United States, Sierra Leone, Sudan, Nepal, and Israel.

OVERVIEW

Sexual slavery and its associated practices create social, economic, and ethical concerns worldwide: between countries, within countries, and on regional, local, familial, and individual levels. Those who are trafficked or enslaved live the nightmare, but those of us who are not primary victims may still be affected, with loved ones suffering as victims of the attitudes or behaviors that condone women's oppression. Many people experience the economic impact, because millions of dollars are spent on law enforcement, investigation, and containment of the problem. Many millions more are allocated to pay for the social and medical services necessary to treat the returned or escaped survivors. In a just world, slavery in any form is untenable; sexual slavery is a particularly heinous type as it continues to violate people in the most fundamental and intimate way.

There are countless immediate as well as long-term physical and emotional consequences suffered by victims and their families. The social consequences break apart families and communities. If a woman is fortunate enough to escape sexual slavery, the physical and social consequences often last throughout her life, and may even impact her children and her descendants for generations.

HEALTH CONSEQUENCES

It is difficult to separate the physical and mental health consequences resulting from sexual slavery. When women are suffering from chronic physical pain, HIV, or infertility as a result of their forced sexual servitude, it often causes mental health problems, such as depression. Conversely, post-traumatic stress disorder (commonly experienced as a result of sexual slavery) often impacts physical health by causing gastrointestinal disorders, ulcers, and heart disease. In the following section we will highlight the most common types of physical and mental health disorders that victims of sexual slavery experience. Of course, these problems are likely to be worse if the women were held for extended periods, or the trauma they experienced while enslaved was extreme.

Physical Health

Most sexual slavery involves some manner of confinement, as well as physical and psychological abuse. For many trafficked women and those forced into prostitution, violence has been a part of their lives since childhood. Farley and colleagues reported that more than half of prostituted women had as children experienced beatings so severe that they resulted in physical injury, and two-thirds of them had been sexually abused as children (2003).

Kahn (Thailand)

Traffickers took Khan, an eleven-year-old girl living in the hills of Laos, to an embroidery factory in Bangkok. There she and other children worked fourteen hours a day for food and clothing, but no wages. After protesting, Khan was beaten. After further protests, Khan was stuffed into a closet where the factory owner's son fired a BB gun pellet into her cheek and industrial chemicals were poured over her. Khan was rescued and is now receiving plastic surgery and counseling at a Thai government shelter.

—Khan, trafficked in Thailand, originally from Laos. (Slavery Still Exists, 2005)

The violence that women experience as slaves often results in neurological symptoms, gastrointestinal problems, back pain, and gynecological infections. These women suffer disproportionately from malnutrition, dehydration, poor personal hygiene (U.S. Department of State, 2004), and injuries sustained from abuse and beatings, including bruises, broken bones, cuts, and mouth and head injuries (Zimmerman, 2006).

Reproductive complications as a result of disease and injury are not uncommon either. These health problems include physical trauma to the genital area, vaginal and rectal fistulas (tears of the vagina and rectum often allowing urine or fecal matter to constantly drain from the vagina), prolapsed uterus or other uterine scarring and infections or complications, infertility, unwanted pregnancies, and complications during pregnancy, birth, or abortion. Postabortion risks such as incomplete abortion, septicemia (blood poisoning), and hemorrhaging are very high among this population. A 2003 study found that these conditions often result in death (U.S. Department of State, 2007b). Infant mortality is high among children born to enslaved women (Human Rights Watch, 2006e).

Untreated sexually transmitted infections may lead to serious consequences for long-term health. Pelvic inflammatory disease (PID) often leads to very serious health problems such as infertility, tubal pregnancy, hysterectomy, and chronic pelvic pain (Willis & Levy, 2002).

19-year-old woman gang raped during the civil war in Sierra Leone

Mosquito was the first person who raped me.... Then he ordered his men to continue the act. Nine other men continued to rape me.... After misusing me to their satisfaction, the rebels left me alone in a very hopeless condition.... Even now the pain is still in me, which is creating problems in my marital home, because my husband drives me from my home and says that I am barren. (Ben-Ari & Harsch, 2005)

Almost half of the millions of women and girls forced into prostitution each year are infected with the human papillomavirus (HPV) (Willis & Levy, 2002). Higher rates of HPV infection are associated with a high number of sexual partners and with first intercourse at an early age (National Cancer Institute (NCI), 2006; Willis & Levy, 2002).

Girls engaged in sex work are susceptible to developing cervical cancer. Sexually transmissible infections and HIV are found at higher levels in women who have been forced into sexual slavery. Armed conflicts in particular are vectors for sexually transmitted infections (STIs). It is not uncommon to find that soldiers have a higher rate (compared to civilians) of STIs and/or HIV, and therefore the women they rape will have much higher rates of diseases and infections, especially if the victims are gang raped or kept as sex slaves.

Abuk (Sudan)

Abuk Deng Akuei is a Christian girl in her early teens. She is the granddaughter of one of the great chiefs of Bahr El Ghazal and the half sister of the former Deputy Prime Minister, the Hon. Aldo Ajou Deng. She was enslaved two years ago during a PDF raid on her village of Bac, near Warawar: "My master was called Mohammed. I never heard he rest of his name. He lives in Aliet. He had eight other slaves. One of them was Adut Tong, a woman from Warawar. He and his wife, Howeya, called me Miriam, and made me do everything like a Muslim. Howeya was an unkind woman. I had to do all kinds of work in their home. During the rainy season, I also had to do a lot of cultivation. Mohammed often beat me. He also raped me many times. I had to sleep outside with the cows and the goats. He would come outside at night and have intercourse with me. Whenever I resisted, I got a bad beating. Mohammed and Howeya wanted me to be a Muslim woman, so they forced me to have my genitals cut (genital excision). A man did it. I don't know who he was. He tied my hands and legs down very tightly. You can still see the marks [scars on wrists visible]. It was so painful. I cried and cried. That was the worst thing they did to me. I am so happy to be here now. I will go back to Warawar and Bac, and I will go back to church again." (American Anti-Slavery Group, 1999)

Women who have been enslaved are often exposed to communicable diseases such as tuberculosis, or suffer from diabetes, arthritis, malaria, anemia, and/or hepatitis due to increased exposure to these diseases and lack of treatment (Farley et al., 2003).

Gita (Nepal)

"Not so long ago, I weighed 126 pounds; now I'm down to just 95 pounds," says 20-year old Gita, who was infected with HIV after being forced to service as many as 50 men a day for the three years she was in sexual servitude. "I know the disease is taking over my body. The diarrhea is constant. So are the sweats and headaches." Gita also has painful bone tuberculosis, a complication of the disease. "I know I don't have long," she says. "But stopping the traffickers is my revenge—the only one I have." (Goodwin, 2003)

In some cases, fear of HIV actually causes more trafficking. Many people in sub-Saharan Africa believe the risk of HIV transmission will be less if they have intercourse with a very young girl. This increases the demand for younger girls in the sex trade (Adepoju, 2005). Because clients will often pay more for unprotected sex, many sex workers do not always insist on condom use, instead seeking the higher price men are willing to pay. This exposes women to a higher risk of HIV infection. A study of sex workers in Togo found that almost 80 percent of the women who were tested were HIV positive (Adepoju, 2005).

In some cases, survivors of sexual slavery are too ashamed or unable to seek medical treatment. Seeking such treatment is especially difficult when there are no health care facilities nearby, and no money or transportation to get to them (Human Rights Watch, 2007b).

Girls and women who are forced into sexual servitude often become pregnant, and are then forced to have abortions. According to Human Rights Watch (2001b), of the 1,862 female sexual abuse victims who were raped and/or abducted during the January 1999 offensive in Freetown, Sierra Leone, and who received medical treatment and counseling from Doctors without Borders, more than half had been gang raped and 200 had become pregnant as a result of these rapes (Human Rights Watch, 2001b).

Kadiatu (Sierra Leone)

All of us arrived at Dankawali checkpoint where rebels told us to stand in line. They were checking whether there were any Guineans among us. They checked our properties and took whatever they could use. They occupied an old school building and asked the women in, one by one. A woman name[d] Fati was called in before me. It took a long time before she came out. Then it was my turn. There were five men inside the room. One of them lifted up my skirt to see whether they liked my thighs. They found my legs smooth. They said that they needed me to have a good time, and ripped my clothes off. The first one, who was called "Hold Me Cap," raped me three times while he was asking all kinds of questions about Guinea. He told me not to worry since they [the rebels] would retaliate. Then the second raped me twice. He was called "Lebanese." I started to feel pain so I offered the third one the little money I had left so he would stop after one time. The fourth man asked me what tribe I was. He then said that he would use me only once since he had a good friend who was a Temne by tribe, just like me. By the time the last one used me, I was dizzy and in a lot of pain. I hardly reacted anymore and I think he noticed because he did it slow to me and got up after a few minutes and left. I was released but could barely walk. All of us were released the same day and were told to move on. In the next village, Fati was complaining about pain in her abdomen. Then of course I knew. There was no chance to hide it from each other. I have a painful infection ever since during that day. (Human Rights Watch, 2001b)

Women who become pregnant under sexual slavery conditions are particularly vulnerable to postabortion risks, such as incomplete abortion, sepsis (infections of the bloodstream), hemorrhaging, and intra-abdominal injury, sometimes resulting in maternal death (U.S. Department of State, 2007b; Zimmerman, 2006). If women who have had abortions are forced to go back to work before they have healed sufficiently, there is a significant risk of postabortion infection. Abortions are often done by untrained individuals in unsanitary conditions, often resulting in infertility or more serious, life-threatening consequences (Barrows, 2006).

Jill (United States)

For three years I was forced to let men rape me for Bruce's profit. During that time, I'd nearly been killed several times, including Bruce's failed attempt to perform an abortion on me after I'd become pregnant. In 1982, I entered a suburban Los Angeles hospital bleeding extensively from my vaginal area. On my wrists, ankles and neck were burns, cuts and scars. Having been hung from the ceiling by my wrists while my pimp attempted to abort a child that I was pregnant with, I was in shock and nearly unconscious when I was brought into the hospital. A broken, long neck beer bottle had been shoved into my vagina as the object to remove the fetus. Needless to say, it didn't work out. The fetus remained in my womb but the abortion attempt nearly killed me. Fearing retaliation from my pimp, I didn't communicate to the doctors what had actually transpired, but instead, remained silent allowing my pimp's explanation of my abortion attempt to go unchallenged. Had these doctors given any thought [to] their ethical oaths it should have occurred to them that the bruises, scars, strangulation marks, etc. were inconsistent with attempting to abort my own child. Exactly how did I destroy my larynx attempting to abort a child? How did I self-inflict leather strap burn marks around my wrists and ankles? Since I was an in-patient for three days, why wasn't a mental health professional sent to talk to me? Why was I questioned only in the presence of my pimp who was masquerading as my older brother, who was pretending to help his psychotic little sister? Had I been questioned alone and placed in the psychiatric ward away from him, perhaps the outcome would have been different.

    —Jill, trafficked in the United States, originally from the United States.

    (Polaris Project, n.d., *Jill*)

Sex trafficking is believed to contribute significantly to the worldwide spread of HIV/AIDS. In South Africa, almost three-quarters of sex slaves and women who were trafficked into sex work are HIV positive. In 1996, the vast majority (between 50 and 90 percent) of children who were rescued from sexual servitude in Southeast Asia were HIV positive (World Congress against Commercial Sexual Exploitation of Children [WCACSEC], 1996). Sex trafficking is contributing to the global dispersion of HIV subtypes and the mutation of the HIV virus, as well as to the development of drug-resistant strains of other sexually transmitted infections (Joesoef, 1998).

Mental Health

For women who have been abducted, confined, manipulated, coerced, and violently forced into sexual slavery, the emotional and mental effects are almost unimaginable. While some physical injuries may heal, the emotional toll from these atrocities has long-term consequences, not just for the victims themselves but for those who know the victims as well. For children whose mothers are abducted, or for mothers whose daughters are trafficked, there are also long-term psychological effects.

Mental health trauma among women, including depression and anxiety, is often the consequence of being trafficked or enslaved. Depression, personality disorders, hopelessness, dissociative disorders, anger, rage, drug dependence, and post-traumatic stress disorder are common; two-thirds of rescued women have contemplated suicide (Farley et al., 2003; Raymond & Hughes, 2001).

Olga (Israel)

If I refused to work, they would not feed me. They beat me, but only across the back near my kidneys, so it would not hurt my appearance. It was very painful. I saw only clients who spoke no Russian, so I couldn't tell them my story. I saw 15–20 customers a day and the brothel owners gave me drugs so that I would work. I began to feel crazy and sick, so he gave me some kind of pills, which he told me were for headaches. I found out later that it was Ecstasy, a drug that makes you relax, and more willing to be intimate. After three weeks, I was dependent on the pills and asked for it every day.
—Olga, trafficked in Israel, originally from Russia; Testimony before the U.S. Senate Foreign Relations Committee, 2000. (Polaris Project, n.d. *Olga*)

Mental health services for survivors of sexual violence are generally unavailable or insufficient to cope with the demand for them. For example, as of 2002, there was only one qualified psychiatrist in all of Sierra Leone, where reports of uncountable and unspeakable atrocities against women have been documented (Human Rights Watch, 2007b).

Rachel (United States)

Seventy to eighty percent of us are diagnosed with post traumatic stress disorder even though we can't articulate or understand why we feel so numb to the pain we experience. We have nightmares in the daytime and terrors in the night. Many of us have STD, some of us can no longer have children. Some of us are infected with HIV or AIDS.

Many of us have physical scars, but all of us have scars that no one will ever see. We know how society feels about us, and we begin to internalize the stigma and we always carry around a sense of shame and self-loathing for the things that we've done. So, what do we need to get out of it? The first thing that we need is the understanding that we are not child prostitutes or teen prostitutes, but we are sexually exploited youth. This is not a choice we've made, it's something that has been done to us, but we are the victims and we should be treated as such. We don't need to be judged or stigmatized or made to feel any worse than we already feel about ourselves. We often come into contact with people or professionals and workers in emergency rooms and shelters and programs that should be able to help us, but because either they don't recognize the signs of what's going on, or they have their own preconceived notions about the type of people that we are, we don't receive the services or the intervention that we need. We need support to leave, it's hard to do it alone, and we need people to understand our fears are real. The people who hurt us are dangerous and we often genuinely are in fear of our lives. We need protection from these people, and sometimes we even need to be protected from our own choices, because we've been so dependent and brainwashed by these people, that sometimes we really do believe that this is our only option. We need a safe place to go, a residential facility that's designed just for us, where we're treated [for] our emotional and physical injuries that we're suffered and where we can begin to heal from our past. We need options, and alternatives, job training, access to education, assistance with basic life skills that often we've been denied. We need funding for programs and services that have been designed just for us because our needs are so unique and we can't be fitted into a lot of traditional programs.

—Testimony of Rachel Lloyd, a survivor of child trafficking, and founder of GEMS in New York City. Here she describes the experience of children trafficked into prostitution to the New York City Council (2002).
(Slavery Still Exists, 2005)

SOCIAL CONSEQUENCES

As a result of sexual slavery, families and communities are often torn apart. If the loss is due to war or armed conflict, the communities and families may already be struggling with disruption of their normal lives, terror, and other atrocities. In the case of girls who are abducted, trafficked, provided as "wives," or sold into sexual servitude outside of armed conflict situations, the loss to the individual family member may be emotionally devastating. Even when women escape or return home, they may be further victimized as their communities find out what they have experienced.

Perhaps one of the most devastating social consequences of forced sexual servitude is the stigma and discrimination these women face once they are freed (Aspler & Queyranne, 2007). Once they attempt the process of medical and psychosocial healing and return to their home communities, they often face rejection by partners, families, and communities (Doctors without Borders, 2004).

In Kosovo, ethnic Albanian women who were repeatedly sexually violated, often in rape camps, rarely speak about the trauma. Some families in these communities have rejected and ostracized these women because of their sexual violation. They are often blamed for shaming and dishonoring the entire family. In Kosovo, as well as in other communities in the region, it is not uncommon for a husband to divorce his wife when he learns or even suspects that his wife has been raped. Furthermore, unmarried women who have been violated in this way have almost no opportunities for marriage in Kosovo or related communities if their fate is known (Bumiller, 1999).

Survivors who do not return to their home communities are forced to survive in isolation. Trafficked women may end up residing in foreign countries, not knowing the language, with few of the skills necessary to work legitimately, and with little social service, medical, or legal support. Instead, they often live with other former slaves who become their families, and they leave behind the lives they knew in an attempt to create a home in a culture that is often not welcoming or understanding.

Women who report their victimization have sometimes been shunned by other victims of sexual violence for making their victimization public (Igric, 1999). This often means that other women will acknowledge that they have been threatened with or witnessed rape or other sexual abuse, but they will often not report having been victimized themselves (United Nations, 2000a). The United Nations Commission on Human Rights recommends that women who have been raped should not be characterized solely as "rape victims," as this term ignores the other violations they may have endured (2000). Women who have been raped and held in sexual slavery during armed conflict need to have services provided to help them with all the traumatic experiences they have had, some of which may be even more difficult to deal with than their sexual slavery.

Without appropriate attention being paid to the needs of women released from bondage, few will want to return to their previous lives, and they will not be welcomed back by their communities. Survivors need a safe place to go once they are free. They also often need job or vocational training, health care, and legal assistance. Once returned or freed, women need marketable skills so they can make a living wage. To that end, some NGOs train women in skills that will allow them to work in their own communities, rather than having to leave to find work. Furthermore, from a safety point of view, they most certainly often require police or community protection from those who enslaved them and believe that they "own" them (Farley et al., 2003).

Ying (Thailand)

Ying was born into a poor family near the Burma/China border. When she was sixteen years old, a neighbor in her village contacted her parents to discuss taking Ying to Thailand to find domestic work. He told her parents that they would receive a big fee for Ying. Everyone agreed to this plan and Ying accompanied the neighbor to the border of Thailand. After they crossed into Thailand, the neighbor handed Ying over to a new agent, a Thai national who told Ying she would stay overnight before going on to Bangkok. She was taken to his house with three other young Burmese girls. That night and for the following two nights, Ying and the other girls were forced to have sex with a series of Thai men. They had no choice. They were prisoners and couldn't escape. After three days, Ying was shipped to Bangkok. When she arrived in Bangkok, she was taken, with 30 other girls, all under 18 years of age, to another house. In the morning, the girls were sent to a local massage parlor and forced to become prostitutes. One of the girls refused, and she was beaten, raped and confined to an unlit room for three days without food or water. This effectively broke the girls. All money from the sex acts went to the manager of the massage parlor. Thus, their conditions amounted to virtually a contemporary form of slavery. In October of 1998, the Thai police raided the massage parlor and arrested Ying along with 22 other girls and the manager. The girls were charged with procuration for the purposes of prostitution. Thailand has no program for survivors of trafficking, and we don't know what happened to Ying and the other girls. In some cases, the girls are deported back to the country from which they came. Usually they are sick, destitute and frightened that the men who trafficked them will find them and traffick them again. Many are ashamed of what has happened to them, and isolated from families and friends because of that shame. Sometimes they are also afraid that the agents will track down their families and demand money from them. In all cases, they are alone, afraid and in need of help to rebuild their lives.

—Ying Chen, trafficked in Thailand, originally from Myanmar.
(Polaris Project, n.d., *Ying Chen*)

CONCLUSION

Cultural social attitudes must be challenged so that the subjugation and objectification of women and girls begins to diminish. The encouragement of education and literacy for girls may in turn lead to marketable skills. These skills help women become more valued and reduce the vulnerability that leads to victimization.

The gender implications of sexual slavery cannot be ignored. Women and girls are subordinated, devalued, and discriminated against worldwide, although to varying degrees. This gender disparity is compounded by the racial, ethnic, religious, or other forms of discrimination that female members of minority groups often face. This not only increases their vulnerability to sexual violence but also creates significant additional obstacles to asserting their rights and seeking redress for violations committed against them.

One way in which gender inequality impacts women disproportionately is that rape and other acts of sexual violence are still to a large extent linked to gender-based concepts of a family's "honor." Often the shame, ostracism, and dishonor that the perpetrator of sexual violence deserves for his actions are instead directed to the survivor. Often, by the time reports of sexual slavery and sexual violence are made public, it is already too late to help the victims. These women are already suffering from physical and emotional trauma as a result of the experience, they are unable to return home or uncomfortable doing so, and they are shunned by communities or families. Even if they are able to escape slavery, these women sometimes commit suicide, while others may die of a disease they contracted during their enslavement. The toll of sexual slavery on humanity is enormous.

10

Initiatives to Stop Sexual Slavery: International, National, and Legislative

OVERVIEW

Over the last three decades, various initiatives have been developed to prevent or minimize sexual slavery, its impact, and its causes. Policy initiatives and recommendations are directed at the international community, national community, and legislative levels. These recommendations are being implemented at an increasing rate by international human rights organizations, as a result of the alarming number of women being forced into sexual slavery. Unfortunately, as the number and types of initiatives to reduce sexual slavery increase, sexual slavery itself has continued to increase. The initiatives are well intentioned and appropriate, but not entirely effective. This is partly because sexual slavery and human trafficking are highly lucrative and secretive businesses; the likelihood of perpetrators being caught is very small; the conditions that make women vulnerable are constantly being created; and cultural assumptions that minimize women's worth persist. A number of initiatives will be highlighted below.

INTERNATIONAL INITIATIVES

There have been several important international milestones in addressing violence against women and girls, but they do not all specifically address the most critical issues that support sexual slavery and its related causes. Several of the most important milestones have been identified by Panos (1998) in *The Intimate Enemy: Gender Violence and Reproductive Health*. The first was the World Conference on Human Rights, Vienna (l993), which affirmed that women's human rights are a fundamental part of all human rights. The second was the International Conference on Population and Development (ICPD), Cairo (1994), which asserted that women's rights are an integral part of all human rights. At this conference, measures were taken to improve the status of women: women's empowerment; recommendations for governments including prohibiting the trafficking of women and children; promoting discussion of the need to protect women from violence through education; and establishing preventative measures and rehabilitation programs for victims of violence. The third milestone was the

UN Fourth World Conference on Women, Beijing (1995). The "Conference Platform for Action" recognized that "all governments, irrespective of their political, economic, and cultural systems, are responsible for the promotion and protection of women's human rights" (Panos, 1998). This document also specifically declared that violence against women is one of the critical areas of concern and is an obstacle to the achievement of women's human rights. In this document, countries were encouraged to integrate mental health services into appropriate primary health care delivery systems, and to develop training programs for primary health care providers, to help them recognize and care for girls and women who have experienced any form of violence (Panos, 1998).

In addition to the three mentioned above, four major international United Nations initiatives were developed and introduced in the hope that they would have a significant impact on violence and discrimination and violence against women and children specifically. The first to be introduced was the Convention on the Elimination of All Forms of Discrimination against Women (CEDAW), which was adopted by the United Nations General Assembly in 1979. It entered into force as an international treaty in 1981 after 20 countries had ratified it. As of 2007, 185 countries have ratified CEDAW (Appendix A, table). However, the United States, although it is a signatory to the convention, has not ratified it. Although President Carter signed CEDAW at its conception, ratification required a positive vote by the U.S. Senate Foreign Relations Committee. This has been the stumbling block, with either inaction or negative votes by conservative senators (Human Rights Watch, 2007). The credibility of the United States is called into question on human rights issues, in part, as a result of its inaction regarding the ratification of CEDAW.

The other three international initiatives are the Convention on the Rights of the Child (Appendix B), introduced in 1990, the Declaration on the Elimination of Violence against Women (Appendix C), introduced in 1993, and the Protocol to Prevent, Suppress and Punish Trafficking in Persons (Appendix D), introduced in 2000. All of these have advanced the global understanding of issues related to the sexual slavery of women and children, but none of them have effectively stopped the practice or factors contributing to it. The international approach is essential, because this is an international problem. However, when one country is successful in eliminating sexual slavery or related practices within its borders, there seems to be an associated increase in surrounding countries. Sweden's example of reducing forced prostitution is laudable, but one of its unintended effects was to increase the trafficking of women to countries bordering Sweden (see chapter 8 for a discussion of Sweden's experience).

Convention on the Elimination of All Forms of Discrimination against Women (CEDAW)

CEDAW brings girls and women into the forefront of human rights attention. This convention focuses the goals of the United Nations on females: to reaffirm "faith in fundamental human rights, in the dignity and worth of the human person and in the equal rights of men and women" (Appendix A). CEDAW is primarily concerned with human reproduction and the impact of cultural factors on gender relations. The legal status of women is central to this document. Additionally, CEDAW addresses the human rights of women, and it provides formal recognition of the influence of culture and tradition on restricting women's ability to access these rights. The implementation of CEDAW is monitored by the Committee on the Elimination of Discrimination against Women. The committee is composed of 23 experts "elected by States Parties" as individuals of "high moral standing and competence in the field covered by the Convention" (Appendix A).

Convention on the Rights of the Child

The Convention on the Rights of the Child was the first *legally binding* international instrument to assign all human rights to children (civil, cultural, economic, political, and social rights). In 1989, this convention was developed in recognition of the fact that people under 18 frequently require special care and protection not required by adults. The framers of the convention intended to make sure that the world recognized that children have human rights too. This convention spells out the basic human rights of children: "the right to survival; to develop to the fullest; to protection from harmful influences, abuse and exploitation; and to participate fully in family, cultural and social life" (United Nations, 2008). The four core principles of the convention are nondiscrimination; devotion to the best interests of the child; the right to life, survival, and development; and respect for the views of the child. Human dignity and the harmonious development of children are central to this convention. Children's rights are assured by the development of standards in health care, education, and legal, civil, and social services. By ratifying this convention, national governments commit themselves to protecting and ensuring children's rights and to hold themselves accountable for this agreement before the international community. States that have ratified the convention promise to develop and undertake all actions and policies set forth in it (UNICEF, 2008). As of 2008, only two members of the United Nations have not ratified this convention, the United States and Somalia (CRC, 2008). This convention is especially pertinent to the issues of child marriage, the sexual slavery of children (for example, *trokosi* and *devadasi*), sex trafficking, and children being forced into prostitution for sex tourism.

Declaration on the Elimination of Violence against Women

The Declaration on the Elimination of Violence against Women (DEVAW) was adopted by the United Nations General Assembly in 1993. It provided a definition of violence that included an acknowledgment of psychological violence (Panos, 1998). This declaration does not create legally binding obligations for nations, but it does clearly state that "violence against women constitutes a violation of the rights and fundamental freedoms of women and impairs or nullifies their enjoyment of those rights and freedoms. . . . The Declaration explains that violence against women is a manifestation of historically unequal power relations between men and women, which have led to domination over and discrimination against women by men and to the prevention of the full advancement of women" (UNIFEM, 2003). Although this declaration acknowledges that violence is rooted in historical power inequalities between men and women, it makes clear that violence against women violates existing universal human rights. This declaration's definition of violence is expansive, including physical, sexual, or psychological harm, and threats and coercion that occur in public as well as private circumstances. Finally, this declaration addresses the obligation of the state to guarantee the prevention of such violence, its investigation when it does occur, and the punishment of all perpetrators, regardless of their relationship to the victim or the circumstance in which the violation occurs (UNIFEM, 2003).

The Protocol to Prevent, Suppress and Punish Trafficking in Persons

Designed to "prevent and combat" trafficking in persons and facilitate international cooperation, this protocol provides for criminalization of traffickers, control and cooperation measures against them, and some measures to protect and help victims of trafficking. "Trafficking in persons" occurs when human beings are exploited by organized crime groups, where there is an element of duress involved and a transnational aspect, such as the movement of people across borders or their exploitation within a country by a transnational organized crime group. According to this protocol, trafficking is defined as the "recruitment, transportation, transfer, harbouring or receipt of persons" by improper means, such as force, abduction, fraud, or coercion, for an improper purpose, like forced or coerced labor, servitude, slavery, or sexual exploitation. Nations that ratify this protocol are required to create laws that criminalize these activities. With the exception of activities involving children, who cannot consent, this protocol differentiates between consensual acts or treatment and cases in which abduction, force, fraud, deception, or coercion are used or threatened. In addition to taking action against traffickers, nations that ratify it are required to protect and help persons who have been trafficked. Trafficked persons must be provided with confidentiality and protection against offenders. Social services, such as housing, medical care, and legal or other counseling must also be provided to trafficked persons. The law enforcement agencies of countries that ratify this protocol are required to cooperate in the identification of offenders and trafficked persons, sharing information about the methods of offenders and the training of investigators, enforcement officers, and victim support personnel. Countries are required to implement security and border controls to detect and prevent trafficking. In most cases, cooperation between states that ratify the protocol is mandatory, while cooperation with states that are not parties to this protocol is encouraged. Social strategies regarding prevention (research, advertising and social or economic support) are required of governments in their collaboration with nongovernmental organizations (World Revolution, n.d.).

Although many countries and regions of the world have attempted to limit sexual slavery and trafficking, none of them has demonstrated tremendous effectiveness, with the exception of Sweden. The United States has introduced the Trafficking in Persons Protection Act to monitor worldwide trafficking, but it is limited in scope and effectiveness. Attempts to thwart the offering of girls to temples in India and shrines in West Africa have had only partial success. Forced marriage is often so entrenched in the culture in which it occurs that it may be fully accepted by those who live there. The atrocities committed against women in armed conflicts have gained a lot of global attention, but this has not diminished their prevalence. The definition of war crimes has expanded to include sexual slavery and rape, but these war crimes continue to occur.

The international community has a responsibility to identify and avert impending conflicts, monitor the conduct of all parties involved in a conflict, and develop more timely and effective responses to reported atrocities. Responses can include a variety of strategies, such as diplomacy; economic, political or public pressure; or humanitarian or development aid.

Of all of the examples of sexual slavery during war highlighted in this book, "only the egregious acts of sexual violence that have occurred in Kosovo are within the jurisdiction of an existing international criminal tribunal, the International Criminal Tribunal for the Former Yugoslavia. The permanent International Criminal Court will have jurisdiction only over those crimes which are committed after the Court is established. Thus, in the vast majority of cases of sexual violence occurring in contemporary armed conflicts, national judicial systems must be relied on to investigate, prosecute and punish the perpetrators" (McDougall, 2000). To remedy this inequity, in 2000 the United Nations Commission on Human Rights prepared a list of recommendations to reduce the incidence and consequences of sexual slavery and violence, which are summarized below under national level, legislative approach, and postconflict recommendations.

NATIONAL LEVEL

National governments should enact legislation incorporating human rights, humanitarian law, and international criminal law into their legal systems. Legislation should provide jurisdiction over all types of slavery (sexual or otherwise), crimes against humanity, genocide, torture, and other international crimes. Criminal laws at the national and international levels should consider the following violations of the Geneva Conventions: slavery, sexual violence, rape, war crimes, forms of torture, crimes against humanity, and genocide, regardless of the location of the crime. National governments should be responsible for pursuing people believed to have committed or to have ordered crimes against humanity, including sexual slavery, genocide, and rape. Military and security force regulations and training materials must specifically address the prohibition of sexual violence during armed conflict, and officers must be mandated to enforce the regulations. Unlawful conduct involving sexual violence on the part of the military or security forces must be quickly contained and punished. Training on human rights, humanitarian law, and international criminal law must be provided for members of legal communities. The effective protection of civilians during armed conflict must address and acknowledge the realities, needs, and circumstances of women and girls (McDougall, 2000).

LEGISLATIVE APPROACH

Governments at all levels must ensure that their legal systems conform to internationally accepted norms without gender bias. Gender considerations should be fully integrated into the deliberations and work of lawmaking bodies and courts. The Office of the United Nations High Commissioner for Human Rights should document sexual violence in conflict situations, with the expectation of prosecution. Female translators and investigators with specific training in appropriate documentation techniques should be recruited and employed to investigate survivors' stories, with the intention of pursuing those responsible when possible. Coordination with all investigators to reduce the trauma of victims and witnesses in recounting their stories is critical. Victims of sexual violence must have their cases thoroughly investigated and carefully prosecuted, and be given access to all appropriate medical, legal, and social services. In addition, victims and witnesses of sex crimes must be protected from intimidation, retaliation, and reprisals at all stages of the proceedings and thereafter (McDougall, 2000).

POSTCONFLICT RECOMMENDATIONS

Human rights must be addressed in every peace treaty to avoid the amnesty that is frequently granted to people who have committed crimes such as sexual slavery, crimes against humanity, genocide, war crimes, and torture. According to the recommendations of the United Nations Commission on Human Rights in 2000, *demands for amnesty should be denied*. The involvement of women in the peace-building process is crucial to maintaining lasting peace, achieving reconciliation, and rebuilding war-torn societies. States must strengthen the role of women and ensure equal representation of women at all decision-making levels in national and international institutions that may make or influence policy with regard to matters related to peacekeeping, preventive diplomacy, and related activities and in all stages of peace mediation and negotiations (McDougall, 2000).

Perhaps the most important recommendations to reduce or eliminate sexual slavery and its related manifestations and causes are the following: "peace agreements should contain provisions designed to break the cycle of impunity and to ensure the effective investigation and redress of sexual slavery and sexual violence, including rape, committed during the armed conflict. Nor should peace treaties attempt to extinguish the rights of victims to reparation and other forms of legal redress. To that end, nations must develop and implement appropriate responses to sexual and other forms of violence against women which often escalate after the cessation of hostilities, in particular, domestic violence, and trafficking of women and girls" (McDougall, 2000).

While these recommendations are not exhaustive, they do acknowledge the difficulty and complexity of creating policies that attempt to address sexual violence against women and girls at local, national, and international levels. While appropriate and necessary as policy, recommendations do little to challenge the root causes of women's sexual enslavement. What is needed is a multifaceted approach related to the causes created by a world that devalues women and exploits their bodies.

There are a few examples that some measures may have an effect. On May 30, 2007 the "*Malaysia General News* reported that Jetsadophorn Chaladone, known as 'Ning,' a former child sex slave, last month was awarded compensation by an Australian court. Chaladone was sold into sex slavery by her father at the age of 13, and was rented out to pay back her debt and beaten for several months. A routine immigration raid discovered her. Chaladone is the first person in Australia to receive compensation for being a victim of sex trafficking" (Malaysia General News, 2007).

CONCLUSION

Structural violence (patriarchy, poverty, illiteracy) contributes to violence against women both by causing it and by preventing society and victims from confronting it effectively (Nikolic-Ristanovic, 2002). Therefore, it is not surprising that in spite of positive political changes and efforts made by civil society and political movements, few substantial legal and institutional reforms have directly addressed violence against women, especially in postcommunist countries (Nikolic-Ristanovic, 2005). The costs of economic change are very high, especially in developing and war-torn countries. A dramatic decrease in the standard of living and an increase in uncertainty, overall fluidity, instability, and war victimization have led to increasing sex trafficking and sexual slavery in the recent past. In addition, national concerns about illegal migration and the reluctance of the international community to address the causes rather than the consequences of sex trafficking make it difficult to establish effective solutions (Nikolic- Ristanovic, 2005). "If the society's structural dynamics continue to produce violence, anti-violence policies and programs are bound to fail" (Cunningham, 2000). The same is true of the failure of most anti-trafficking programs. Only by critically addressing and eradicating structural violence will causal problems related to sex trafficking in postconflict societies be eliminated (Nikolic-Ristanovic, 2005).

The reduction and eradication of the varied forms of sexual slavery depend on the most comprehensive attention to attitudes and behaviors that promote women's subjugation and oppression. These are incredibly complex problems.

This issue needs to be brought into the personal arena. Individuals need to consider how exploitation, gender bias, and discrimination affect their own lives. In February 2008, the United Nations held a forum in Vienna on fighting human trafficking, in which 1,400 delegates from 116 countries worked to develop a coordinated strategy to combat human trafficking. They called for businesses and civil society to take practical steps to prevent trafficking. They recommended self-certification by businesses to take slave-made products off their shelves; the development of technology to identify, monitor, and disrupt human trafficking routes; the tracking and blocking of credit card payments for Internet human trafficking transactions; and the development of international codes of conduct to curb sex tourism (United Nations, 2008). These ideas include recommendations from the macro to the micro level. But most importantly, they point the way to thinking creatively and comprehensively in an effort to employ different strategies to stem the tide of the human flesh trade. We need to think creatively to change the status quo. The lives of millions of victimized women and girls depend on it. If we are not part of the solution, we are part of the problem.

Appendices

Appendix A: Convention on the Elimination of All Forms of Discrimination against Women

THE STATES PARTIES TO THE PRESENT CONVENTION

Noting that the Charter of the United Nations reaffirms faith in fundamental human rights, in the dignity and worth of the human person and in the equal rights of men and women,

Noting that the Universal Declaration of Human Rights affirms the principle of the inadmissibility of discrimination and proclaims that all human beings are born free and equal in dignity and rights and that everyone is entitled to all the rights and freedoms set forth therein, without distinction of any kind, including distinction based on sex,

Noting that the States Parties to the International Covenants on Human Rights have the obligation to ensure the equal rights of men and women to enjoy all economic, social, cultural, civil and political rights,

Considering the international conventions concluded under the auspices of the United Nations and the specialized agencies promoting equality of rights of men and women,

Noting also the resolutions, declarations and recommendations adopted by the United Nations and the specialized agencies promoting equality of rights of men and women,

Concerned, however, that despite these various instruments extensive discrimination against women continues to exist,

Recalling that discrimination against women violates the principles of equality of rights and respect for human dignity, is an obstacle to the participation of women, on equal terms with men, in the political, social, economic and cultural life of their countries, hampers the growth of the prosperity of society and the family and makes more difficult the full development of the potentialities of women in the service of their countries and of humanity,

Concerned that in situations of poverty women have the least access to food, health, education, training and opportunities for employment and other needs,

Convinced that the establishment of the new international economic order based on equity and justice will contribute significantly towards the promotion of equality between men and women,

Emphasizing that the eradication of apartheid, all forms of racism, racial discrimination, colonialism, neo-colonialism, aggression, foreign occupation and domination and interference in the internal affairs of States is essential to the full enjoyment of the rights of men and women,

Affirming that the strengthening of international peace and security, the relaxation of international tension, mutual co-operation among all States irrespective of their social and economic systems, general and complete disarmament, in particular nuclear disarmament under strict and effective international control, the affirmation of the principles of justice, equality and mutual benefit in relations among countries and the realization of the right of peoples under alien and colonial domination and foreign occupation to self-determination and independence, as well as respect for national sovereignty and territorial integrity, will promote social progress and development and as a consequence will contribute to the attainment of full equality between men and women,

Convinced that the full and complete development of a country, the welfare of the world and the cause of peace require the maximum participation of women on equal terms with men in all fields,

Bearing in mind the great contribution of women to the welfare of the family and to the development of society, so far not fully recognized, the social significance of maternity and the role of both parents in the family and in the upbringing of children, and aware that the role of women in procreation should not be a basis for discrimination but that the upbringing of children requires a sharing of responsibility between men and women and society as a whole,

Aware that a change in the traditional role of men as well as the role of women in society and in the family is needed to achieve full equality between men and women,

Determined to implement the principles set forth in the Declaration on the Elimination of Discrimination against Women and, for that purpose, to adopt the measures required for the elimination of such discrimination in all its forms and manifestations,

Have agreed on the following:

PART I

Article 1

For the purposes of the present Convention, the term "discrimination against women" shall mean any distinction, exclusion or restriction made on the basis of sex which has the effect or purpose of impairing or nullifying the recognition, enjoyment or exercise by women, irrespective of their marital status, on a basis of equality of men and women, of human rights and fundamental freedoms in the political, economic, social, cultural, civil or any other field.

Article 2

States Parties condemn discrimination against women in all its forms, agree to pursue by all appropriate means and without delay a policy of eliminating discrimination against women and, to this end, undertake:

(a) To embody the principle of the equality of men and women in their national constitutions or other appropriate legislation if not yet incorporated therein and to ensure, through law and other appropriate means, the practical realization of this principle;

(b) To adopt appropriate legislative and other measures, including sanctions where appropriate, prohibiting all discrimination against women;

(c) To establish legal protection of the rights of women on an equal basis with men and to ensure through competent national tribunals and other public institutions the effective protection of women against any act of discrimination;

(d) To refrain from engaging in any act or practice of discrimination against women and to ensure that public authorities and institutions shall act in conformity with this obligation;

(e) To take all appropriate measures to eliminate discrimination against women by any person, organization or enterprise;

(f) To take all appropriate measures, including legislation, to modify or abolish existing laws, regulations, customs and practices which constitute discrimination against women;

(g) To repeal all national penal provisions which constitute discrimination against women.

Article 3

States Parties shall take in all fields, in particular in the political, social, economic and cultural fields, all appropriate measures, including legislation, to ensure the full development and advancement of women, for the purpose of guaranteeing them the exercise and enjoyment of human rights and fundamental freedoms on a basis of equality with men.

Article 4

1. Adoption by States Parties of temporary special measures aimed at accelerating de facto equality between men and women shall not be considered discrimination as defined in the present Convention, but shall in no way entail as a consequence the maintenance of unequal or separate standards; these measures shall be discontinued when the objectives of equality of opportunity and treatment have been achieved.

2. Adoption by States Parties of special measures, including those measures contained in the present Convention, aimed at protecting maternity shall not be considered discriminatory.

Article 5

States Parties shall take all appropriate measures:

(a) To modify the social and cultural patterns of conduct of men and women, with a view to achieving the elimination of prejudices and customary and all other practices which are based on the idea of the inferiority or the superiority of either of the sexes or on stereotyped roles for men and women;

(b) To ensure that family education includes a proper understanding of maternity as a social function and the recognition of the common responsibility of men and women in the upbringing and development of their children, it being understood that the interest of the children is the primordial consideration in all cases.

Article 6

States Parties shall take all appropriate measures, including legislation, to suppress all forms of traffic in women and exploitation of prostitution of women.

PART II

Article 7

States Parties shall take all appropriate measures to eliminate discrimination against women in the political and public life of the country and, in particular, shall ensure to women, on equal terms with men, the right:

(a) To vote in all elections and public referenda and to be eligible for election to all publicly elected bodies;

(b) To participate in the formulation of government policy and the implementation thereof and to hold public office and perform all public functions at all levels of government;

(c) To participate in non-governmental organizations and associations concerned with the public and political life of the country.

Article 8

States Parties shall take all appropriate measures to ensure to women, on equal terms with men and without any discrimination, the opportunity to represent their Governments at the international level and to participate in the work of international organizations.

Article 9

1. States Parties shall grant women equal rights with men to acquire, change or retain their nationality. They shall ensure in particular that neither marriage to an alien nor change of nationality by the husband during marriage shall automatically change the nationality of the wife, render her stateless or force upon her the nationality of the husband.

2. States Parties shall grant women equal rights with men with respect to the nationality of their children.

PART III

Article 10

States Parties shall take all appropriate measures to eliminate discrimination against women in order to ensure to them equal rights with men in the field of education and in particular to ensure, on a basis of equality of men and women:

(a) The same conditions for career and vocational guidance, for access to studies and for the achievement of diplomas in educational establishments of all categories in rural as well as in urban areas; this equality shall be ensured in pre-school, general, technical, professional and higher technical education, as well as in all types of vocational training;

(b) Access to the same curricula, the same examinations, teaching staff with qualifications of the same standard and school premises and equipment of the same quality;

(c) The elimination of any stereotyped concept of the roles of men and women at all levels and in all forms of education by encouraging coeducation and other types of education which will help to achieve this aim and, in particular, by the revision of textbooks and school programmes and the adaptation of teaching methods;

(d) The same opportunities to benefit from scholarships and other study grants;

(e) The same opportunities for access to programmes of continuing education, including adult and functional literacy programmes, particularly those aimed at reducing, at the earliest possible time, any gap in education existing between men and women;

(f) The reduction of female student drop-out rates and the organization of programmes for girls and women who have left school prematurely;

(g) The same opportunities to participate actively in sports and physical education;

(h) Access to specific educational information to help to ensure the health and well-being of families, including information and advice on family planning.

Article 11

1. States Parties shall take all appropriate measures to eliminate discrimination against women in the field of employment in order to ensure, on a basis of equality of men and women, the same rights, in particular:

   (a) The right to work as an inalienable right of all human beings;

   (b) The right to the same employment opportunities, including the application of the same criteria for selection in matters of employment;

   (c) The right to free choice of profession and employment, the right to promotion, job security and all benefits and conditions of service and the right to receive vocational training and retraining, including apprenticeships, advanced vocational training and recurrent training;

   (d) The right to equal remuneration, including benefits, and to equal treatment in respect of work of equal value, as well as equality of treatment in the evaluation of the quality of work;

(e) The right to social security, particularly in cases of retirement, unemployment, sickness, invalidity and old age and other incapacity to work, as well as the right to paid leave;

(f) The right to protection of health and to safety in working conditions, including the safeguarding of the function of reproduction.

2. In order to prevent discrimination against women on the grounds of marriage or maternity and to ensure their effective right to work, States Parties shall take appropriate measures:

(a) To prohibit, subject to the imposition of sanctions, dismissal on the grounds of pregnancy or of maternity leave and discrimination in dismissals on the basis of marital status;

(b) To introduce maternity leave with pay or with comparable social benefits without loss of former employment, seniority or social allowances;

(c) To encourage the provision of the necessary supporting social services to enable parents to combine family obligations with work responsibilities and participation in public life, in particular through promoting the establishment and development of a network of child-care facilities;

(d) To provide special protection to women during pregnancy in types of work proved to be harmful to them.

3. Protective legislation relating to matters covered in this article shall be reviewed periodically in the light of scientific and technological knowledge and shall be revised, repealed or extended as necessary.

Article 12

1. States Parties shall take all appropriate measures to eliminate discrimination against women in the field of health care in order to ensure, on a basis of equality of men and women, access to health care services, including those related to family planning.

2. Notwithstanding the provisions of paragraph 1 of this article, States Parties shall ensure to women appropriate services in connection with pregnancy, confinement and the post-natal period, granting free services where necessary, as well as adequate nutrition during pregnancy and lactation.

Article 13

States Parties shall take all appropriate measures to eliminate discrimination against women in other areas of economic and social life in order to ensure, on a basis of equality of men and women, the same rights, in particular:

(a) The right to family benefits;

(b) The right to bank loans, mortgages and other forms of financial credit;

(c) The right to participate in recreational activities, sports and all aspects of cultural life.

Article 14

1. States Parties shall take into account the particular problems faced by rural women and the significant roles which rural women play in the economic survival of their families, including their work in the non-monetized sectors of the economy, and shall take all appropriate measures to ensure the application of the provisions of the present Convention to women in rural areas.

2. States Parties shall take all appropriate measures to eliminate discrimination against women in rural areas in order to ensure, on a basis of equality of men and women, that they participate in and benefit from rural development and, in particular, shall ensure to such women the right:

   (a) To participate in the elaboration and implementation of development planning at all levels;
   (b) To have access to adequate health care facilities, including information, counselling and services in family planning;
   (c) To benefit directly from social security programmes;
   (d) To obtain all types of training and education, formal and non-formal, including that relating to functional literacy, as well as, inter alia, the benefit of all community and extension services, in order to increase their technical proficiency;
   (e) To organize self-help groups and co-operatives in order to obtain equal access to economic opportunities through employment or self employment;
   (f) To participate in all community activities;
   (g) To have access to agricultural credit and loans, marketing facilities, appropriate technology and equal treatment in land and agrarian reform as well as in land resettlement schemes;
   (h) To enjoy adequate living conditions, particularly in relation to housing, sanitation, electricity and water supply, transport and communications.

PART IV

Article 15

1. States Parties shall accord to women equality with men before the law.
2. States Parties shall accord to women, in civil matters, a legal capacity identical to that of men and the same opportunities to exercise that capacity. In particular, they shall give women equal rights to conclude contracts and to administer property and shall treat them equally in all stages of procedure in courts and tribunals.
3. States Parties agree that all contracts and all other private instruments of any kind with a legal effect which is directed at restricting the legal capacity of women shall be deemed null and void.
4. States Parties shall accord to men and women the same rights with regard to the law relating to the movement of persons and the freedom to choose their residence and domicile.

Article 16

1. States Parties shall take all appropriate measures to eliminate discrimination against women in all matters relating to marriage and family relations and in particular shall ensure, on a basis of equality of men and women:

   (a) The same right to enter into marriage;

   (b) The same right freely to choose a spouse and to enter into marriage only with their free and full consent;

   (c) The same rights and responsibilities during marriage and at its dissolution;

   (d) The same rights and responsibilities as parents, irrespective of their marital status, in matters relating to their children; in all cases the interests of the children shall be paramount;

   (e) The same rights to decide freely and responsibly on the number and spacing of their children and to have access to the information, education and means to enable them to exercise these rights;

   (f) The same rights and responsibilities with regard to guardianship, wardship, trusteeship and adoption of children, or similar institutions where these concepts exist in national legislation; in all cases the interests of the children shall be paramount;

   (g) The same personal rights as husband and wife, including the right to choose a family name, a profession and an occupation;

   (h) The same rights for both spouses in respect of the ownership, acquisition, management, administration, enjoyment and disposition of property, whether free of charge or for a valuable consideration.

2. The betrothal and the marriage of a child shall have no legal effect, and all necessary action, including legislation, shall be taken to specify a minimum age for marriage and to make the registration of marriages in an official registry compulsory.

PART V

Article 17

1. For the purpose of considering the progress made in the implementation of the present Convention, there shall be established a Committee on the Elimination of Discrimination against Women (hereinafter referred to as the Committee) consisting, at the time of entry into force of the Convention, of eighteen and, after ratification of or accession to the Convention by the thirty-fifth State Party, of twenty-three experts of high moral standing and competence in the field covered by the Convention. The experts shall be elected by States Parties from among their nationals and shall serve in their personal capacity, consideration being given to equitable geographical distribution and to the representation of the different forms of civilization as well as the principal legal systems.

2. The members of the Committee shall be elected by secret ballot from a list of persons nominated by States Parties. Each State Party may nominate one person from among its own nationals.

3. The initial election shall be held six months after the date of the entry into force of the present Convention. At least three months before the date of each election the Secretary-General of the United Nations shall address a letter to the States Parties inviting them to submit their nominations within two months. The Secretary-General shall prepare a list in alphabetical order of all persons thus nominated, indicating the States Parties which have nominated them, and shall submit it to the States Parties.

4. Elections of the members of the Committee shall be held at a meeting of States Parties convened by the Secretary-General at United Nations Headquarters. At that meeting, for which two thirds of the States Parties shall constitute a quorum, the persons elected to the Committee shall be those nominees who obtain the largest number of votes and an absolute majority of the votes of the representatives of States Parties present and voting.

5. The members of the Committee shall be elected for a term of four years. However, the terms of nine of the members elected at the first election shall expire at the end of two years; immediately after the first election the names of these nine members shall be chosen by lot by the Chairman of the Committee.

6. The election of the five additional members of the Committee shall be held in accordance with the provisions of paragraphs 2, 3 and 4 of this article, following the thirty-fifth ratification or accession. The terms of two of the additional members elected on this occasion shall expire at the end of two years, the names of these two members having been chosen by lot by the Chairman of the Committee.

7. For the filling of casual vacancies, the State Party whose expert has ceased to function as a member of the Committee shall appoint another expert from among its nationals, subject to the approval of the Committee.

8. The members of the Committee shall, with the approval of the General Assembly, receive emoluments from United Nations resources on such terms and conditions as the Assembly may decide, having regard to the importance of the Committee's responsibilities.

9. The Secretary-General of the United Nations shall provide the necessary staff and facilities for the effective performance of the functions of the Committee under the present Convention.

Article 18

1. States Parties undertake to submit to the Secretary-General of the United Nations, for consideration by the Committee, a report on the legislative, judicial, administrative or other measures which they have adopted to give effect to the provisions of the present Convention and on the progress made in this respect:

   (a) Within one year after the entry into force for the State concerned;

   (b) Thereafter at least every four years and further whenever the Committee so requests.

2. Reports may indicate factors and difficulties affecting the degree of fulfilment of obligations under the present Convention.

Article 19

1. The Committee shall adopt its own rules of procedure.
2. The Committee shall elect its officers for a term of two years.

Article 20

1. The Committee shall normally meet for a period of not more than two weeks annually in order to consider the reports submitted in accordance with article 18 of the present Convention.
2. The meetings of the Committee shall normally be held at United Nations Headquarters or at any other convenient place as determined by the Committee.

Article 21

1. The Committee shall, through the Economic and Social Council, report annually to the General Assembly of the United Nations on its activities and may make suggestions and general recommendations based on the examination of reports and information received from the States Parties. Such suggestions and general recommendations shall be included in the report of the Committee together with comments, if any, from States Parties.
2. The Secretary-General of the United Nations shall transmit the reports of the Committee to the Commission on the Status of Women for its information.

Article 22

The specialized agencies shall be entitled to be represented at the consideration of the implementation of such provisions of the present Convention as fall within the scope of their activities. The Committee may invite the specialized agencies to submit reports on the implementation of the Convention in areas falling within the scope of their activities.

PART VI

Article 23

Nothing in the present Convention shall affect any provisions that are more conducive to the achievement of equality between men and women which may be contained:

(a) In the legislation of a State Party; or
(b) In any other international convention, treaty or agreement in force for that State.

Article 24

States Parties undertake to adopt all necessary measures at the national level aimed at achieving the full realization of the rights recognized in the present Convention.

Article 25

1. The present Convention shall be open for signature by all States.
2. The Secretary-General of the United Nations is designated as the depositary of the present Convention.
3. The present Convention is subject to ratification. Instruments of ratification shall be deposited with the Secretary-General of the United Nations.
4. The present Convention shall be open to accession by all States. Accession shall be effected by the deposit of an instrument of accession with the Secretary-General of the United Nations.

Article 26

1. A request for the revision of the present Convention may be made at any time by any State Party by means of a notification in writing addressed to the Secretary-General of the United Nations.
2. The General Assembly of the United Nations shall decide upon the steps, if any, to be taken in respect of such a request.

Article 27

1. The present Convention shall enter into force on the thirtieth day after the date of deposit with the Secretary-General of the United Nations of the twentieth instrument of ratification or accession.
2. For each State ratifying the present Convention or acceding to it after the deposit of the twentieth instrument of ratification or accession, the Convention shall enter into force on the thirtieth day after the date of the deposit of its own instrument of ratification or accession.

Article 28

1. The Secretary-General of the United Nations shall receive and circulate to all States the text of reservations made by States at the time of ratification or accession.
2. A reservation incompatible with the object and purpose of the present Convention shall not be permitted.
3. Reservations may be withdrawn at any time by notification to this effect addressed to the Secretary-General of the United Nations, who shall then inform all States thereof. Such notification shall take effect on the date on which it is received.

Article 29

1. Any dispute between two or more States Parties concerning the interpretation or application of the present Convention which is not settled by negotiation shall, at the request of one of them, be submitted to arbitration. If within six months from the date of the request for arbitration the parties are unable to agree on the organization of the arbitration, any one of those parties may refer the dispute to the International Court of Justice by request in conformity with the Statute of the Court.

2. Each State Party may at the time of signature or ratification of the present Convention or accession thereto declare that it does not consider itself bound by paragraph 1 of this article. The other States Parties shall not be bound by that paragraph with respect to any State Party which has made such a reservation.
3. Any State Party which has made a reservation in accordance with paragraph 2 of this article may at any time withdraw that reservation by notification to the Secretary-General of the United Nations.

Article 30

The present Convention, the Arabic, Chinese, English, French, Russian and Spanish texts of which are equally authentic, shall be deposited with the Secretary-General of the United Nations.

IN WITNESS WHEREOF the undersigned, duly authorized, have signed the present Convention (United Nations, 2007).

STATES PARTIES

Currently, 185 countries—over 90 percent of the members of the United Nations—have ratified the convention (latest signature: San Marino, September 26, 2003; latest accession: Cook Islands, August 11, 2006). An additional state has signed but not ratified the treaty; therefore it is not bound to put the provisions of the Convention into practice.

State Ratifications

State	Date of Signature	Date of Receipt of the Instrument of Ratification, Accession, or Succession
Afghanistan	August 14, 1980	March 5, 2003 a
Albania		May 11, 1994 a
Algeria		May 22, 1996 a; b
Andorra		January 15, 1997 a
Angola		September 17, 1986 a
Antigua and Barbuda		August 1, 1989 a
Argentina	July 17, 1980	July 15, 1985 b
Armenia		September 13, 1993 a
Australia	July 17, 1980	July 28, 1983 b
Austria	July 17, 1980	March 31, 1982 b
Azerbaijan		July 10, 1995 a
Bahamas		October 6, 1993 a; b

State	Date of Signature	Date of Receipt of the Instrument of Ratification, Accession, or Succession
Bahrain		June 18, 2002 a
Bangladesh		November 6, 1984 a; b/
Barbados	July 24, 1980	October 16, 1980
Belarus	July 17, 1980	February 4, 1981 c
Belgium	July 17, 1980	July 10, 1985 b
Belize	March 7, 1990	May 16, 1990
Benin	November 11, 1981	March 12, 1992
Bhutan	July 17, 1980	August 31, 1981
Bolivia	May 30, 1980	June 8, 1990
Bosnia & Herzegovina		September 1, 1993 d
Botswana		August 13, 1996 a
Brazil	March 31, 1981 b	February 1, 1984 b
Brunei Darussalam		May 24, 2006 a
Bulgaria	July 17, 1980	February 8, 1982 c
Burkina Faso		October 14, 1987 a
Burundi	July 17, 1980	January 8, 1992
Cambodia	October 17, 1980	October 15, 1992 a
Cameroon	June 6, 1983	August 23, 1994 a
Canada	July 17, 1980	December 10, 1981 c
Cape Verde		December 5, 1980 a
Central African Republic		June 21, 1991 a
Chad		June 9, 1995 a
Chile	July 17, 1980	December 7, 1989 b
China	July 17, 1980 b	November 4, 1980 b
Colombia	July 17, 1980	January 19, 1982
Comoros		October 31, 1994 a
Congo	July 29, 1980	July 26, 1982
Cook Islands		August 11, 2006 a
Costa Rica	July 17, 1980	April 4, 1986
Côte d'Ivoire	July 17, 1980	December 18, 1995 a
Croatia		September 9, 1992 d
Cuba	March 6, 1980	July 17, 1980 b

State	Date of Signature	Date of Receipt of the Instrument of Ratification, Accession, or Succession
Cyprus		July 23, 1985 a; b
Czech Republic		February 22, 1993 c; d
Democratic People's Republic of Korea		February 27, 2001 a
Democratic Republic of the Congo	October 17, 1986	November 16, 1986
Denmark	July 17, 1980	April 21, 1983
Djibouti		December 2, 1998 a
Dominica	September 15, 1980	September 15, 1980
Dominican Republic	July 17, 1980	September 2, 1982
Ecuador	July 17, 1980	November 9, 1981
Egypt	July 16, 1980 b	September 18, 1981 b
El Salvador	November 14, 1980 b	August 19, 1981 b
Equatorial Guinea		October 23, 1984 a
Eritrea		September 5, 1995 a
Estonia		October 21, 1991 a
Ethiopia	July 8, 1980	December 10, 1981 b
Fiji		August 28, 1995 a; b
Finland	July 17, 1980	September 4, 1986
France	July 17, 1980 b	December 14, 1983 b; c
Gabon	July 17, 1980	January 21, 1983
Gambia	July 29, 1980	April 16, 1993
Georgia		October 26, 1994 a;
Germany	July 17, 1980	July 10, 1985 b
Ghana	July 17, 1980	January 2, 1986
Greece	March 2, 1982	June 7, 1983
Grenada	July 17, 1980	August 30, 1990
Guatemala	June 8, 1981	August 12, 1982
Guinea	July 17, 1980	August 9, 1982
Guinea-Bissau	July 17, 1980	August 23, 1985
Guyana	July 17, 1980	July 17, 1980
Haiti	July 17, 1980	July 20, 1981
Honduras	June 11, 1980	March 3, 1983

State	Date of Signature	Date of Receipt of the Instrument of Ratification, Accession, or Succession
Hungary	June 6, 1980	December 22, 1980 c
Iceland	July 24, 1980	June 18, 1985
India	July 30, 1980 b	July 9, 1993 b
Indonesia	July 29, 1980	September 13, 1984 b
Iraq		August 13, 1986 a; b
Ireland		December 23, 1985 a; b; c
Israel	July 17, 1980	October 3, 1991 b
Italy	July 17, 1980 b	June 10, 1985
Jamaica	July 17, 1980	October 19, 1984 b
Japan	July 17, 1980	June 25, 1985
Jordan	December 3, 1980 b	July 1, 1992 b
Kazakhstan		August 26, 1998 a
Kenya		March 9, 1984 a
Kiribati		March 17, 2004 a/
Kuwait		September 2, 1994 a; b
Kyrgyzstan		February 10, 1997 a
Lao People's Democratic Republic	July 17, 1980	August 14, 1981
Latvia		April 14, 1992 a
Lebanon		April 21, 1997 a; b
Lesotho	July 17, 1980	August 22, 1995 a; b
Liberia		July 17, 1984 a
Libyan A. Jamahiriya		May 16, 1989 a; b
Liechtenstein		December 22, 1995 a; b
Lithuania		January 18, 1994 a
Luxembourg	July 17, 1980	February 2, 1989 b
Madagascar	July 17, 1980	March 17, 1989
Malawi		March 12, 1987 a; c
Malaysia		July 5, 1995 a; b
Maldives		July 1, 1993 a; b
Mali	February 5, 1985	September 10, 1985
Malta		March 8, 1991 a; b
Marshall Islands		March 2, 2006 a

State	Date of Signature	Date of Receipt of the Instrument of Ratification, Accession, or Succession
Mauritania		May 10, 2001 *a*
Mauritius		July 9, 1984 *a*; *b*
Mexico	July 17, 1980 *b*	March 23, 1981
Micronesia		September 1, 2004 *a*
Monaco		March 18, 2005 *a*
Mongolia	July 17, 1980	July 20, 1981 *c*
Montenegro		October 23, 2006 *d*
Morocco		June 21, 1993 *a*; *b*
Mozambique		April 16, 1997 *a*
Myanmar		July 22, 1997 *a*; *b*
Namibia		November 23, 1992 *a*
Nepal	February 5, 1991	April 22, 1991
Netherlands	July 17, 1980	July 23, 1991 *b*
New Zealand	July 17, 1980	January 10, 1985 *b*; *c*
Nicaragua	July 17, 1980	October 27, 1981
Niger		October 8, 1999 *a*
Nigeria	April 23, 1984	June 13, 1985
Norway	July 17, 1980	May 21, 1981
Oman		February 7, 2006 *a*
Pakistan		March 12, 1996 *a*; *b*
Panama	June 26, 1980	October 29, 1981
Papua New Guinea		January 12, 1995 *a*
Paraguay		April 6, 1987 *a*
Peru	July 23, 1981	September 13, 1982
Philippines	July 15, 1980	August 5, 1981
Poland	May 29, 1980	July 30, 1980 *b*
Portugal	April 24, 1980	July 30, 1980
Republic of Korea	May 25, 1983 *b*	December 27, 1984 *b*; *c*
Republic of Moldova		July 1, 1994 *a*
Romania	September 4, 1980 *b*	January 7, 1982 *b*
Russian Federation	July 17, 1980	January 23, 1981 *c*
Rwanda	May 1, 1980	March 2, 1981

State	Date of Signature	Date of Receipt of the Instrument of Ratification, Accession, or Succession
Saint Kitts & Nevis		April 25, 1985 *a*
Saint Lucia		October 8, 1982 *a*
Saint Vincent & the Grenadines		August 4, 1981 *a*
Samoa		September 25, 1992 *a*
San Marino	September 26, 2003	December 10, 2003
São Tomé and Principe	October 31, 1995	June 3, 2003
Saudi Arabia	September 7, 2000	September 7, 2000 *b*
Senegal	July 29, 1980	February 5, 1985
Serbia		March 12, 2001 *d*
Seychelles		May 5, 1992 *a*
Sierra Leone	September 21, 1988	November 11, 1988
Singapore		October 5, 1995 *a*; *b*
Slovakia		May 28, 1993 *d*
Slovenia		July 6, 1992 *d*
Solomon Islands		May 6, 2002
South Africa	January 29, 1993	December 15, 1995 *a*
Spain	July 17, 1980	January 5, 1984 *b*
Sri Lanka	July 17, 1980	October 5, 1981
Suriname		March 1, 1993 *a*
Swaziland		March 26, 2004 *a*
Sweden	March 7, 1980	July 2, 1980
Switzerland	January 23, 1987	March 27, 1997 *a*; *b*
Syrian Arab Republic		March 28, 2003 *a*
Tajikistan		October 26, 1993 *a*
Thailand		August 9, 1985 *a*; *b*; *c*
The former Yugoslav Republic of Macedonia		January 18, 1994 *d*
Timor-Leste		April 16, 2003 *a*
Togo		September 26, 1983 *a*
Trinidad and Tobago	June 27, 1985 *b*	January 12, 1990 *b*
Tunisia	July 24, 1980	September 20, 1985 *b*

State	Date of Signature	Date of Receipt of the Instrument of Ratification, Accession, or Succession
Turkey		December 20, 1985 a; b
Turkmenistan		May 1, 1997 a
Tuvalu		October 6, 1999 a
Uganda	July 30, 1980	July 22, 1985
Ukraine	July 17, 1980	March 12, 1981 c
United Arab Emirates		October 6, 2004 a
United Kingdom of Great Britain & Northern Ireland	July 22, 1981	April 7, 1986 b
United Republic of Tanzania	July 17, 1980	August 20, 1985
United States of America	July 17, 1980	
Uruguay	March 30, 1981	October 9, 1981
Uzbekistan		July 19, 1995 a
Vanuatu		September 8, 1995 a
Venezuela	July 17, 1980	May 2, 1983 b
Viet Nam	July 29, 1980	February 17, 1982 b
Yemen		May 30, 1984 a; b
Zambia	July 17, 1980	June 21, 1985
Zimbabwe		May 13, 1991 a

a: accession; b: declarations or reservations; c: reservation subsequently withdrawn; d: succession.

Source: http://www.un.org/womenwatch/daw/cedaw/states.htm.

Appendix B: Convention on the Rights of the Child

Adopted and opened for signature, ratification and accession by General Assembly resolution 44/25 of 20 November 1989; entry into force 2 September 1990, in accordance with article 49

The States Parties to the present Convention,

Considering that, in accordance with the principles proclaimed in the Charter of the United Nations, recognition of the inherent dignity and of the equal and inalienable rights of all members of the human family is the foundation of freedom, justice and peace in the world,

Bearing in mind that the peoples of the United Nations have, in the Charter, reaffirmed their faith in fundamental human rights and in the dignity and worth of the human person, and have determined to promote social progress and better standards of life in larger freedom,

Recognizing that the United Nations has, in the Universal Declaration of Human Rights and in the International Covenants on Human Rights, proclaimed and agreed that everyone is entitled to all the rights and freedoms set forth therein, without distinction of any kind, such as race, colour, sex, language, religion, political or other opinion, national or social origin, property, birth or other status,

Recalling that, in the Universal Declaration of Human Rights, the United Nations has proclaimed that childhood is entitled to special care and assistance,

Convinced that the family, as the fundamental group of society and the natural environment for the growth and well-being of all its members and particularly children, should be afforded the necessary protection and assistance so that it can fully assume its responsibilities within the community,

Recognizing that the child, for the full and harmonious development of his or her personality, should grow up in a family environment, in an atmosphere of happiness, love and understanding,

Considering that the child should be fully prepared to live an individual life in society, and brought up in the spirit of the ideals proclaimed in the Charter of the United Nations, and in particular in the spirit of peace, dignity, tolerance, freedom, equality and solidarity,

Bearing in mind that the need to extend particular care to the child has been stated in the Geneva Declaration of the Rights of the Child of 1924 and in the Declaration of the Rights of the Child adopted by the General Assembly on 20 November 1959 and recognized in the Universal Declaration of Human Rights, in the International Covenant on Civil and Political Rights (in particular in articles 23 and 24), in the International

Covenant on Economic, Social and Cultural Rights (in particular in article 10) and in the statutes and relevant instruments of specialized agencies and international organizations concerned with the welfare of children,

Bearing in mind that, as indicated in the Declaration of the Rights of the Child, "the child, by reason of his physical and mental immaturity, needs special safeguards and care, including appropriate legal protection, before as well as after birth,"

Recalling the provisions of the Declaration on Social and Legal Principles relating to the Protection and Welfare of Children, with Special Reference to Foster Placement and Adoption Nationally and Internationally; the United Nations Standard Minimum Rules for the Administration of Juvenile Justice (The Beijing Rules); and the Declaration on the Protection of Women and Children in Emergency and Armed Conflict,

Recognizing that, in all countries in the world, there are children living in exceptionally difficult conditions, and that such children need special consideration,

Taking due account of the importance of the traditions and cultural values of each people for the protection and harmonious development of the child,

Recognizing the importance of international co-operation for improving the living conditions of children in every country, in particular in the developing countries,

Have agreed as follows:

PART I

Article 1

For the purposes of the present Convention, a child means every human being below the age of eighteen years unless under the law applicable to the child, majority is attained earlier.

Article 2

1. States Parties shall respect and ensure the rights set forth in the present Convention to each child within their jurisdiction without discrimination of any kind, irrespective of the child's or his or her parent's or legal guardian's race, colour, sex, language, religion, political or other opinion, national, ethnic or social origin, property, disability, birth or other status.
2. States Parties shall take all appropriate measures to ensure that the child is protected against all forms of discrimination or punishment on the basis of the status, activities, expressed opinions, or beliefs of the child's parents, legal guardians, or family members.

Article 3

1. In all actions concerning children, whether undertaken by public or private social welfare institutions, courts of law, administrative authorities or legislative bodies, the best interests of the child shall be a primary consideration.
2. States Parties undertake to ensure the child such protection and care as is necessary for his or her well-being, taking into account the rights and duties of his or her parents, legal guardians, or other individuals legally responsible for him or her, and, to this end, shall take all appropriate legislative and administrative measures.

3. States Parties shall ensure that the institutions, services and facilities responsible for the care or protection of children shall conform with the standards established by competent authorities, particularly in the areas of safety, health, in the number and suitability of their staff, as well as competent supervision.

Article 4

States Parties shall undertake all appropriate legislative, administrative, and other measures for the implementation of the rights recognized in the present Convention. With regard to economic, social and cultural rights, States Parties shall undertake such measures to the maximum extent of their available resources and, where needed, within the framework of international co-operation.

Article 5

States Parties shall respect the responsibilities, rights and duties of parents or, where applicable, the members of the extended family or community as provided for by local custom, legal guardians or other persons legally responsible for the child, to provide, in a manner consistent with the evolving capacities of the child, appropriate direction and guidance in the exercise by the child of the rights recognized in the present Convention.

Article 6

1. States Parties recognize that every child has the inherent right to life.
2. States Parties shall ensure to the maximum extent possible the survival and development of the child.

Article 7

1. The child shall be registered immediately after birth and shall have the right from birth to a name, the right to acquire a nationality and. as far as possible, the right to know and be cared for by his or her parents.
2. States Parties shall ensure the implementation of these rights in accordance with their national law and their obligations under the relevant international instruments in this field, in particular where the child would otherwise be stateless.

Article 8

1. States Parties undertake to respect the right of the child to preserve his or her identity, including nationality, name and family relations as recognized by law without unlawful interference.
2. Where a child is illegally deprived of some or all of the elements of his or her identity, States Parties shall provide appropriate assistance and protection, with a view to re-establishing speedily his or her identity.

Article 9

1. States Parties shall ensure that a child shall not be separated from his or her parents against their will, except when competent authorities subject to judicial

review determine, in accordance with applicable law and procedures, that such separation is necessary for the best interests of the child. Such determination may be necessary in a particular case such as one involving abuse or neglect of the child by the parents, or one where the parents are living separately and a decision must be made as to the child's place of residence.

2. In any proceedings pursuant to paragraph 1 of the present article, all interested parties shall be given an opportunity to participate in the proceedings and make their views known.

3. States Parties shall respect the right of the child who is separated from one or both parents to maintain personal relations and direct contact with both parents on a regular basis, except if it is contrary to the child's best interests.

4. Where such separation results from any action initiated by a State Party, such as the detention, imprisonment, exile, deportation or death (including death arising from any cause while the person is in the custody of the State) of one or both parents or of the child, that State Party shall, upon request, provide the parents, the child or, if appropriate, another member of the family with the essential information concerning the whereabouts of the absent member(s) of the family unless the provision of the information would be detrimental to the well-being of the child. States Parties shall further ensure that the submission of such a request shall of itself entail no adverse consequences for the person(s) concerned.

Article 10

1. In accordance with the obligation of States Parties under article 9, paragraph 1, applications by a child or his or her parents to enter or leave a State Party for the purpose of family reunification shall be dealt with by States Parties in a positive, humane and expeditious manner. States Parties shall further ensure that the submission of such a request shall entail no adverse consequences for the applicants and for the members of their family.

2. A child whose parents reside in different States shall have the right to maintain on a regular basis, save in exceptional circumstances personal relations and direct contacts with both parents. Towards that end and in accordance with the obligation of States Parties under article 9, paragraph 1, States Parties shall respect the right of the child and his or her parents to leave any country, including their own, and to enter their own country. The right to leave any country shall be subject only to such restrictions as are prescribed by law and which are necessary to protect the national security, public order (ordre public), public health or morals or the rights and freedoms of others and are consistent with the other rights recognized in the present Convention.

Article 11

1. States Parties shall take measures to combat the illicit transfer and non-return of children abroad.

2. To this end, States Parties shall promote the conclusion of bilateral or multilateral agreements or accession to existing agreements.

Article 12

1. States Parties shall assure to the child who is capable of forming his or her own views the right to express those views freely in all matters affecting the child, the views of the child being given due weight in accordance with the age and maturity of the child.
2. For this purpose, the child shall in particular be provided the opportunity to be heard in any judicial and administrative proceedings affecting the child, either directly, or through a representative or an appropriate body, in a manner consistent with the procedural rules of national law.

Article 13

1. The child shall have the right to freedom of expression; this right shall include freedom to seek, receive and impart information and ideas of all kinds, regardless of frontiers, either orally, in writing or in print, in the form of art, or through any other media of the child's choice.
2. The exercise of this right may be subject to certain restrictions, but these shall only be such as are provided by law and are necessary:

   (a) For respect of the rights or reputations of others; or
   (b) For the protection of national security or of public order (ordre public), or of public health or morals.

Article 14

1. States Parties shall respect the right of the child to freedom of thought, conscience and religion.
2. States Parties shall respect the rights and duties of the parents and, when applicable, legal guardians, to provide direction to the child in the exercise of his or her right in a manner consistent with the evolving capacities of the child.
3. Freedom to manifest one's religion or beliefs may be subject only to such limitations as are prescribed by law and are necessary to protect public safety, order, health or morals, or the fundamental rights and freedoms of others.

Article 15

1. States Parties recognize the rights of the child to freedom of association and to freedom of peaceful assembly.
2. No restrictions may be placed on the exercise of these rights other than those imposed in conformity with the law and which are necessary in a democratic society in the interests of national security or public safety, public order (ordre public), the protection of public health or morals or the protection of the rights and freedoms of others.

Article 16

1. No child shall be subjected to arbitrary or unlawful interference with his or her privacy, family, home or correspondence, nor to unlawful attacks on his or her honour and reputation.

2. The child has the right to the protection of the law against such interference or attacks.

Article 17

States Parties recognize the important function performed by the mass media and shall ensure that the child has access to information and material from a diversity of national and international sources, especially those aimed at the promotion of his or her social, spiritual and moral well-being and physical and mental health. To this end, States Parties shall:

(a) Encourage the mass media to disseminate information and material of social and cultural benefit to the child and in accordance with the spirit of article 29;

(b) Encourage international co-operation in the production, exchange and dissemination of such information and material from a diversity of cultural, national and international sources;

(c) Encourage the production and dissemination of children's books;

(d) Encourage the mass media to have particular regard to the linguistic needs of the child who belongs to a minority group or who is indigenous;

(e) Encourage the development of appropriate guidelines for the protection of the child from information and material injurious to his or her well-being, bearing in mind the provisions of articles 13 and 18.

Article 18

1. States Parties shall use their best efforts to ensure recognition of the principle that both parents have common responsibilities for the upbringing and development of the child. Parents or, as the case may be, legal guardians, have the primary responsibility for the upbringing and development of the child. The best interests of the child will be their basic concern.

2. For the purpose of guaranteeing and promoting the rights set forth in the present Convention, States Parties shall render appropriate assistance to parents and legal guardians in the performance of their child-rearing responsibilities and shall ensure the development of institutions, facilities and services for the care of children.

3. States Parties shall take all appropriate measures to ensure that children of working parents have the right to benefit from child-care services and facilities for which they are eligible.

Article 19

1. States Parties shall take all appropriate legislative, administrative, social and educational measures to protect the child from all forms of physical or mental violence, injury or abuse, neglect or negligent treatment, maltreatment or exploitation, including sexual abuse, while in the care of parent(s), legal guardian(s) or any other person who has the care of the child.

2. Such protective measures should, as appropriate, include effective procedures for the establishment of social programmes to provide necessary support for the child and for those who have the care of the child, as well as for other forms of

prevention and for identification, reporting, referral, investigation, treatment and follow-up of instances of child maltreatment described heretofore, and, as appropriate, for judicial involvement.

Article 20

1. A child temporarily or permanently deprived of his or her family environment, or in whose own best interests cannot be allowed to remain in that environment, shall be entitled to special protection and assistance provided by the State.
2. States Parties shall in accordance with their national laws ensure alternative care for such a child.
3. Such care could include, inter alia, foster placement, kafalah of Islamic law, adoption or if necessary placement in suitable institutions for the care of children. When considering solutions, due regard shall be paid to the desirability of continuity in a child's upbringing and to the child's ethnic, religious, cultural and linguistic background.

Article 21

States Parties that recognize and/or permit the system of adoption shall ensure that the best interests of the child shall be the paramount consideration and they shall:

(a) Ensure that the adoption of a child is authorized only by competent authorities who determine, in accordance with applicable law and procedures and on the basis of all pertinent and reliable information, that the adoption is permissible in view of the child's status concerning parents, relatives and legal guardians and that, if required, the persons concerned have given their informed consent to the adoption on the basis of such counselling as may be necessary;
(b) Recognize that inter-country adoption may be considered as an alternative means of child's care, if the child cannot be placed in a foster or an adoptive family or cannot in any suitable manner be cared for in the child's country of origin;
(c) Ensure that the child concerned by inter-country adoption enjoys safeguards and standards equivalent to those existing in the case of national adoption;
(d) Take all appropriate measures to ensure that, in inter-country adoption, the placement does not result in improper financial gain for those involved in it;
(e) Promote, where appropriate, the objectives of the present article by concluding bilateral or multilateral arrangements or agreements, and endeavour, within this framework, to ensure that the placement of the child in another country is carried out by competent authorities or organs.

Article 22

1. States Parties shall take appropriate measures to ensure that a child who is seeking refugee status or who is considered a refugee in accordance with applicable international or domestic law and procedures shall, whether unaccompanied or accompanied by his or her parents or by any other person, receive appropriate protection and humanitarian assistance in the enjoyment of applicable rights

set forth in the present Convention and in other international human rights or humanitarian instruments to which the said States are Parties.

2. For this purpose, States Parties shall provide, as they consider appropriate, co-operation in any efforts by the United Nations and other competent inter-governmental organizations or non-governmental organizations co-operating with the United Nations to protect and assist such a child and to trace the parents or other members of the family of any refugee child in order to obtain information necessary for reunification with his or her family. In cases where no parents or other members of the family can be found, the child shall be accorded the same protection as any other child permanently or temporarily deprived of his or her family environment for any reason, as set forth in the present Convention.

Article 23

1. States Parties recognize that a mentally or physically disabled child should enjoy a full and decent life, in conditions which ensure dignity, promote self-reliance and facilitate the child's active participation in the community.
2. States Parties recognize the right of the disabled child to special care and shall encourage and ensure the extension, subject to available resources, to the eligible child and those responsible for his or her care, of assistance for which application is made and which is appropriate to the child's condition and to the circumstances of the parents or others caring for the child.
3. Recognizing the special needs of a disabled child, assistance extended in accordance with paragraph 2 of the present article shall be provided free of charge, whenever possible, taking into account the financial resources of the parents or others caring for the child, and shall be designed to ensure that the disabled child has effective access to and receives education, training, health care services, rehabilitation services, preparation for employment and recreation opportunities in a manner conducive to the child's achieving the fullest possible social integration and individual development, including his or her cultural and spiritual development.
4. States Parties shall promote, in the spirit of international cooperation, the exchange of appropriate information in the field of preventive health care and of medical, psychological and functional treatment of disabled children, including dissemination of and access to information concerning methods of rehabilitation, education and vocational services, with the aim of enabling States Parties to improve their capabilities and skills and to widen their experience in these areas. In this regard, particular account shall be taken of the needs of developing countries.

Article 24

1. States Parties recognize the right of the child to the enjoyment of the highest attainable standard of health and to facilities for the treatment of illness and rehabilitation of health. States Parties shall strive to ensure that no child is deprived of his or her right of access to such health care services.
2. States Parties shall pursue full implementation of this right and, in particular, shall take appropriate measures:

(a) To diminish infant and child mortality;

(b) To ensure the provision of necessary medical assistance and health care to all children with emphasis on the development of primary health care;

(c) To combat disease and malnutrition, including within the framework of primary health care, through, inter alia, the application of readily available technology and through the provision of adequate nutritious foods and clean drinking-water, taking into consideration the dangers and risks of environmental pollution;

(d) To ensure appropriate pre-natal and post-natal health care for mothers;

(e) To ensure that all segments of society, in particular parents and children, are informed, have access to education and are supported in the use of basic knowledge of child health and nutrition, the advantages of breastfeeding, hygiene and environmental sanitation and the prevention of accidents;

(f) To develop preventive health care, guidance for parents and family planning education and services.

3. States Parties shall take all effective and appropriate measures with a view to abolishing traditional practices prejudicial to the health of children.

4. States Parties undertake to promote and encourage international co-operation with a view to achieving progressively the full realization of the right recognized in the present article. In this regard, particular account shall be taken of the needs of developing countries.

Article 25

States Parties recognize the right of a child who has been placed by the competent authorities for the purposes of care, protection or treatment of his or her physical or mental health, to a periodic review of the treatment provided to the child and all other circumstances relevant to his or her placement.

Article 26

1. States Parties shall recognize for every child the right to benefit from social security, including social insurance, and shall take the necessary measures to achieve the full realization of this right in accordance with their national law.

2. The benefits should, where appropriate, be granted, taking into account the resources and the circumstances of the child and persons having responsibility for the maintenance of the child, as well as any other consideration relevant to an application for benefits made by or on behalf of the child.

Article 27

1. States Parties recognize the right of every child to a standard of living adequate for the child's physical, mental, spiritual, moral and social development.

2. The parent(s) or others responsible for the child have the primary responsibility to secure, within their abilities and financial capacities, the conditions of living necessary for the child's development.

3. States Parties, in accordance with national conditions and within their means, shall take appropriate measures to assist parents and others responsible for the

child to implement this right and shall in case of need provide material assistance and support programmes, particularly with regard to nutrition, clothing
and housing.

4. States Parties shall take all appropriate measures to secure the recovery of
maintenance for the child from the parents or other persons having financial
responsibility for the child, both within the State Party and from abroad. In
particular, where the person having financial responsibility for the child lives
in a State different from that of the child, States Parties shall promote the
accession to international agreements or the conclusion of such agreements, as
well as the making of other appropriate arrangements.

Article 28

1. States Parties recognize the right of the child to education, and with a view to
achieving this right progressively and on the basis of equal opportunity, they
shall, in particular:

    (a) Make primary education compulsory and available free to all;

    (b) Encourage the development of different forms of secondary education, in-
    cluding general and vocational education, make them available and acces-
    sible to every child, and take appropriate measures such as the introduction
    of free education and offering financial assistance in case of need;

    (c) Make higher education accessible to all on the basis of capacity by every
    appropriate means;

    (d) Make educational and vocational information and guidance available and
    accessible to all children;

    (e) Take measures to encourage regular attendance at schools and the reduc-
    tion of drop-out rates.

2. States Parties shall take all appropriate measures to ensure that school discipline is administered in a manner consistent with the child's human dignity
and in conformity with the present Convention.

3. States Parties shall promote and encourage international cooperation in matters relating to education, in particular with a view to contributing to the
elimination of ignorance and illiteracy throughout the world and facilitating
access to scientific and technical knowledge and modern teaching methods.
In this regard, particular account shall be taken of the needs of developing
countries.

Article 29

1. States Parties agree that the education of the child shall be directed to:

    (a) The development of the child's personality, talents and mental and physi-
    cal abilities to their fullest potential;

    (b) The development of respect for human rights and fundamental freedoms,
    and for the principles enshrined in the Charter of the United Nations;

    (c) The development of respect for the child's parents, his or her own cultural
    identity, language and values, for the national values of the country in

which the child is living, the country from which he or she may originate, and for civilizations different from his or her own;

(d) The preparation of the child for responsible life in a free society, in the spirit of understanding, peace, tolerance, equality of sexes, and friendship among all peoples, ethnic, national and religious groups and persons of indigenous origin;

(e) The development of respect for the natural environment.

2. No part of the present article or article 28 shall be construed so as to interfere with the liberty of individuals and bodies to establish and direct educational institutions, subject always to the observance of the principle set forth in paragraph 1 of the present article and to the requirements that the education given in such institutions shall conform to such minimum standards as may be laid down by the State.

Article 30

In those States in which ethnic, religious or linguistic minorities or persons of indigenous origin exist, a child belonging to such a minority or who is indigenous shall not be denied the right, in community with other members of his or her group, to enjoy his or her own culture, to profess and practise his or her own religion, or to use his or her own language.

Article 31

1. States Parties recognize the right of the child to rest and leisure, to engage in play and recreational activities appropriate to the age of the child and to participate freely in cultural life and the arts.

2. States Parties shall respect and promote the right of the child to participate fully in cultural and artistic life and shall encourage the provision of appropriate and equal opportunities for cultural, artistic, recreational and leisure activity.

Article 32

1. States Parties recognize the right of the child to be protected from economic exploitation and from performing any work that is likely to be hazardous or to interfere with the child's education, or to be harmful to the child's health or physical, mental, spiritual, moral or social development.

2. States Parties shall take legislative, administrative, social and educational measures to ensure the implementation of the present article. To this end, and having regard to the relevant provisions of other international instruments, States Parties shall in particular:

   (a) Provide for a minimum age or minimum ages for admission to employment;

   (b) Provide for appropriate regulation of the hours and conditions of employment;

   (c) Provide for appropriate penalties or other sanctions to ensure the effective enforcement of the present article.

Article 33

States Parties shall take all appropriate measures, including legislative, administrative, social and educational measures, to protect children from the illicit use of narcotic drugs and psychotropic substances as defined in the relevant international treaties, and to prevent the use of children in the illicit production and trafficking of such substances.

Article 34

States Parties undertake to protect the child from all forms of sexual exploitation and sexual abuse. For these purposes, States Parties shall in particular take all appropriate national, bilateral and multilateral measures to prevent:

(a) The inducement or coercion of a child to engage in any unlawful sexual activity;
(b) The exploitative use of children in prostitution or other unlawful sexual practices;
(c) The exploitative use of children in pornographic performances and materials.

Article 35

States Parties shall take all appropriate national, bilateral and multilateral measures to prevent the abduction of, the sale of or traffic in children for any purpose or in any form.

Article 36

States Parties shall protect the child against all other forms of exploitation prejudicial to any aspects of the child's welfare.

Article 37

States Parties shall ensure that:

(a) No child shall be subjected to torture or other cruel, inhuman or degrading treatment or punishment. Neither capital punishment nor life imprisonment without possibility of release shall be imposed for offences committed by persons below eighteen years of age;
(b) No child shall be deprived of his or her liberty unlawfully or arbitrarily. The arrest, detention or imprisonment of a child shall be in conformity with the law and shall be used only as a measure of last resort and for the shortest appropriate period of time;
(c) Every child deprived of liberty shall be treated with humanity and respect for the inherent dignity of the human person, and in a manner which takes into account the needs of persons of his or her age. In particular, every child deprived of liberty shall be separated from adults unless it is considered in the child's best interest not to do so and shall have the right to maintain contact with his or her family through correspondence and visits, save in exceptional circumstances;

(d) Every child deprived of his or her liberty shall have the right to prompt access to legal and other appropriate assistance, as well as the right to challenge the legality of the deprivation of his or her liberty before a court or other competent, independent and impartial authority, and to a prompt decision on any such action.

Article 38

1. States Parties undertake to respect and to ensure respect for rules of international humanitarian law applicable to them in armed conflicts which are relevant to the child.
2. States Parties shall take all feasible measures to ensure that persons who have not attained the age of fifteen years do not take a direct part in hostilities.
3. States Parties shall refrain from recruiting any person who has not attained the age of fifteen years into their armed forces. In recruiting among those persons who have attained the age of fifteen years but who have not attained the age of eighteen years, States Parties shall endeavour to give priority to those who are oldest.
4. In accordance with their obligations under international humanitarian law to protect the civilian population in armed conflicts, States Parties shall take all feasible measures to ensure protection and care of children who are affected by an armed conflict.

Article 39

States Parties shall take all appropriate measures to promote physical and psychological recovery and social reintegration of a child victim of: any form of neglect, exploitation, or abuse; torture or any other form of cruel, inhuman or degrading treatment or punishment; or armed conflicts. Such recovery and reintegration shall take place in an environment which fosters the health, self-respect and dignity of the child.

Article 40

1. States Parties recognize the right of every child alleged as, accused of, or recognized as having infringed the penal law to be treated in a manner consistent with the promotion of the child's sense of dignity and worth, which reinforces the child's respect for the human rights and fundamental freedoms of others and which takes into account the child's age and the desirability of promoting the child's reintegration and the child's assuming a constructive role in society.
2. To this end, and having regard to the relevant provisions of international instruments, States Parties shall, in particular, ensure that:
   (a) No child shall be alleged as, be accused of, or recognized as having infringed the penal law by reason of acts or omissions that were not prohibited by national or international law at the time they were committed;
   (b) Every child alleged as or accused of having infringed the penal law has at least the following guarantees:
      (i) To be presumed innocent until proven guilty according to law;

(ii)   To be informed promptly and directly of the charges against him or her, and, if appropriate, through his or her parents or legal guardians, and to have legal or other appropriate assistance in the preparation and presentation of his or her defence;

(iii)   To have the matter determined without delay by a competent, independent and impartial authority or judicial body in a fair hearing according to law, in the presence of legal or other appropriate assistance and, unless it is considered not to be in the best interest of the child, in particular, taking into account his or her age or situation, his or her parents or legal guardians;

(iv)   Not to be compelled to give testimony or to confess guilt; to examine or have examined adverse witnesses and to obtain the participation and examination of witnesses on his or her behalf under conditions of equality;

(v)   If considered to have infringed the penal law, to have this decision and any measures imposed in consequence thereof reviewed by a higher competent, independent and impartial authority or judicial body according to law;

(vi)   To have the free assistance of an interpreter if the child cannot understand or speak the language used;

(vii)   To have his or her privacy fully respected at all stages of the proceedings.

3. States Parties shall seek to promote the establishment of laws, procedures, authorities and institutions specifically applicable to children alleged as, accused of, or recognized as having infringed the penal law, and, in particular:

(a) The establishment of a minimum age below which children shall be presumed not to have the capacity to infringe the penal law;

(b) Whenever appropriate and desirable, measures for dealing with such children without resorting to judicial proceedings, providing that human rights and legal safeguards are fully respected.

4. A variety of dispositions, such as care, guidance and supervision orders; counselling; probation; foster care; education and vocational training programmes and other alternatives to institutional care shall be available to ensure that children are dealt with in a manner appropriate to their well-being and proportionate both to their circumstances and the offence.

Article 41

Nothing in the present Convention shall affect any provisions which are more conducive to the realization of the rights of the child and which may be contained in:

(a) The law of a State party; or
(b) International law in force for that State.

PART II

Article 42

States Parties undertake to make the principles and provisions of the Convention widely known, by appropriate and active means, to adults and children alike.

Article 43

1. For the purpose of examining the progress made by States Parties in achieving the realization of the obligations undertaken in the present Convention, there shall be established a Committee on the Rights of the Child, which shall carry out the functions hereinafter provided.
2. The Committee shall consist of ten experts of high moral standing and recognized competence in the field covered by this Convention. The members of the Committee shall be elected by States Parties from among their nationals and shall serve in their personal capacity, consideration being given to equitable geographical distribution, as well as to the principal legal systems.
3. The members of the Committee shall be elected by secret ballot from a list of persons nominated by States Parties. Each State Party may nominate one person from among its own nationals.
4. The initial election to the Committee shall be held no later than six months after the date of the entry into force of the present Convention and thereafter every second year. At least four months before the date of each election, the Secretary-General of the United Nations shall address a letter to States Parties inviting them to submit their nominations within two months. The Secretary-General shall subsequently prepare a list in alphabetical order of all persons thus nominated, indicating States Parties which have nominated them, and shall submit it to the States Parties to the present Convention.
5. The elections shall be held at meetings of States Parties convened by the Secretary-General at United Nations Headquarters. At those meetings, for which two thirds of States Parties shall constitute a quorum, the persons elected to the Committee shall be those who obtain the largest number of votes and an absolute majority of the votes of the representatives of States Parties present and voting.
6. The members of the Committee shall be elected for a term of four years. They shall be eligible for re-election if renominated. The term of five of the members elected at the first election shall expire at the end of two years; immediately after the first election, the names of these five members shall be chosen by lot by the Chairman of the meeting.
7. If a member of the Committee dies or resigns or declares that for any other cause he or she can no longer perform the duties of the Committee, the State Party which nominated the member shall appoint another expert from among its nationals to serve for the remainder of the term, subject to the approval of the Committee.
8. The Committee shall establish its own rules of procedure.
9. The Committee shall elect its officers for a period of two years.

10. The meetings of the Committee shall normally be held at United Nations Headquarters or at any other convenient place as determined by the Committee. The Committee shall normally meet annually. The duration of the meetings of the Committee shall be determined, and reviewed, if necessary, by a meeting of the States Parties to the present Convention, subject to the approval of the General Assembly.

11. The Secretary-General of the United Nations shall provide the necessary staff and facilities for the effective performance of the functions of the Committee under the present Convention.

12. With the approval of the General Assembly, the members of the Committee established under the present Convention shall receive emoluments from United Nations resources on such terms and conditions as the Assembly may decide.

Article 44

1. States Parties undertake to submit to the Committee, through the Secretary-General of the United Nations, reports on the measures they have adopted which give effect to the rights recognized herein and on the progress made on the enjoyment of those rights:

   (a) Within two years of the entry into force of the Convention for the State Party concerned;

   (b) Thereafter every five years.

2. Reports made under the present article shall indicate factors and difficulties, if any, affecting the degree of fulfilment of the obligations under the present Convention. Reports shall also contain sufficient information to provide the Committee with a comprehensive understanding of the implementation of the Convention in the country concerned.

3. A State Party which has submitted a comprehensive initial report to the Committee need not, in its subsequent reports submitted in accordance with paragraph 1 (b) of the present article, repeat basic information previously provided.

4. The Committee may request from States Parties further information relevant to the implementation of the Convention.

5. The Committee shall submit to the General Assembly, through the Economic and Social Council, every two years, reports on its activities.

6. States Parties shall make their reports widely available to the public in their own countries.

Article 45

In order to foster the effective implementation of the Convention and to encourage international co-operation in the field covered by the Convention:

   (a) The specialized agencies, the United Nations Children's Fund, and other United Nations organs shall be entitled to be represented at the consideration of the implementation of such provisions of the present Convention as fall within the scope of their mandate. The Committee may invite the specialized agencies, the United Nations Children's Fund and other competent bodies as it may consider appropriate to provide expert advice on the implementation of the

Convention in areas falling within the scope of their respective mandates. The Committee may invite the specialized agencies, the United Nations Children's Fund, and other United Nations organs to submit reports on the implementation of the Convention in areas falling within the scope of their activities;

(b) The Committee shall transmit, as it may consider appropriate, to the specialized agencies, the United Nations Children's Fund and other competent bodies, any reports from States Parties that contain a request, or indicate a need, for technical advice or assistance, along with the Committee's observations and suggestions, if any, on these requests or indications;

(c) The Committee may recommend to the General Assembly to request the Secretary-General to undertake on its behalf studies on specific issues relating to the rights of the child;

(d) The Committee may make suggestions and general recommendations based on information received pursuant to articles 44 and 45 of the present Convention. Such suggestions and general recommendations shall be transmitted to any State Party concerned and reported to the General Assembly, together with comments, if any, from States Parties.

PART III

Article 46

The present Convention shall be open for signature by all States.

Article 47

The present Convention is subject to ratification. Instruments of ratification shall be deposited with the Secretary-General of the United Nations.

Article 48

The present Convention shall remain open for accession by any State. The instruments of accession shall be deposited with the Secretary-General of the United Nations.

Article 49

1. The present Convention shall enter into force on the thirtieth day following the date of deposit with the Secretary-General of the United Nations of the twentieth instrument of ratification or accession.

2. For each State ratifying or acceding to the Convention after the deposit of the twentieth instrument of ratification or accession, the Convention shall enter into force on the thirtieth day after the deposit by such State of its instrument of ratification or accession.

Article 50

1. Any State Party may propose an amendment and file it with the Secretary-General of the United Nations. The Secretary-General shall thereupon

communicate the proposed amendment to States Parties, with a request that they indicate whether they favour a conference of States Parties for the purpose of considering and voting upon the proposals. In the event that, within four months from the date of such communication, at least one third of the States Parties favour such a conference, the Secretary-General shall convene the conference under the auspices of the United Nations. Any amendment adopted by a majority of States Parties present and voting at the conference shall be submitted to the General Assembly for approval.

2. An amendment adopted in accordance with paragraph 1 of the present article shall enter into force when it has been approved by the General Assembly of the United Nations and accepted by a two-thirds majority of States Parties.

3. When an amendment enters into force, it shall be binding on those States Parties which have accepted it, other States Parties still being bound by the provisions of the present Convention and any earlier amendments which they have accepted.

Article 51

1. The Secretary-General of the United Nations shall receive and circulate to all States the text of reservations made by States at the time of ratification or accession.

2. A reservation incompatible with the object and purpose of the present Convention shall not be permitted.

3. Reservations may be withdrawn at any time by notification to that effect addressed to the Secretary-General of the United Nations, who shall then inform all States. Such notification shall take effect on the date on which it is received by the Secretary-General.

Article 52

A State Party may denounce the present Convention by written notification to the Secretary-General of the United Nations. Denunciation becomes effective one year after the date of receipt of the notification by the Secretary-General.

Article 53

The Secretary-General of the United Nations is designated as the depositary of the present Convention.

Article 54

The original of the present Convention, of which the Arabic, Chinese, English, French, Russian and Spanish texts are equally authentic, shall be deposited with the Secretary-General of the United Nations. (United Nations, 2003)

Appendix C: Declaration on the Elimination of Violence against Women

ARTICLE 1

For the purposes of this Declaration, the term "violence against women" means any act of gender-based violence that results in, or is likely to result in, physical, sexual or psychological harm or suffering to women, including threats of such acts, coercion or arbitrary deprivation of liberty, whether occurring in public or in private life.

ARTICLE 2

Violence against women shall be understood to encompass, but not be limited to, the following:

(a) Physical, sexual and psychological violence occurring in the family, including battering, sexual abuse of female children in the household, dowry-related violence, marital rape, female genital mutilation and other traditional practices harmful to women, non-spousal violence and violence related to exploitation;
(b) Physical, sexual and psychological violence occurring within the general community, including rape, sexual abuse, sexual harassment and intimidation at work, in educational institutions and elsewhere, trafficking in women and forced prostitution;
(c) Physical, sexual and psychological violence perpetrated or condoned by the State, wherever it occurs.

ARTICLE 3

Women are entitled to the equal enjoyment and protection of all human rights and fundamental freedoms in the political, economic, social, cultural, civil or any other field. These rights include, inter alia:

(a) The right to life;
(b) The right to equality;

(c) The right to liberty and security of person;

(d) The right to equal protection under the law;

(e) The right to be free from all forms of discrimination;

(f) The right to the highest standard attainable of physical and mental health;

(g) The right to just and favourable conditions of work;

(h) The right not to be subjected to torture, or other cruel, inhuman or degrading treatment or punishment.

ARTICLE 4

States should condemn violence against women and should not invoke any custom, tradition or religious consideration to avoid their obligations with respect to its elimination. States should pursue by all appropriate means and without delay a policy of eliminating violence against women and, to this end, should:

(a) Consider, where they have not yet done so, ratifying or acceding to the Convention on the Elimination of All Forms of Discrimination against Women or withdrawing reservations to that Convention;

(b) Refrain from engaging in violence against women;

(c) Exercise due diligence to prevent, investigate and, in accordance with national legislation, punish acts of violence against women, whether those acts are perpetrated by the State or by private persons;

(d) Develop penal, civil, labour and administrative sanctions in domestic legislation to punish and redress the wrongs caused to women who are subjected to violence; women who are subjected to violence should be provided with access to the mechanisms of justice and, as provided for by national legislation, to just and effective remedies for the harm that they have suffered; States should also inform women of their rights in seeking redress through such mechanisms;

(e) Consider the possibility of developing national plans of action to promote the protection of women against any form of violence, or to include provisions for that purpose in plans already existing, taking into account, as appropriate, such cooperation as can be provided by non-governmental organizations, particularly those concerned with the issue of violence against women;

(f) Develop, in a comprehensive way, preventive approaches and all those measures of a legal, political, administrative and cultural nature that promote the protection of women against any form of violence, and ensure that the revictimization of women does not occur because of laws insensitive to gender considerations, enforcement practices or other interventions;

(g) Work to ensure, to the maximum extent feasible in the light of their available resources and, where needed, within the framework of international cooperation, that women subjected to violence and, where appropriate, their children have specialized assistance, such as rehabilitation, assistance in child care and maintenance, treatment, counselling, and health and social services, facilities and programmes, as well as support structures, and should take all other appropriate measures to promote their safety and physical and psychological rehabilitation;

(h) Include in government budgets adequate resources for their activities related to the elimination of violence against women;

(i) Take measures to ensure that law enforcement officers and public officials responsible for implementing policies to prevent, investigate and punish violence against women receive training to sensitize them to the needs of women;

(j) Adopt all appropriate measures, especially in the field of education, to modify the social and cultural patterns of conduct of men and women and to eliminate prejudices, customary practices and all other practices based on the idea of the inferiority or superiority of either of the sexes and on stereotyped roles for men and women;

(k) Promote research, collect data and compile statistics, especially concerning domestic violence, relating to the prevalence of different forms of violence against women and encourage research on the causes, nature, seriousness and consequences of violence against women and on the effectiveness of measures implemented to prevent and redress violence against women; those statistics and findings of the research will be made public;

(l) Adopt measures directed towards the elimination of violence against women who are especially vulnerable to violence;

(m) Include, in submitting reports as required under relevant human rights instruments of the United Nations, information pertaining to violence against women and measures taken to implement the present Declaration;

(n) Encourage the development of appropriate guidelines to assist in the implementation of the principles set forth in the present Declaration;

(o) Recognize the important role of the women's movement and non-governmental organizations world wide in raising awareness and alleviating the problem of violence against women;

(p) Facilitate and enhance the work of the women's movement and non-governmental organizations and cooperate with them at local, national and regional levels;

(q) Encourage intergovernmental regional organizations of which they are members to include the elimination of violence against women in their programmes, as appropriate.

ARTICLE 5

The organs and specialized agencies of the United Nations system should, within their respective fields of competence, contribute to the recognition and realization of the rights and the principles set forth in the present Declaration and, to this end, should, inter alia:

(a) Foster international and regional cooperation with a view to defining regional strategies for combating violence, exchanging experiences and financing programmes relating to the elimination of violence against women;

(b) Promote meetings and seminars with the aim of creating and raising awareness among all persons of the issue of the elimination of violence against women;

(c) Foster coordination and exchange within the United Nations system between human rights treaty bodies to address the issue of violence against women effectively;

(d) Include in analyses prepared by organizations and bodies of the United Nations system of social trends and problems, such as the periodic reports on the world social situation, examination of trends in violence against women;

(e) Encourage coordination between organizations and bodies of the United Nations system to incorporate the issue of violence against women into ongoing programmes, especially with reference to groups of women particularly vulnerable to violence;

(f) Promote the formulation of guidelines or manuals relating to violence against women, taking into account the measures referred to in the present Declaration;

(g) Consider the issue of the elimination of violence against women, as appropriate, in fulfilling their mandates with respect to the implementation of human rights instruments;

(h) Cooperate with non-governmental organizations in addressing the issue of violence against women.

ARTICLE 6

Nothing in the present Declaration shall affect any provision that is more conducive to the elimination of violence against women that may be contained in the legislation of a State or in any international convention, treaty or other instrument in force in a State. United Nations (1994).

Appendix D: Protocol to Prevent, Suppress, and Punish Trafficking in Persons, Especially Women and Children, Supplementing the United Nations Convention against Transnational Organized Crime

PREAMBLE

The States Parties to this Protocol,

Declaring that effective action to prevent and combat trafficking in persons, especially women and children, requires a comprehensive international approach in the countries of origin, transit and destination that includes measures to prevent such trafficking, to punish the traffickers and to protect the victims of such trafficking, including by protecting their internationally recognized human rights,

Taking into account the fact that, despite the existence of a variety of international instruments containing rules and practical measures to combat the exploitation of persons, especially women and children, there is no universal instrument that addresses all aspects of trafficking in persons,

Concerned that, in the absence of such an instrument, persons who are vulnerable to trafficking will not be sufficiently protected,

Recalling General Assembly resolution 53/111 of 9 December 1998, in which the Assembly decided to establish an open-ended intergovernmental ad hoc committee for the purpose of elaborating a comprehensive international convention against transnational organized crime and of discussing the elaboration of, inter alia, an international instrument addressing trafficking in women and children,

Convinced that supplementing the United Nations Convention against Transnational Organized Crime with an international instrument for the prevention, suppression and punishment of trafficking in persons, especially women and children, will be useful in preventing and combating that crime,

Have agreed as follows:

I. GENERAL PROVISIONS

Article 1

Relation with the United Nations Convention against Transnational Organized Crime

1. This Protocol supplements the United Nations Convention against Transnational Organized Crime. It shall be interpreted together with the Convention.

2. The provisions of the Convention shall apply, mutatis mutandis, to this Protocol unless otherwise provided herein.
3. The offences established in accordance with article 5 of this Protocol shall be regarded as offences established in accordance with the Convention.

Article 2

Statement of Purpose

The purposes of this Protocol are:

(a) To prevent and combat trafficking in persons, paying particular attention to women and children;
(b) To protect and assist the victims of such trafficking, with full respect for their human rights; and
(c) To promote cooperation among States Parties in order to meet those objectives.

Article 3

Use of Terms

For the purposes of this Protocol:

(a) "Trafficking in persons" shall mean the recruitment, transportation, transfer, harbouring or receipt of persons, by means of the threat or use of force or other forms of coercion, of abduction, of fraud, of deception, of the abuse of power or of a position of vulnerability or of the giving or receiving of payments or benefits to achieve the consent of a person having control over another person, for the purpose of exploitation. Exploitation shall include, at a minimum, the exploitation of the prostitution of others or other forms of sexual exploitation, forced labour or services, slavery or practices similar to slavery, servitude or the removal of organs;
(b) The consent of a victim of trafficking in persons to the intended exploitation set forth in subparagraph (a) of this article shall be irrelevant where any of the means set forth in subparagraph (a) have been used;
(c) The recruitment, transportation, transfer, harbouring or receipt of a child for the purpose of exploitation shall be considered "trafficking in persons" even if this does not involve any of the means set forth in subparagraph (a) of this article;
(d) "Child" shall mean any person under eighteen years of age.

Article 4

Scope of Application

This Protocol shall apply, except as otherwise stated herein, to the prevention, investigation and prosecution of the offences established in accordance with article 5 of this Protocol, where those offences are transnational in nature and involve an organized criminal group, as well as to the protection of victims of such offences.

Article 5

Criminalization

1. Each State Party shall adopt such legislative and other measures as may be necessary to establish as criminal offences the conduct set forth in article 3 of this Protocol, when committed intentionally.

2. Each State Party shall also adopt such legislative and other measures as may be necessary to establish as criminal offences:

    (a) Subject to the basic concepts of its legal system, attempting to commit an offence established in accordance with paragraph 1 of this article;

    (b) Participating as an accomplice in an offence established in accordance with paragraph 1 of this article; and

    (c) Organizing or directing other persons to commit an offence established in accordance with paragraph 1 of this article.

II. PROTECTION OF VICTIMS OF TRAFFICKING IN PERSONS

Article 6

Assistance to and Protection of Victims of Trafficking in Persons

1. In appropriate cases and to the extent possible under its domestic law, each State Party shall protect the privacy and identity of victims of trafficking in persons, including, inter alia, by making legal proceedings relating to such trafficking confidential.

2. Each State Party shall ensure that its domestic legal or administrative system contains measures that provide to victims of trafficking in persons, in appropriate cases:

    (a) Information on relevant court and administrative proceedings;

    (b) Assistance to enable their views and concerns to be presented and considered at appropriate stages of criminal proceedings against offenders, in a manner not prejudicial to the rights of the defence.

3. Each State Party shall consider implementing measures to provide for the physical, psychological and social recovery of victims of trafficking in persons, including, in appropriate cases, in cooperation with non-governmental organizations, other relevant organizations and other elements of civil society, and, in particular, the provision of:

    (a) Appropriate housing;

    (b) Counselling and information, in particular as regards their legal rights, in a language that the victims of trafficking in persons can understand;

    (c) Medical, psychological and material assistance; and

    (d) Employment, educational and training opportunities.

4. Each State Party shall take into account, in applying the provisions of this article, the age, gender and special needs of victims of trafficking in persons, in particular the special needs of children, including appropriate housing, education and care.

5. Each State Party shall endeavour to provide for the physical safety of victims of trafficking in persons while they are within its territory.
6. Each State Party shall ensure that its domestic legal system contains measures that offer victims of trafficking in persons the possibility of obtaining compensation for damage suffered.

Article 7

Status of Victims of Trafficking in Persons in Receiving States

1. In addition to taking measures pursuant to article 6 of this Protocol, each State Party shall consider adopting legislative or other appropriate measures that permit victims of trafficking in persons to remain in its territory, temporarily or permanently, in appropriate cases.
2. In implementing the provision contained in paragraph 1 of this article, each State Party shall give appropriate consideration to humanitarian and compassionate factors.

Article 8

Repatriation of Victims of Trafficking in Persons

1. The State Party of which a victim of trafficking in persons is a national or in which the person had the right of permanent residence at the time of entry into the territory of the receiving State Party shall facilitate and accept, with due regard for the safety of that person, the return of that person without undue or unreasonable delay.
2. When a State Party returns a victim of trafficking in persons to a State Party of which that person is a national or in which he or she had, at the time of entry into the territory of the receiving State Party, the right of permanent residence, such return shall be with due regard for the safety of that person and for the status of any legal proceedings related to the fact that the person is a victim of trafficking and shall preferably be voluntary.
3. At the request of a receiving State Party, a requested State Party shall, without undue or unreasonable delay, verify whether a person who is a victim of trafficking in persons is its national or had the right of permanent residence in its territory at the time of entry into the territory of the receiving State Party.
4. In order to facilitate the return of a victim of trafficking in persons who is without proper documentation, the State Party of which that person is a national or in which he or she had the right of permanent residence at the time of entry into the territory of the receiving State Party shall agree to issue, at the request of the receiving State Party, such travel documents or other authorization as may be necessary to enable the person to travel to and re-enter its territory.
5. This article shall be without prejudice to any right afforded to victims of trafficking in persons by any domestic law of the receiving State Party.
6. This article shall be without prejudice to any applicable bilateral or multilateral agreement or arrangement that governs, in whole or in part, the return of victims of trafficking in persons.

III. PREVENTION, COOPERATION AND OTHER MEASURES

Article 9

Prevention of Trafficking in Persons

1. States Parties shall establish comprehensive policies, programmes and other measures:

   (a) To prevent and combat trafficking in persons; and

   (b) To protect victims of trafficking in persons, especially women and children, from revictimization.

2. States Parties shall endeavour to undertake measures such as research, information and mass media campaigns and social and economic initiatives to prevent and combat trafficking in persons.

3. Policies, programmes and other measures established in accordance with this article shall, as appropriate, include cooperation with non-governmental organizations, other relevant organizations and other elements of civil society.

4. States Parties shall take or strengthen measures, including through bilateral or multilateral cooperation, to alleviate the factors that make persons, especially women and children, vulnerable to trafficking, such as poverty, underdevelopment and lack of equal opportunity.

5. States Parties shall adopt or strengthen legislative or other measures, such as educational, social or cultural measures, including through bilateral and multilateral cooperation, to discourage the demand that fosters all forms of exploitation of persons, especially women and children, that leads to trafficking.

Article 10

Information Exchange and Training

1. Law enforcement, immigration or other relevant authorities of States Parties shall, as appropriate, cooperate with one another by exchanging information, in accordance with their domestic law, to enable them to determine:

   (a) Whether individuals crossing or attempting to cross an international border with travel documents belonging to other persons or without travel documents are perpetrators or victims of trafficking in persons;

   (b) The types of travel document that individuals have used or attempted to use to cross an international border for the purpose of trafficking in persons; and

   (c) The means and methods used by organized criminal groups for the purpose of trafficking in persons, including the recruitment and transportation of victims, routes and links between and among individuals and groups engaged in such trafficking, and possible measures for detecting them.

2. States Parties shall provide or strengthen training for law enforcement, immigration and other relevant officials in the prevention of trafficking in persons. The training should focus on methods used in preventing such trafficking, prosecuting the traffickers and protecting the rights of the victims, including protecting the victims from the traffickers. The training should also take into

account the need to consider human rights and child- and gender-sensitive issues and it should encourage cooperation with non-governmental organizations, other relevant organizations and other elements of civil society.

3. A State Party that receives information shall comply with any request by the State Party that transmitted the information that places restrictions on its use.

Article 11

Border Measures

1. Without prejudice to international commitments in relation to the free movement of people, States Parties shall strengthen, to the extent possible, such border controls as may be necessary to prevent and detect trafficking in persons.
2. Each State Party shall adopt legislative or other appropriate measures to prevent, to the extent possible, means of transport operated by commercial carriers from being used in the commission of offences established in accordance with article 5 of this Protocol.
3. Where appropriate, and without prejudice to applicable international conventions, such measures shall include establishing the obligation of commercial carriers, including any transportation company or the owner or operator of any means of transport, to ascertain that all passengers are in possession of the travel documents required for entry into the receiving State.
4. Each State Party shall take the necessary measures, in accordance with its domestic law, to provide for sanctions in cases of violation of the obligation set forth in paragraph 3 of this article.
5. Each State Party shall consider taking measures that permit, in accordance with its domestic law, the denial of entry or revocation of visas of persons implicated in the commission of offences established in accordance with this Protocol.
6. Without prejudice to article 27 of the Convention, States Parties shall consider strengthening cooperation among border control agencies by, inter alia, establishing and maintaining direct channels of communication.

Article 12

Security and Control of Documents

Each State Party shall take such measures as may be necessary, within available means:

(a) To ensure that travel or identity documents issued by it are of such quality that they cannot easily be misused and cannot readily be falsified or unlawfully altered, replicated or issued; and
(b) To ensure the integrity and security of travel or identity documents issued by or on behalf of the State Party and to prevent their unlawful creation, issuance and use.

Article 13

Legitimacy and Validity of Documents

At the request of another State Party, a State Party shall, in accordance with its domestic law, verify within a reasonable time the legitimacy and validity of travel or identity documents issued or purported to have been issued in its name and suspected of being used for trafficking in persons.

IV. FINAL PROVISIONS

Article 14

Saving Clause

1. Nothing in this Protocol shall affect the rights, obligations and responsibilities of States and individuals under international law, including international humanitarian law and international human rights law and, in particular, where applicable, the 1951 Convention and the 1967 Protocol relating to the Status of Refugees and the principle of non-refoulement as contained therein.
2. The measures set forth in this Protocol shall be interpreted and applied in a way that is not discriminatory to persons on the ground that they are victims of trafficking in persons. The interpretation and application of those measures shall be consistent with internationally recognized principles of non-discrimination.

Article 15

Settlement of Disputes

1. States Parties shall endeavour to settle disputes concerning the interpretation or application of this Protocol through negotiation.
2. Any dispute between two or more States Parties concerning the interpretation or application of this Protocol that cannot be settled through negotiation within a reasonable time shall, at the request of one of those States Parties, be submitted to arbitration. If, six months after the date of the request for arbitration, those States Parties are unable to agree on the organization of the arbitration, any one of those States Parties may refer the dispute to the International Court of Justice by request in accordance with the Statute of the Court.
3. Each State Party may, at the time of signature, ratification, acceptance or approval of or accession to this Protocol, declare that it does not consider itself bound by paragraph 2 of this article. The other States Parties shall not be bound by paragraph 2 of this article with respect to any State Party that has made such a reservation.
4. Any State Party that has made a reservation in accordance with paragraph 3 of this article may at any time withdraw that reservation by notification to the Secretary-General of the United Nations.

Article 16

Signature, Ratification, Acceptance, Approval and Accession

1. This Protocol shall be open to all States for signature from 12 to 15 December 2000 in Palermo, Italy, and thereafter at United Nations Headquarters in New York until 12 December 2002.
2. This Protocol shall also be open for signature by regional economic integration organizations provided that at least one member State of such organization has signed this Protocol in accordance with paragraph 1 of this article.

3. This Protocol is subject to ratification, acceptance or approval.

   Instruments of ratification, acceptance or approval shall be deposited with the Secretary-General of the United Nations. A regional economic integration organization may deposit its instrument of ratification, acceptance or approval if at least one of its member States has done likewise. In that instrument of ratification, acceptance or approval, such organization shall declare the extent of its competence with respect to the matters governed by this Protocol. Such organization shall also inform the depositary of any relevant modification in the extent of its competence.

4. This Protocol is open for accession by any State or any regional economic integration organization of which at least one member State is a Party to this Protocol. Instruments of accession shall be deposited with the Secretary-General of the United Nations. At the time of its accession, a regional economic integration organization shall declare the extent of its competence with respect to matters governed by this Protocol. Such organization shall also inform the depositary of any relevant modification in the extent of its competence.

Article 17

Entry into Force

1. This Protocol shall enter into force on the ninetieth day after the date of deposit of the fortieth instrument of ratification, acceptance, approval or accession, except that it shall not enter into force before the entry into force of the Convention. For the purpose of this paragraph, any instrument deposited by a regional economic integration organization shall not be counted as additional to those deposited by member States of such organization.

2. For each State or regional economic integration organization ratifying, accepting, approving or acceding to this Protocol after the deposit of the fortieth instrument of such action, this Protocol shall enter into force on the thirtieth day after the date of deposit by such State or organization of the relevant instrument or on the date this Protocol enters into force pursuant to paragraph 1 of this article, whichever is the later.

Article 18

Amendment

1. After the expiry of five years from the entry into force of this Protocol, a State Party to the Protocol may propose an amendment and file it with the Secretary-General of the United Nations, who shall thereupon communicate the proposed amendment to the States Parties and to the Conference of the Parties to the Convention for the purpose of considering and deciding on the proposal. The States Parties to this Protocol meeting at the Conference of the Parties shall make every effort to achieve consensus on each amendment. If all efforts at consensus have been exhausted and no agreement has been reached, the amendment shall, as a last resort, require for its adoption a two-thirds majority vote of the States Parties to this Protocol present and voting at the meeting of the Conference of the Parties.

2. Regional economic integration organizations, in matters within their competence, shall exercise their right to vote under this article with a number of votes equal to the number of their member States that are Parties to this Protocol. Such organizations shall not exercise their right to vote if their member States exercise theirs and vice versa.

3. An amendment adopted in accordance with paragraph 1 of this article is subject to ratification, acceptance or approval by States Parties.

4. An amendment adopted in accordance with paragraph 1 of this article shall enter into force in respect of a State Party ninety days after the date of the deposit with the Secretary-General of the United Nations of an instrument of ratification, acceptance or approval of such amendment.

5. When an amendment enters into force, it shall be binding on those States Parties which have expressed their consent to be bound by it. Other States Parties shall still be bound by the provisions of this Protocol and any earlier amendments that they have ratified, accepted or approved.

Article 19

Denunciation

1. A State Party may denounce this Protocol by written notification to the Secretary-General of the United Nations. Such denunciation shall become effective one year after the date of receipt of the notification by the Secretary-General.

2. A regional economic integration organization shall cease to be a Party to this Protocol when all of its member States have denounced it.

Article 20

Depositary and Languages

1. The Secretary-General of the United Nations is designated depositary of this Protocol.

2. The original of this Protocol, of which the Arabic, Chinese, English, French, Russian and Spanish texts are equally authentic, shall be deposited with the Secretary-General of the United Nations.

IN WITNESS WHEREOF, the undersigned plenipotentiaries, being duly authorized thereto by their respective Governments, have signed this Protocol (United Nations, 2000a).

Glossary

Bai: Currency from Romania.

Bhat: Currency from Thailand.

Breaking in: The repeated beating, drugging, and raping of women until they become compliant sex slaves.

Comfort women: Sex slaves in World War II who were forced to service Japanese soldiers.

Customary marriage: Marriage that is other than traditional marriage in a culture but is accepted on some level by the culture.

Dalit: The untouchable caste (India).

Debt bondage (bonded labor):   A person's labor demanded as a means of repayment for a loan.

Ethnic cleansing: Rape to tarnish the pure ethnic stock of a group.

Feticide: The systematic elimination of part of a population group by the aborting of one type of fetus (such as the female fetus).

Genital excision: A form of female genital mutilation in which typically the clitoris and labia minora are removed.

Janjawid: Armed men on horses, armed fighters in the Sudan conflict.

Jirga: Tribal council.

John: A male customer of prostitutes.

La Strada: A European network against human trafficking.

Madam: A woman who runs a brothel and organizes prostitutes.

Natasha: A generic term used to refer to female Russian prostitutes.

One-child policy: The population control policy instituted in China in the early 1980s.

Pottu thali: Wedlock.

Rape camps: Detention facilities where women are held and raped repeatedly, often during wars, for the purpose of carrying out ethnic cleansing.

Sacred prostitution: Sexual slavery based on the ancient worship of fertility and goddesses.

Snack bars: A euphemism for brothels in Japan.

Trokosi: Virgin girls committed to shrines, often as sex slaves, in West Africa.

Voodoo: An animistic or shamanic belief system.

References

Adepoju, A. (2005). Review of research and data on human trafficking in sub-Saharan Africa. *International Migration, 43*(1/2).

Aird, S. C. (2000). Ghana's slaves to the gods. *Human Rights Brief*. Retrieved January 15, 2008, from http://www.wcl.american.edu/hrbrief/v7il/ghana.htm.

Alfredson, L. (2001). *Sexual exploitation of child soldiers: An exploration and analysis of global dimensions and trends*. Retrieved February 22, 2008, from http://www.reliefweb.int/rw/lib.nsf/db900SID/LGEL-5RPBPA/$FILE/csusc-exploit.pdf?OpenElement.

Allen, J., & Schaeffer, P. (2001, March 16). Reports of abuse: AIDS exacerbates sexual exploitation of nuns, reports allege. *National Catholic Reporter*. Retrieved October 30, 2007, from http://www.natcath.org/NCR_Online/archives/031601/031601a.htm.

American Anti-Slavery Group. (1999). *Christian Solidarity International (CSI) visits Northern Bahr El Ghazal, Sudan: Focusing on slavery, including personal testimonies, and military mobilization*. Retrieved February 27, 2008, from http://www.iabolish.org/slavery_today/sudan/csi.html.

American Antislavery Group. (2008). *Country report: Ghana*. Retrieved February 24, 2008, from http://www.iabolish.org/slavery_today/country_reports/gh.html.

Aminova, A. (2004, June 18). *Uzbekistan: No love lost in Karakalpak bride thefts: The old practice of abducting women persists despite opposition from Uzbek laws, Muslim clerics and the forced brides themselves*. Retrieved January 3, 2008, from Institute for War and Peace Reporting Web site: http://iwpr.net/?p=rca&s=f&o=175889&apc_state=henirca2004.

Amnesty International. (2004, July 19). *Sudan: Darfur: Rape as a weapon of war: Sexual violence and its consequences*. Retrieved November 30, 2007, from http://www.amnesty.org/en/report/info/AFR54/076/2004.

Amnesty International. (2007a, December 21). *Breakthrough in battle for justice for "comfort women."* Retrieved January 3, 2008, from http://www.amnesty.org/en/news-and-updates/good-news/breakthrough-battle-justice-comfort-women-20071221.

Amnesty International. (2007b). *Still waiting after 60 years: Justice for survivors of Japan's military sexual slavery system*. Retrieved January 3, 2008, from http://www.amnestyusa.org/document.php?lang=e&id=ENGASA220122005.

Amsler, S., & Kleinbach, R. (1999). Bride kidnapping in the Kyrgyz Republic. *International Journal of Central Asian Studies, 4*, 185–216.

Anti-Slavery International. (1999). *Bonded labour*. Retrieved January 3, 2008, from http://www.antislavery.org/homepage/campaign/bondedinfo.htm.

Asia Foundation. (2001, August). *Trafficking and human rights in Nepal: Community perceptions and policy program responses*. Population Council. Retrieved April 21, 2008 from the Population Council Web site: http://www.popcouncil.org/pdfs/horizons/traffickingsum1.pdf.

Aspler, A., & Queyranne, G. (2007). Conflict and sexual violence in the Democratic Republic of the Congo. *The Lancet Student*. Retrieved January 3, 2008, from http://www.thelancetstudent.com/2007/11/16/conflict-and-sexual-violence-in-the-democratic-republic-of-the-congo/.

Associated Press. (2003, June 10). *Man pleads guilty in sex slave case*. Retrieved April 21, 2008 from http://www.wtop.com/?nid=25&sid=1361431.

Bales, K. (2004). *Disposable people: New slavery in the global economy*. Berkeley: University of California Press.

Banerjee, P. (2008). *Trafficking and migration*. Paper presented at the International Women, Leadership and Community conference, Delhi, India.

Bangladesh National Women Lawyers Association. (2001). *Forced marriages: A blot in women's freedom of expression*. Dhaka: Creative Canvas.

Barrows, J. (2006, August 15). *Introduction to human trafficking: The slavery of the 21st century*. Christian Medical and Dental Associations. Retrieved January 3, 2008, from http://www.cmawashington.org/index.cgi?cat=100284&BISKIT=1244688284&CONTEXT=cat.

BBC News. (2006, November 30). *UN troops face child abuse claims*. Retrieved February 2, 2008, from http://news.bbc.co.uk/2/hi/americas/6195830.stm.

BBC News. (2007, February 8). *Sweden's prostitution solution: Why hasn't anyone tried this before?* Retrieved April 21, 2008, from http://news.bbc.co.uk/go/pr/fr/-/2/hi/uk_news/6343325.stm. 2007/02/08.

Beeks, K., & Amir, D. (2006). *Trafficking and the global sex industry*. Lanham, MD: Lexington Books.

Belair, K. (2006). Unearthing the customary law foundations of "forced marriages" during Sierra Leone's civil war: The possible impact of international criminal law on customary marriage and women's rights in post-conflict Sierra Leone. *Columbia Journal of Gender and Law*. 15: 551. Retrieved February 22, 2008, from http://www.accessmylibrary.com/coms2/summary_0286-25736595_ITM.

Ben-Ari, N., & Harsch, E. (2005, January). Sexual violence, an "invisible war crime" *Africa Renewal, 18*(4). Retrieved February 28, 2008, from http://www.un.org/ecosocdev/geninfo/afrec/vol18no4/184sierraleone.htm.

Berry, J. (2001, April 10). A problem for the Pope: Recent reports of the sexual violation of African nuns recall past stories of abuse in Louisiana and elsewhere; An increasing number of critics are saying the blame extends to the Vatican. *Gambit Weekly, 22*(15), 5. Retrieved February 26, 2008, from http://proquest.umi.com.proxy.library.cornell.edu/pqdweb?index=0&did=582130201&SrchMode=1&sid=1&Fmt=3&VInst=PROD&VType=PQD&RQT=309&VName=PQD&TS=1204163814&clientId=8424.

Bertell, R. (2000). Victims of the nuclear age. *Ambassador Online Magazine, 3*(2).

Boaten, A. B. (2001). The trokosi system in Ghana: Discrimination against women and children. In A. Rwomire (Ed.), *African women and children: Crisis and response*. Westport, CT: Praeger.

Brettingham, M. (2007, March 9). Married in shackles: Pupils' horror stories. *The Times Educational Supplement*, 12.

Brown, L. (2001). *Sex slaves: The trafficking of women in Asia.* London, UK: Virago Press.

Bumiller, E. (1999, June 22). Kosovo victims must choose to deny rape or be hated. *The New York Times.* Retrieved January 3, 2008, from http://partners.nytimes.com/library/world/europe/062299kosovo-rape-attitudes.html.

Butcher, T. (2003, January 17). UN troops accused of "systematic" rape in Sierra Leone. *Telegraph.* Retrieved January 3, 2008, from http://www.prisonplanet.com/un_troops_accused_of_systematic_rape_in_sierra_leone.html.

Calandruccio, G. (2005). A review of recent research on human trafficking in the Middle East. *Immigration International, 43*(1/2).

Card, C. (1996). Rape as a weapon of war. *Hypatia, 11*(4). Retrieved December 13, 2007, from http://iupjournals.org/hypatia/hyp11-4.html.

CBS News. (2005, June 22). War rape trauma lingers in Congo: As a weapon of war, sexual violence leaves lasting pains. Retrieved February 15, 2008, from http://www.cbsnews.com/stories/2005/06/22/world/main703577.shtml.

CBS News. (2008, January 13). War against women: The use of rape as a weapon in Congo's civil war. Retrieved February 12, 2008, from http://www.cbsnews.com/stories/2008/01/11/60minutes/main3701249.shtml.

Child Brides. (2008). Retrieved February 27, 2008, from about.com Web site: http://marriage.about.com/od/arrangedmarriages/a/childbride.htm.

Chuang, J. (2005). The United States as global sheriff: Using unilateral sanctions to combat human trafficking. *Michigan Journal of International Law, 27*(437).

Cole, J. (2006). Reducing the damage: Dilemmas of Anti-Trafficking Efforts Among Nigerian Prostitutes in Palermo. *Anthropoligica 48*(2), 217–228.

Corrin, C. (2005). Transitional road for traffic: Analysing trafficking in women from and through Central and Eastern Europe. *Europe-Asia Studies, 57*(4), 543–560.

CRC. (2008). *What is the Convention on the Rights of the Child?* Retrieved February 28, 2008, from www.childrightscampaign.org.

Cuffe, J. (2008, April 15) Child Brides "sold" in Afghanistan. BBC News. Retrieved April 16, 2008, from http://news.bbc.co.uk/2/hi/programmes/7342902.stm.

Cunningham, S. (2000). What we teach about when we teach about violence. *The HFG Review, 1*, 4–9.

Derdian, K. (2005). Common fate, different experience: Gender-specific aspects of the Armenian genocide, 1915–1917. *Holocaust and Genocide Studies, 19*(1), 1–25.

De Santis, M. (2005). *Opposing prostitution as a form of male violence: The Swedish model.* Women's Justice Center. Retrieved April 21, 2008, from http://www.peaceworkmagazine.org/pwork/0506/050616.htm.

Doctors without Borders. (2004). *Medical, psychosocial, and socioeconomic consequences of sexual violence in eastern DRC.* Retrieved January 12, 2008, from http://www.msf.org/source/countries/africa/drc/2004/drcreport-nojoy.pdf.

Dogar, R. (1999, April 5). After a life of slavery: Julie Dogbadzi escaped. Now she's freeing others. *Newsweek.* Retrieved February 26, 2008, from http://www.newsweek.com/id/87930/page/1.

Ebrahim, Z. T. (2006, September 19). *Pakistan: Girls as sacrificial lambs.* Women's Feature Service. Retrieved January 11, 2007, from http://proquest.umi.com/pqdweb?did=1167646791&Fmt=7&clientId=8424&RQT=309&VName=PQD&cfc=1.

Empowering Women and Girls. (2007). *Child marriages now banned in Afghanistan.* Retrieved January 24, 2008, from http://thirdworldorphans.org/gpage.html58.html.

Expressindia. (2008, April 3). Cambodia stops "human trafficking" through marriages. Retrieved May 1, 2008, from http://www.expressindia.com/latest-news/Cambodia-stops-human-trafficking-through-marriages/292049/.

Farley, M., Cotton, A., Lynne, J., Zumbeck, S., Spiwak, F., Reyes, M. E., et al. (2003). Prostitution and trafficking in nine countries: An update on violence and posttraumatic stress disorder. *Journal of Trauma Practice, 2*, 33–74.

Fawthrop, T. (2005, July 15). *Lao tribes suffer from drug crackdown.* Retrieved January 5, 2008, from BBC News Web site: http://news.bbc.co.uk/2/hi/asia-pacific/4673109.stm.

Feingold, D. (September/October 2005). *Think again: Human trafficking.* Foreign Policy. Retrieved April 21, 2008, from http://www.foreignpolicy.com/users/login.php?story_id=3157&URL=http://www.foreignpolicy.com/story/cms.php?story_id=3157.

Fried, J. P. (2004, January 25). House has history, just not the right kind. *The New York Times.* Retrieved February 22, 2008, from http://query.nytimes.com/gst/fullpage.html?res=9903E4DC1638F936A15752C0A9629C8B63.

Friedman, R. (1996, April 8). India's shame: Sexual slavery and political corruption are leading to an AIDS catastrophe. *The Nation.*

Gibb, J. (2003). Sex and slavery. *The Guardian.* Retrieved December 17, 2007, from http://observer.guardian.co.uk/magazine/story/0,11913,901001,00.html.

Goodwin, J. (2003, July). Rescued from hell. *Marie Claire Magazine.* Retrieved February 25, 2008, from http://friendsofmaitinepal.org/html/mc703.htm.

Gozdiak, E. M., & Collett, E. A. (2005). Research on human trafficking in North America: A review of literature. *International Migration, 43*(1/2).

Grammaticas, D. (2007, June 8). *Slaves to the goddess of fertility.* Retrieved February 27, 2008, from BBC News Web site: http://news.bbc.co.uk/2/hi/south_asia/6729927.stm.

Graves, G. (2003). Post-traumatic stress syndrome and related disorders among civilian victims of sexual trauma and exploitation in Southeast Asia. In Krippner, S., & McIntyre, T. (Eds.), *The psychological impact of war trauma on civilians: An international perspective (Psychological dimensions to war and peace).* Westport, CT: Praeger.

Grey, M. (2005). Dalit women and the struggle for justice in a world of global capitalism. *Feminist Theology, 14*(1), 127–149.

Group for the Convention on the Rights of the Child and EPCAT. (2001). *In the name of culture and tradition.* Briefing note to the 2nd World Congress against Commercial Sexual Exploitation of Children. Retrieved February 26, 2008, from http://www.stopdemand.com/wa.asp?idWebPage=8109&idDetails=140.

Halli, S. S., Ramesh, B. M., O'Neil, J., Moses, S., & Blanchard, J. F. (2006, October). The role of collectives in STI and HIV/AIDS prevention among female sex workers in Karnataka, India. *AIDS Care, 18*(7), 739–749.

Hamlyn, E., Peer, A., & Easterbrook, P. (2007) Sexual health and HIV in travelers and expatriates. *Occupational Medicine 57*(5), 313–321.

Handrahan, L. M. (2000a, January 28). International human rights law and bride kidnapping in Kyrgyzstan. *Eurasia Insight.* Retrieved January 3, 2008, from http://www.eurasianet.org/departments/insight/articles/eav012400.shtml.

Handrahan, L. M. (2000b, March). Kidnapping brides in Kyrgyzstan: Prescriptive human rights measures. *Human Rights Tribune, 7*(1). Retrieved January 3, 2008, from http://www.hri.ca/cftribune/templates/article.cfm?IssueIDj16&Sectionj1&Articlej256.

Harvard School of Public Health Press Release. (2007, July 31). *High rates of HIV infection documented among young Nepalese girls sex-trafficked to India.* Retrieved September

5, 2007, from http://www.hsph.harvard.edu/news/press-releases/2007-releases/press 07312007.html.

Hassan, S. R. (2007). *Victim of parental neglect and child marriage*. Retrieved February 26, 2008, from Ansar Burney Trust Web site: http://www.ansarburney.org/news/n144 .html.

Holmes, S. (2008). *Trafficking: A very modern slavery*. Retrieved February 15, 2008, from BBC News Web site: http://newsvote.bbc.co.uk/mpapps/pagetools/print/news. bbc.co.uk/hi/europe/7243612.stm.

Hossain, S. & Turner, S. (2001). Abduction for forced marriage—Rights and remedies in Bangladesh and Pakistan. *International Family Law, 1*(64), 15–24.

Hughes, D. (2000a). The "Natasha" trade: The transnational shadow market of trafficking in women. *Journal of International Affairs, 53*(2), 635, 651.

Hughes, D. (2000b). "Welcome to the rape camp": Sexual exploitation and the internet in Cambodia. *Journal of Sexual Aggression, 6*(1–2).

Human Rights Watch. (1994, March). *Interview: Japan*. Retrieved April 21, 2008 from http://www.hrw.org/reports/2000/japan/4-profiles.htm.

Human Rights Watch. (1995a, October). *Human Rights Watch and FOWIA interview: Chiang Mai province, Thailand*. Retrieved April 21, 2008 from http://www.hrw.org/re ports/2000/japan/4-profiles.htm.

Human Rights Watch. (1995b). *Rape for profit: Trafficking of Nepali girls and women to India's brothels*. Retrieved January 10, 2008, from http://www.hrw.org/reports/1995/ India.htm.

Human Rights Watch. (1996a). *Rwanda's genocide: Human rights abuses against women*. Retrieved December 20, 2007, from http://hrw.org/english/docs/1996/09/24/rwanda4161. htm.

Human Rights Watch. (1996b). *Shattered lives: Sexual violence during the Rwandan genocide and its aftermath*. Retrieved November 30, 2007, from http://www.hrw.org/reports/ pdfs/r/rwanda/rwanda969.pdf.

Human Rights Watch. (1999, March). *Broken people, caste violence against India's untouchables*. Retrieved January 8, 2008, from http://www.hrw.org/reports/1999/india/ India994–09.htm#P1695_354939.

Human Rights Watch. (2000). *Owed justice: Thai women trafficked into debt bondage in Japan*. Retrieved February 25, 2008, from http://www.hrw.org/reports/2000/japan/6-sec -6-7-8.htm.

Human Rights Watch. (2001a). *Bosnia: Landmark verdicts for rape, torture, and sexual enslavement: Criminal tribunal convicts Bosnian Serbs for crimes against humanity*. Retrieved February 20, 2008, from http://hrw.org/english/docs/2001/02/22/bosher256.htm.

Human Rights Watch. (2001b). *Human Rights Watch world report 2001: Sierra Leone: Sexual violence within the Sierra Leone conflict*. Retrieved February 28, 2008, from http:// www.hrw.org/backgrounder/africa/sl-bck0226.htm.

Human Rights Watch. (2001c). *World report 2001: Women in conflict and refugees*. Retrieved February 22, 2008, from http://www.hrw.org/wr2k1/women/women3.html.

Human Rights Watch. (2002). *The war within the war: Sexual violence against women and girls in Eastern Congo*. Retrieved February 12, 2008, from http://www.hrw.org/reports/2002/ drc/.

Human Rights Watch. (2003a). *Gender based violence in refugee camps*. Retrieved February 15, 2008, from http://www.hrw.org/reports/2003/nepal0903/8.htm#_Toc51386793.

Human Rights Watch. (2003b, January 15). *Interview with Sara K., Naguru, Uganda*. Retrieved April 21, 2008, from http://www.hrw.org/reports/2003/africa1203/4.htm#_ftnref63.

Human Rights Watch. (2003c). Killing you is a very easy thing for us: Human rights abuses in Southeast Afghanistan. *Human Rights Watch, 15*(5)(C). Retrieved April 21, 2008, from http://www.hrw.org/reports/2003/afghanistan0703/afghanistan0703.pdf.

Human Rights Watch. (2003d). *Risk to girls and women in long term unions*. Retrieved February 25, 2008, from http://www.hrw.org/reports/2003/africa1203/4.htm.

Human Rights Watch. (2003e, July). Uganda: Abducted and abused: Renewed conflict in northern Uganda. *Human Rights Watch, 15*(12)(A). Retrieved February 22, 2008, from http://www.hrw.org/reports/2003/uganda0703/uganda0703a-04.htm#P608_100047.

Human Rights Watch. (2003f). We'll kill you if you cry: Sexual violence in the Sierra Leone Conflict. *Human Rights Watch, 15*(1)(A). Retrieved December 17, 2007, from http://www.hrw.org/reports/2003/sierraleone/sierleon0103–06.htm#P849_179644.

Human Rights Watch. (2004a). Darfur in flames: Atrocities in Western Sudan. *Human Rights Watch, 16*(5)(A). Retrieved February 20, 2008, from http://hrw.org/reports/2004/sudan0404/.

Human Rights Watch. (2004b, December 29). *D.R. Congo: Civilians at risk*. Retrieved January 18, 2005, from http://hrw.org/english/docs/2004/12/29/congo9936.htm.

Human Rights Watch. (2005). *No protection: Rape and sexual violence following displacement*. Retrieved February 27, 2008, from http://www.hrw.org/backgrounder/africa/darfur0505/3.htm.

Human Rights Watch. (2006a). *Annex: Definition of terms*. Retrieved December 17, 2007, from http://hrw.org/reports/2007/cdi0807/11.htm.

Human Rights Watch. (2006b, September 27). *Kyrgyzstan: Bride kidnapping, domestic abuse rampant*. Retrieved January 3, 2008, from http://hrw.org/english/docs/2006/09/27/kyrgyz14261_txt.htm.

Human Rights Watch. (2006c). *Reconciled to violence: State failure to stop domestic abuse and abduction of women in Kyrgystan*. Retrieved February 22, 2008, from http://hrw.org/reports/2006/kyrgyzstan0906/.

Human Rights Watch. (2006d). *Stolen voices: Firsthand stories of women abducted for forced marriage in Kyrgyzstan*. Retrieved January 3, 2008, from http://hrw.org/reports/2006/kyrgyzstan0906/testimonies.htm.

Human Rights Watch. (2006e). *Burma: Army forces thousands to flee: Attacks and abuses displace civilians in Eastern Burma*. Retrieved May 30, 2008, from http://www.hrw.org/english/docs/2006/11/30/burma14718.htm.

Human Rights Watch. (2007). *CEDAW: The women's rights treaty*. Retrieved February 28, 2008, from http://www.hrw.org/campaigns/cedaw/.

Human Rights Watch. (2007b). *Effects of sexual violence on survivors and the need for services*. http://hrw.org/reports/2007/cdi0807/7.htm.

Human Rights Watch. (2008, February 19). *Uganda: New accord provides for war crimes trials: Prosecuting rights abusers will require political will, legal reforms*. Retrieved February 28, 2008, from http://hrw.org/english/docs/2008/02/19/uganda18094.htm.

iAbolish. (1999). *Christian Solidarity International (CSI) visits Northern Bahr El Ghazal, Sudan. January 8–13*. Retrieved February 28, 2008, from http://www.iabolish.org/slavery_today/sudan/csi.html.

Igric, G. (1999, June 18). *Kosovo rape victims suffer twice*. Institute for War and Peace Reporting. Retrieved January 6, 2008, from http://www.motherjones.com/news/special_reports/total_coverage/kosovo/victims.html.

Independent Catholic News. (2008, February 20). *Cambodia: Campaigners welcome new law to fight sex trafficking*. Retrieved February 25, 2008, from http://www.ungift.org/index.php?option=com_content&task=view&id=844&Itemid=1136.

IN Network. (2007, November 12). *Trokosi of West Africa*. Retrieved February 23, 2008, from http://www.innetwork.org/index.php?option=com_content&task=view&id=39&Itemid=45.

INTERIGHTS, Ain o Salish Kendra (ASK), & Shirkat Gah. (2000). *Home Office Working Group—Information gathering exercise on forced marriages*. London: Home Office.

International Center for Research on Women (ICRW). (2005). *Too young to wed: Education and action toward ending child marriages*. Retrieved January 3, 2008, from http://www.icrw.org/docs/2005_brief_childmarriage.pdf.

International Center for Research on Women (ICRW). (2007). *New insights on preventing child marriage: A global analysis of factors and programs*. Retrieved May 30, 2008, from http://www.icrw.org/docs/2007-new-insights-preventing-child-marriage.pdf

International Criminal Court. (2007). *The state parties to the Rome Statute*. Retrieved January 31, 2008, from http://www.icc-cpi.int/statesparties.html.

International Labour Conference. (1998). *Child labour: Targeting the intolerable*. Geneva: International Labour Office.

Jain, S., & Kurz, K. (2007). *New insights on preventing child marriage: A global analysis of factors and programs*. Retrieved January 25, 2008, from http://www.icrw.org/docs/2007-new-insights-preventing-child-marriage.pdf.

Joesoef, M. R., et al. (1998). Risk profile of female sex workers who participate in a routine penicillin prophylaxis programme in Surabaya, Indonesia. *International Journal of STD and AIDS, 9*, 756–60.

Jeffreys, S. (1999). Globalizing sexual exploitation: Sex tourism and the traffic in women. *Leisure Studies, 18*, 179–196.

Kandathil, R. (2005). Global sex trafficking and the Trafficking Victims Protection Act of 2000: Legislative responses to the problem of modern slavery. *Michigan Journal of Gender and Law, 12*(1).

Kempadoo, K., & Doezema, J. (1998). *Global sex workers: Rights, resistance and redefinition*. New York: Routledge.

Kennedy, F. (2001). Vatican confirms report of sexual abuse and rape of nuns by priests. *The Independent* (London). Retrieved January 2, 2008, from http://findarticles.com/p/articles/mi_qn4158/is_20010321/ai_n14367971.

Kimani, M. (2007). Congolese women confront legacy of rape: War and sexual violence leave survivors in desperate need. *Africa Renewal, 20*(4), 4. Retrieved February 15, 2008, from http://www.un.org/ecosocdev/geninfo/afrec/vol20no4/204-congolese-women.html.

Kirloskar, S., & Cameroon-Moore, S. (1997). Cult supplies child sex trade. *India Times, 27*, 22–29.

Kleinbach, R. (2003). Frequency of non-consensual bride kidnapping in the Kyrgyz Republic. *International Journal of Central Asian Studies, 8*(1), 108–128.

Kleinbach, R., Ablezova, M., & Aitieva, M. (2005). Kidnapping for marriage (Ala Kachuu) in a Kyrgyz village. *Central Asian Survey, 24*(2), 191–202.

Kuehnast, K. (1998). From pioneers to entrepreneurs: Young women, consumerism, and the "world picture" in Kyrgyzstan. *Central Asian Survey, 17*(4), 639–654.

Kurlantzick, J. (2007, October 21). China's future: A nation of single men? *Los Angeles Times*. Retrieved February 19, 2008, from http://www.latimes.com/news/printedition/opinion/la-op-kurlantzick21oct21,1,6759831.story?coll=la-news-comment.

La Strada International. (2007). *Root causes*. Retrieved January 19, 2008, from http://www.lastradainternational.org/?main=traffickinghumanbeings&section=rootcauses.

Lederer, L. (2007). *In modern bondage: An international perspective on human trafficking in the 21st century*. Remarks at the Federal Acquisition Regulation Compliance Training for Government Contractors, Washington DC. Retrieved January 12, 2008, from http://www.state.gov/g/tip/rls/rm/07/96276.html.

Lerner, G. (1986). The origin of prostitution in ancient Mesopotamia. *Signs, 11*(2), 236–254.

MacKinnon, C. (2005). Pornography as trafficking. *Michigan Journal of International Law, 26*, 993–1012.

Maiti Nepal. (2006). Retrieved on April 22, 2008, from http://www.maitinepal.org/abtus/index.php.

Mattar, M. (2002, July 9). *The International Criminal Court (ICC) becomes a reality: When will the court prosecute the first trafficking in persons case?* Retrieved December 17, 2007, from the Protection Project Web site: http://www.protectionproject.org.

May, M. (2006, October 6). Sex trafficking: San Francisco is a major center for international crime networks that smuggle and enslave. *San Francisco Chronicle*. Retrieved on April 22, 2008, from http://www.sfgate.com/cgi-bin/article.cgi?f=/c/a/2006/10/06/MNGR1LGUQ41.DTL.

McDougall, G. J. (2000, June). *Contemporary forms of slavery: Systematic rape, sexual slavery and slavery-like practices during armed conflict*. United Nations Commission on Human Rights Sub-Commission on the Promotion and Protection of Human Rights, fifty-second session. Retrieved January 24, 2007, from http://www.unhchr.ch/huridocda/huridoca.nsf/0/3d25270b5fa3ea998025665f0032f220.

McGirk, T. (2002, February 10). Lifting the veil on Taliban sex slavery. *Time Magazine*. Retrieved January 2, 2008, from http://www.time.com/time/magazine/article/0,9171,1101020218-201892,00.html.

McKinsey, K. (1993, January 23). Mass rape in Bosnia: 20,000 women, mostly Muslims, have been abused by Serb soldiers. *Southam News*. Retrieved February 28, 2008, from http://www.peacewomen.org/news/BosniaHerzegovina/newsarchive/massrape.html.

Mealer, B. (2005). *War rape trauma lingers in Congo; As a weapon of war, sexual violence leaves lasting pains*. Associated Press. Retrieved February 20, 2008, from CBS Web site: http://www.cbsnews.com/stories/2005/06/22/world/main703577.shtml.

Mendenhall, P. (2002, May). *Escaping brutal bondage in Europe: Few sex slaves survive to tell a tale of forced sex and torture*. Retrieved February 15, 2008, from MSNBC Web site: http://www.msnbc.msn.com/id/3071966/.

Miller, J. (2006, February 15). *Human trafficking and transnational organized crime*. Retrieved February 22, 2008, from U.S. Department of State Web site: http://www.state.gov/g/tip/rls/rm/62072.htm.

Narula, S. (1999). *Broken people: Caste violence against India's untouchables*. New York: Human Rights Watch.

National Cancer Institute. (2006, August 21). *Human papilloma viruses and cancer: Q & A*. Retrieved January 6, 2008, from http://www.nci.nih.gov/cancertopics/factsheet/Risk/HPV.

National Catholic Reporter. (2001, March 9). The problem of the sexual abuse of African religious in Africa and Rome. *National Catholic* Reporter Online. Retrieved January 24, 2008, from http://ncronline.org/NCR_Online/documents/McDonaldAFRICAreport.htm.

Neill, G. (2000). Duty, honor, rape: Sexual assault against women during war. *International Journal of Women's Studies, 2*(1). Retrieved February 21, 2008 from http://www. bridgew.edu/SoAS/jiws/fall01/index.htm.

Nikolic-Ristanovic, V. (2002). *Social change, gender and violence: Post-communist and war-affected societies*. Boston: Kluwer.

Nikolic-Ristanovic, V. (2005). Sex trafficking: The impact of war, militarism and globalization in Eastern Europe. *Globalizacija.com: Journal for Political Theory and Research on Globalization, Development, and Gender Issues*. Retrieved January 16, 2008, from http://www.globalizacija.com/doc_en/e0058sim.htm.

Ocansey, R., & Hayhoe, A. (2004). *Practice of trokosi still hurting girls in Ghana*. Retrieved February 20, 2007, from Worldwide Religious News Web site: http://www.wwrn.org/ article.php?idd=7760&sec=73&con=63.

Pallen, D. (2003). Sexual slavery in Bosnia: Negative externality of the market for peace. *Swords and Ploughshares, 13*(1).

Panos Institute. (1998). *The intimate enemy: Gender violence and reproductive health*. Panos Briefing No. 27, Panos, London.

Parrot, A. (2008, January 11). *Successful strategies for reducing violence against women worldwide*. Paper presented at the International Women, Leadership and Community conference, New Delhi, India.

Parrot, A., & Cummings, N. (2006). *Forsaken females: The global brutalization of women*. New York: Rowman and Littlefield.

Peace Pledge Union. (2003, February 26). *War index*. Retrieved January 18, 2005, from http://www.ppu.org.uk/war/countries/africa_index.html.

Polaris Project. (n.d.). *Bopha, trafficked in Cambodia*. Retrieved February 28, 2008, from http://www.humantrafficking.com/humantrafficking/features_ht3/Testimonies/testi monies_mainframe.htm.

Polaris Project. (n.d.). *Chen, trafficked in Thailand*. Retrieved February 28, 2008, from http://www.humantrafficking.com/humantrafficking/features_ht3/Testimonies/testi monies_mainframe.htm.

Polaris Project. (n.d.). *Dawn, trafficked in Canada*. Retrieved February 18, 2008, from http://www.humantrafficking.com/humantrafficking/features_ht3/Testimonies/testi monies_mainframe.htm.

Polaris Project. (n.d.). *Elena, trafficked in Montenegro*. Retrieved February 28, 2008, from http://www.humantrafficking.com/humantrafficking/features_ht3/Testimonies/testi monies_mainframe.htm.

Polaris Project. (n.d.). *Eleni, trafficked in Bosnia*. Retrieved February 20, 2008, from http:// www.humantrafficking.com/humantrafficking/features_ht3/Testimonies/testimo nies_mainframe.htm.

Polaris Project. (n.d.). *I, trafficked in Sierra Leone*. Retrieved February 28, 2008, from http:// www.humantrafficking.com/humantrafficking/features_ht3/Testimonies/testimonies _mainframe.htm.

Polaris Project. (n.d.). *Inez, trafficked in the US*. Retrieved February 28, 2008, from http:// www.humantrafficking.com/humantrafficking/features_ht3/Testimonies/testimo nies_mainframe.htm.

Polaris Project. (n.d.). *Jill, trafficked in the US*. Retrieved January 10, 2008, from http:// www.humantrafficking.com/humantrafficking/features_ht3/Testimonies/testimon ies_mainframe.htm.

Polaris Project. (n.d.). *Juliana Dogbadzi*. Retrieved February 20, 2008, from http://www.hu mantrafficking.com/humantrafficking/features_ht3/Testimonies/testimonies_mainf rame.htm.

Polaris Project. (n.d.). *Julie, trafficked in Ghana*. Retrieved February 28, 2008, from http:// www.humantrafficking.com/humantrafficking/features_ht3/Testimonies/testimon ies_mainframe.htm.

Polaris Project. (n.d.). *Maria, trafficked in Mexico*. Retrieved February 28, 2008, from http://www.humantrafficking.com/humantrafficking/features_ht3/Testimonies/testi monies_mainframe.htm.

Polaris Project. (n.d.). *Marsha, trafficked in Germany, originally from Russia; Testimony before U.S. Senate Foreign Relations Committee, 2000*. Retrieved February 15, 2008, from http://www.humantrafficking.com/humantrafficking/features_ht3/Testimonies/testi monies_mainframe.htm.

Polaris Project. (n.d.). *Olga, trafficked in Israel*. Retrieved February 28, 2008, from http:// www.humantrafficking.com/humantrafficking/features_ht3/Testimonies/testimo nies_mainframe.htm.

Polaris Project. (n.d.). *Natalia, trafficked in Congo*. Retrieved February 28, 2008, from http://www.humantrafficking.com/humantrafficking/features_ht3/Testimonies/testi monies_mainframe.htm.

Polaris Project. (n.d.). *Patricia, trafficked in China*. Retrieved February 28, 2008, from http://www.humantrafficking.com/humantrafficking/features_ht3/Testimonies/testi monies_mainframe.htm.

Polaris Project. (n.d.). *Seema, trafficked in India*. Retrieved February 28, 2008, from http:// www.humantrafficking.com/humantrafficking/features_ht3/Testimonies/testimo nies_mainframe.htm.

Polaris Project. (n.d.). *Shahnara, trafficked in the UAE*. Retrieved February 28, 2008, from http://www.humantrafficking.com/humantrafficking/features_ht3/Testimonies/testi monies_mainframe.htm.

Polaris Project. (n.d.). *Tatyana, trafficked in the UAE*. Retrieved February 28, 2008, from http://www.humantrafficking.com/humantrafficking/features_ht3/Testimonies/testi monies_mainframe.htm.

Polaris Project. (n.d.). *Ying Chen trafficked in Thailand*. Retrieved February 28, 2008, from http://www.humantrafficking.com/humantrafficking/features_ht3/Testimonies/testi monies_mainframe.htm.

Power, C. (2000, June 25). Becoming a "Servant of God." Devadasis are Dalit women sold into sexual slavery. Is this the end of a cruel tradition? *Newsweek*. Retrieved January 22, 2008, from http://www.hartford-hwp.com/archives/52a/013.html.

Protection Project. (2007). *International child sex tourism: Scope of the problem and comparative case studies*. Johns Hopkins University's Paul H. Nitze School of Advanced International Studies. Retrieved December 17, 2007, from http://www.kmk-studio .com/JHU/JHU_Report.pdf.

Protection Project. (2007b). Trafficking of Persons, Especially Women and Children: USA Routes. Retrieved April 30, 2008, from http://www.protectionproject.org/pro grams/us_training/us_map.htm.

Protection Report. (2006). *Trafficking in persons in central Asia: The scope of the problem and the appropriate responses*. Regional Central Asia Conference, "Combating Trafficking in Human Beings—Regional Response," Paper presented at the Regional Central Asia Conference in Astana, Kazakhstan from May 18–19. Retrieved December 21, 2007, from http://www.protectionproject.org/.

Protection Report. (2007). *Survivor stories: Maria*. Retrieved February 20, 2008, from http://www.protectionproject.org/programs/us_training/survivor_maria.htm.

Push Journal. (2007). *Former child sex slave wins compensation in Malaysia*. Retrieved May 30, 2008, from http://www.planetwire.org/details/7334.

Raymond, J., & Hughes, D. (2001). *Sex trafficking of women in the United States*. Coalition against Trafficking in Women. Retrieved December 13, 2007, from http://www.uri.edu/artsci/wms/hughes/sex_traff_us.pdf.

Robinson, B. A. (2007, March 4). *Human slavery: Japanese sex slavery before, during and after World War II*. Ontario Consultants on Religious Tolerance. Retrieved January 3, 2008, from http://www.religioustolerance.org/sla_japa.htm.

Rosenthal, E. (2001, June 25). Harsh Chinese realities feed market in women. *The New York Times*. Retrieved February 19, 2008, from http://query.nytimes.com/gst/fullpage.html?res=950CE5DE1030F936A15755C0A9679C8B63.

Salopek, P. (2004, December 12). The bride was 7: In the heart of Ethiopia, child marriage takes a brutal toll. *The Chicago Tribune*. Retrieved January 3, 2008, from http://www.chicagotribune.com/news/nationworld/chi-0412120360dec12,1,2974333.story.

Sang-hun, C. (2007, December 23). South Korea, where boys were kings, revalues its girls. *New York Times*, 1, 14. Retrieved April 28, 2008, from http://www.nytimes.com/2007/12/23/world/asia/23skorea.html.

Scanlon, T. J. (2002, August 24). Child labour: Vast problem whose effects on children's health remain largely unstudied. *British Medical Journal, 325*, (7361): 401–403.

Schuckman, E. E. (Winter 2006). Antitrafficking policies in Asia and the Russian Far East: A comparative perspective. *Demokratizatsiya*. Retrieved January 27, 2008, from http://findarticles.com/p/articles/mi_qa3996/is_200601/ai_n16537201/print.

Schurman-Kauflin, D. (2006). *Profiling sex trafficking: Illegal immigrants at risk*. Violent Crimes Institute. Retrieved January 14, 2008, from http://www.drdsk.com/articles.html#SexTrafficking.

Sexually transmitted infections. (n.d.). Retrieved January 3, 2008, from Joint United Nations Programme on HIV/AIDS (UNAIDS) Web site: http://www.unaids.org/en/Issues/Prevention_treatment/sexually_transmitted_infections.asp.

Shankar, J. (1990). *Devadasi cult: A sociological analysis*. New Delhi: Ashish Publishing House.

Shanks, L., Ford, N., Schull, M., & de Jong, K. (2001, January 27). Responding to rape. *The Lancet, 357*(9252), 304.

Silverman, J. G., Decker, M. R., Gupta, J., Maheshwari, A., Willis, B. M., & Raj, A. (2007). HIV prevalence and predictors of infection in sex-trafficked Nepalese girls and women. *Journal of the American Medical Association 298*, 536–542.

Simkhada, P. P. (2003). *Context, process and determinants of trafficking and health-seeking behavior of trafficked women and girls in Nepal: Implications for social and public health policy*. Paper presented on *Trafficking in Persons Conference*, June 27–28, 2003, Nottingham, UK.

Sklair, L. (1991). *Sociology of the global system*. Baltimore, MD: Johns Hopkins University Press.

Slavery Still Exists. (2005). *Victim testimonies, Polaris Project*. http://www.slaverystillexists.org/slaverystillexists/about/testimonies.htm.

Stiglmayer, A. (1994). The Rapes in Bosnia-Herzegovina. In Stiglmayer, A. (Ed.), *Mass rape: The war against women in Bosnia-Herzogivna*. University of Nebraska Press.

Stritof, B., & Stritof, S. (2007). *About marriage: Child brides*. Retrieved January 10, 2007, from about.com Web site: http://marriage.about.com/od/arrangedmarriages/a/childbride.htm.

UN troops face child abuse claims. (2006, November 30). Retrieved January 24, 2008, from BBC News Web site: http://news.bbc.co.uk/2/hi/americas/6195830.stm.

UNESCO Trafficking Project. (2003). *Data comparison sheet #1: Worldwide trafficking estimates by organizations*. Retrieved December 19, 2007, from http://www.unescobkk.org/fileadmin/user_upload/culture/Trafficking/project/Graph_Worldwide_Sept_2004.pdf.

UNICEF. (2005). *United Nations Children's Fund, Early Marriage: A Harmful traditional practice: A statistical exploration*. Retrieved February 22, 2008, from http://64.233.169.104/search?q=cache:w-dxKk6zhWMJ:www.unicef.org/protection/files/Child_Marriage.pdf+UNICEF+2005+child+marriage&hl=en&ct=clnk&cd=3&gl=us&client=safari.

UNICEF. (2006). *Child protection information sheet: Child marriage*. Retrieved February 27, 2008, from http://www.unicef.org/protection/files/Child-marriage.pdf.

UNICEF. (2008). *United Nations convention on the rights of the child*. Retrieved May 30, 2008, from http://www.unicef.org.uk/pages.asp?page=92.

UNIFEM. (2008). *Declaration on the elimination of violence against women*. Retrieved May 30, 2008, from http://www.stopvaw.org/Declaration_on_the_Elimination_of_Violence_Against_Women3.html.

United Nations. (1994, February 23). *Declaration on the Elimination of Violence against Women*. Retreived April 27, 2008, from http://www.unhchr.ch/huridocda/huridoca.nsf/(Symbol)/A.RES.48.104.En.

United Nations. (2000a). *Protocol to Prevent, Suppress and Punish Trafficking in Persons, Especially Women and Children, Supplementing the United Nations Convention against Transnational Organized Crime*. Retrieved April 28, 2008, from http://www.uncjin.org/Documents/Conventions/dcatoc/final_documents_2/convention_%20traff_eng.pdf.

United Nations. (2000b, February). *New global treaty to combat "sex slavery" of women and girls*. Retrieved February 12, 2008, from United Nations Department of Public Information Web site: http://www.un.org/events/10thcongress/2098.htm.

United Nations. (2003). *Convention on the Rights of the Child*. Retrieved April 27, 2008, from http://www.unhchr.ch/html/menu3/b/k2crc.htm.

United Nations. (2006). *Opium poppy cultivation in the golden triangle: Lao PDR, Myanmar, Thailand*. Central Committee for Drug Abuse Control, Lao National Commission for Drug Control and Supervision Office of the Narcotics Control Board. Retrieved February 22, 2008, from http://www.shaps.hawaii.edu/drugs/golden/.

United Nations. (2007a). *Convention on the Elimination of All Forms of Discrimination Against Women*. Retrieved April 28, 2008, from http://www.un.org/womenwatch/daw/cedaw/.

United Nations. (2007b). *State Parties*. Retrieved April 28, 2008, from http://www.un.org/womenwatch/daw/cedaw/states.htm.

United Nations. (2008, February 18). *Vienna forum strengthens global fight against human trafficking: New measures outlined to combat a crime that "shames us all."* Retrieved February 25, 2008, from United Nations Office from Geneva Web site: http://www.unog.ch/80256EDD006B9C2E/(httpNewsByYear_en)/BF5DB811BC9645F6C12573F3003BC173?OpenDocument.

United Nations Development Programme. (2005). *Trafficking in human beings in South Eastern Europe*. UNICEF (United Nations Children's Fund)/UNOHCHR (United Nations Office of the High Commission of Human Rights)/OSCE/ODIHR (Organization for Security and Cooperation in Europe/Office for Democratic Institutions and Human Rights). Retrieved November 30, 2007, from http://www.unicef.org/ceecis/Trafficking.Report.2005.pdf.

United Nations High Commissioner for Human Rights. (1996, January 17). *Rights of the child: Report of the special rapporteur on the sale of children, child prostitution and child pornography*. Retrieved April 28, 2008, from http://www.unhchr.ch/Huridocda/Huridoca.nsf/0/eee276066375879b8025689600531c70?Opendocument.

United Nations High Commissioner for Human Rights. (2000). *Report of the United Nations High Commissioner for Human Rights*. Retrieved May 30, 2008, from http://www.un.org/documents/ga/docs/55/a5536.pdf.

United Nations Office on Drugs and Crime. (2006). *Trafficking in persons: Global patterns*. Retrieved January 3, 2008, from http://www.unodc.org/documents/human-trafficking/HT-globalpatterns-en.pdf.

United Nations Population Fund (UNFPA). (2007). Ghana: Liberating slaves and changing minds, starting at the grass roots. *Ending violence: Violence against women case studies*. Retrieved February 23, 2008, from http://www.unfpa.org/endingviolence/html/pdf/chapter_ghana.pdf.

U.S. Department of Justice. (2007). *Child exploitation and obscenity section*. Retrieved January 21, 2008, from http://www.usdoj.gov/criminal/ceos/sextour.html.

U.S. Department of State. (2004, November 24). *The link between prostitution and sex trafficking*. Bureau of Public Affairs, Washington, D.C. Retrieved April 29, 2008, from http://www.state.gov/r/pa/ei/rls/38790.htm.

U.S. Department of State. (2005). *The facts about child sex tourism. Office to Monitor and Combat Trafficking in Persons*. Retrieved January 30, 2008, from http://www.state.gov/g/tip/rls/fs/2005/51351.htm.

U.S. Department of State. (2006, June 8). *Trafficking in persons report*. Retrieved January 13, 2008, from http://www.state.gov/g/tip/rls/tiprpt/2006/65983.htm.

U.S. Department of State. (2007a, March 6). *Bosnia and Herzegovina country reports on human rights practices—2006, Bureau of Democracy, Human Rights, and Labor*. Retrieved April 28, 2008, from http://www.state.gov/g/drl/rls/hrrpt/2006/78804.htm.

U.S. Department of State. (2007b). *Health consequences of trafficking in persons. Office to Monitor and Combat Trafficking in Persons*. Retrieved January 2, 2008 from http://www.state.gov/g/tip/rls/fs/07/91418.htm.

U.S. Department of State. (2007c). *Trafficking in Persons Report: Topics of Special Interest. Office to Monitor and Combat Trafficking in Persons*. Retrieved April 21, 2008, from http://www.state.gov/g/tip/rls/tiprpt/2007/82808.htm.

USINFO. (2007). *2007 trafficking in persons report*. Retrieved May 30, 2008, from http://usinfo.state.gov/gi/global_issues/human_trafficking/traffick_report.html.

Vandeberg, M. (2002). *Hopes betrayed: Trafficking of women and girls in post-conflict Bosnia and Herzegovina for forced prostitution*. New York: Human Rights Watch Press.

van Dijk, R. (2001). "Voodoo" on the doorstep: Young Nigerian prostitutes and magic policing in the Netherlands. *Journal of the International African Institute, 71*(4), 558–586.

Walsh, D., & Byrne, N. (2002, December 22). UN peacekeepers criticized. *The Scotsman*. Edinburgh, Scotland. Retrieved January 30, 2008, from http://www.globalpolicy.org/security/peacekpg/general/2002/1223peace.htm.

Ward, J., & Marsh, M. (2006). *Sexual violence against women and girls in war and its aftermath: Realities, responses and required resources*. Paper presented at the Symposium on Sexual Violence in Conflict and Beyond, Brussels, Belgium.

Wescott, K. (2003, June 25). *Sex slavery awaits Ugandan schoolgirls*. Retrieved February 22, 2008, from BBC News Web site: http://news.bbc.co.uk/2/hi/africa/3019838.stm.

Williams, C., & Stein, A. (2002). *Sexuality and Gender*. Malden, MA: Blackwell.

Williams, P. (1999). *Illegal immigration and commercial sex: The new slave trade*. London: Frank Cass.

Willis, B. M., & Levy, B. S. (2002). Child prostitution: Global health burden, research needs, and interventions. *The Lancet, 359*, 1419.

Wolte, S. (2004). *Armed conflict and trafficking in women*. Eschborn, Germany: Deutsche Gesellschaft für Technische Zusammenarbeit.

Women's International Network. (2002). *Ghana: Finally the terrible tradition of "trokosi" is challenged*. Retrieved January 29, 2008, from http://findarticles.com/p/articles/mi_m2872/is_2_28/ai_86049655.

Wood, E. (2006). Variation in sexual violence during war. *Politics and Society, 34*(3), 307–341.

World Congress against Commercial Sexual Exploitation of Children. (1996). *Impact statement*. Stockholm: WCACSEC.

World Revolution. (n.d.). *Human Trafficking*. Retrieved February 28, 2008, from http://www.worldrevolution.org/Projects/Webguide/GuideArticle.asp?ID=1448.

Zimmerman, C. (2006, August 28). *The health risks and consequences of trafficking in women and adolescents: Findings from a European study*. Retrieved April 28, 2008 from London School of Hygiene and Tropical Medicine Web site: http://www.lshtm.ac.uk/hpu/docs/traffickingfinal.pdf.

Index

About the Authors

ANDREA PARROT is a Professor of Human Ecology at Cornell University and a board certified Sex Educator. She has received more than $1.5 million in funding for 15 studies focused on sexuality (including sexual violence/assault and sex education) since 1990. Parrot has authored, co-authored, or edited five books. She is a member of the Board of Directors for the Foundation for the Scientific Study of Sexuality and a current member/past officer of the Society for the Scientific Study of Sex. She has been interviewed widely for radio, television, and newspapers, including two appearances on *Oprah* as well as *Larry King Live*, *Good Morning America*, *CBS This Morning*, *The Learning Channel* and on NPR with Diane Rehm.

NINA CUMMINGS is a PhD candidate at Cornell and an Adjunct Faculty member at Ithaca College. She is also a University Victim Advocate and a Cornell Advocate for Rape Education, as well as a Certified Health Educator. She coauthored with Parrot the book *Forsaken Females: The Brutalization of Women*. Cummings and Parrot also coauthored articles that have been published in the *Journal of American College Health*, *Vital Signs*, and *RESPONSE: Journal of the Center for Women's Policy Studies*. In 2001, Cummings won the Cornell University Presidential Advisory Committee on the Status of Women Award.

About the Series Editor

JUDY KURIANSKY, PhD, is a licensed clinical psychologist, and an adjunct faculty member in the Department of Clinical Psychology at Columbia University Teachers College and the Department of Psychiatry at Columbia University College of Physicians and Surgeons. Kuriansky is a United Nations representative for the International Association of Applied Psychology and for the World Council for Psychotherapy. She is also a visiting professor at the Peking University Health Sciences Center, a fellow of the American Psychological Association, founder of the APA Media Psychology Division, and a widely known journalist for CBS, CNBC, Lifetime, and A&E, as well as a regular weekly columnist for the *New York Daily News*. She has been a syndicated radio talk show host for more than 20 years.